ROUTLEDGE LIBRARY EDITIONS: POLITICAL THOUGHT AND POLITICAL PHILOSOPHY

Volume 18

LIBERTY AND JUSTICE

LIBERTY AND JUSTICE

J. P. DAY

Routledge
Taylor & Francis Group

LONDON AND NEW YORK

First published in 1987 by Croom Helm Ltd

This edition first published in 2020
by Routledge
2 Park Square, Milton Park, Abingdon, Oxon OX14 4RN

and by Routledge
52 Vanderbilt Avenue, New York, NY 10017

Routledge is an imprint of the Taylor & Francis Group, an informa business

British Library Cataloguing in Publication Data
A catalogue record for this book is available from the British Library

ISBN: 978-0-367-21961-1 (Set)
ISBN: 978-0-429-35434-2 (Set) (ebk)
ISBN: 978-0-367-22022-8 (Volume 18) (hbk)
ISBN: 978-0-367-22023-5 (Volume 18) (pbk)
ISBN: 978-0-429-27034-5 (Volume 18) (ebk)

Publisher's Note
The publisher has gone to great lengths to ensure the quality of this reprint but points out that some imperfections in the original copies may be apparent.

Disclaimer
The publisher has made every effort to trace copyright holders and would welcome correspondence from those they have been unable to trace.

LIBERTY AND JUSTICE

J.P. Day

CROOM HELM
London • Sydney • Wolfeboro, New Hampshire

© J.P. Day 1987
Croom Helm Ltd, Provident House, Burrell Row,
Beckenham, Kent BR3 1AT
Croom Helm Australia Pty Ltd, Suite 4, 6th Floor,
64-76 Kippax Street, Surry Hills, NSW 2010, Australia

British Library Cataloguing in Publication Data

Day, J.P.
  Liberty and justice
  1. Liberty   2. Justice
  I. Title
  323.44   JC585
  ISBN 0-7099-4523-X

Croom Helm US, 27 South Main Street,
Wolfeboro, New Hampshire 03894-2069

Library of Congress Cataloging-in-Publication Data

Day, J.P. (John Patrick), 1919-
  Liberty and justice.

  Includes index.
  1. Liberty. 2. Justice. I. Title.
JC585.D38 1986   323.44   86-16827
ISBN 0-7099-4523-X

Printed and bound in Great Britain
by Billing & Sons Limited, Worcester.

CONTENTS

To Herbert Hart

PREFACE

'Justice and liberty are the central concepts of social and political thought.'[1] These true words of Raphael's indicate the importance of these concepts, which resides in the fact that they are significantly linked to most of the other key notions in this field of thought, so that an understanding of them is indispensable for an adequate grasp of Social Philosophy. The Philosophies of Justice and of Liberty occupy accordingly the same sort of dominant position in Ethics and Social Philosophy as the Philosophy of Probability occupies in Epistemology and Philosophy of Science. Thus, Justice is conceptually connected with the following leading ideas among others: Law, Compensation, Intention, Right, Wrong, Virtue, Vice, Equality, Chance, Reciprocity, Distribution, Punishment, Discrimination, Exploitation, Impartiality, Due, Contribution, Need, Truth, Judgement, Dignity, Indignation, Righteousness, Persecution, Public Good. Similarly, Liberty is conceptually connected with the following leading ideas among others: Desire, Power, Coercion, Deterrence, Threat, Law, Determinism, Paternalism, Chance, Right, Intention, Manipulation, Public Good, Liberalism, Constitutionalism. It will be seen that Justice and Liberty are themselves connected by being linked to a number of the same notions, for example, Law, Intention, Chance, Right, Public Good.[2]

The essays make a book, because they have been composed as such, and so possess an intended unity. Thus, there are many cross-references between them. Again, Nos. 4 and 5 are companion pieces as are also Nos. 6, 11 and 12; and Nos. 8 and 9. Nos. 1, 3, 6, 7, 10, 11 and 12 develop a single and mainly consistent view of Freedom. Unlike the essays on Fairness, however, there is a significant difference between the first two and the later ones. In Nos. 1 and 3 Freedom is defined as a matter of *B* not *preventing A* from doing *X*. Prevention in turn is seen as the physical process of *B* making *A* unable to do *X*, a process which may be either intentional or unintentional. In the later essays, however, Freedom is defined as Bentham defined it, namely, as a matter of *B* not *restraining A* from doing *X*. Restraint (Coercion) is a process which (like Injustice) is mental as well as physical, because it is necessarily intentional. This is conceptually connected with the fact that Freedom (like Fairness) is a negative, general, moral right; for violation of a moral right is necessarily intentional.

The question of the relations between Fairness and Freedom, mentioned above, is another leading one about which a good deal is said in what follows. For example, Plato held that the free man is *identical with* the just (or virtuous) man (Essay 10, Appendix I). Again, classical economists hold that economic liberty is *the means to* economic justice (Essay 12). There are many important *resemblances* between them, such as that (as just said) both are negative, general, moral rights. Similarly, there are significant *differences* between them, one of which it is pertinent to mention here because it is relevant to the plan of the book. The problems of Freedom are best divided into those of Individual Liberty (Essay 6) and those of Collective Liberty (Essays 11 and 12). The latter are interorganisational problems about the coercion of one organisation, such as a church or a business, by another organisation, notably a state (government). They are problems of the greatest consequence. But the problems of Fairness are not best divided similarly. For the problems about unfair treatment of one organisation by another are not so pressing, though there are indeed interesting questions about justice between states (Essay 8, Subsec. 2.1).[3] In this connexion, it is necessary to mention a distinction which is much used and discussed in Essay 11, namely, that between an (unorganised) social set and a social organisation (= an organised social set). The persecution of Christians by the Roman Empire is not an example of Collective Injustice because Christians, unlike the Roman Church, are a social set and not a social organisation. Injustice to a social set is to be interpreted distributively and not collectively, and so reduces to injustice to the members of that set, that is, to Individual Injustice.

The essays have been published previously as follows:

No. 1. 'On Liberty and The Real Will', *Philosophy*, Vol. 45, No. 173 (July 1970), pp. 177-92.
No. 2. 'Fairness and Fortune', *Ratio*, Vol. 19, No. 1 (June 1977), pp. 70-84. Reprinted with corrections in *The Philosopher's Annual*, I. D.L. Boyer, P. Grim and J.T. Sanders (eds.) (Rowman and Littlefield, Towota, 1978), pp. 33-52. The corrected version is reproduced here.
No. 3. 'Threats, Offers, Law, Opinion and Liberty', the *American Philosophical Quarterly*, Vol. 14, No. 4 (October 1977), pp. 257-72.
No. 4. 'Retributive Punishment', *Mind*, Vol. 87, No. 348 (October 1978), pp. 498-516.
No. 5. 'Compensatory Discrimination', *Philosophy*, Vol. 56, No. 215 (January 1981), pp. 55-72.
No. 6, 'Individual Liberty' in *Of Liberty*, A. Phillips Griffiths (ed.)

(University Press, Cambridge, 1983), pp. 17-29.

No. 7. 'Civil Liberty and the Rule of Law', *Political Studies*, Vol. 31 (June 1983), pp. 194-204.

No. 8, 'The Indefeasibility of Justice', *Cogito*, Vol. 3, No. 1 (March 1985), pp. 55-90.

No. 9, 'Procedural Equality' in *Equality and Discrimination*, Stephen Guest and Alan Milne (eds) (Franz Steiner Verlag Wiesbaden Gmbh, 1985), pp. 51-9.

No. 10. 'Is the Concept of Freedom Essentially Contestable?', *Philosophy*, Vol. 61, No. 235 (January 1986), pp. 116-23.

No. 11. 'Collective Liberty and Religious Liberty', the *American Philosophical Quarterly*, Vol. 23, No. 3 (July 1986).

No. 12. 'Economic Liberty and Economic Justice', *Cogito*, Vol. 3, No. 4 (December 1985), pp. 35-59.

I am grateful to the editors of these publications for their permission to reprint the essays here. I also wish to make a general acknowledgement of the assistance which I have received in writing this book from the friends, colleagues and fellow-students who have commented on the essays either privately or in the seminars at which they have been discussed. Individual acknowledgements will be found at the ends of some of the essays.

I have taken advantage of the republication of the essays in book form to make corrections, additions and deletions, and to add material which makes even clearer the connections between them, that is, the unity of the book.

Notes

1. D.D. Raphael, *Justice and Liberty* (Athlone Press, London, 1980), p.v.

2. The *importance* of Justice and Liberty in the sense just explained must not be confused with their *value* (or justification). The latter is indeed a main question about both of them which receives extended treatment in the essays which follow. But it is a quite different question.

3. See also J.R. Lucas, *On Justice* (Clarendon Press, Oxford, 1980), Ch. 15.

A Note on the Jacket

The statues depicted on the jacket are the Statue of Liberty and the Lady of Justice. The Statue of Liberty (originally Liberty Enlightening the World) stands on Liberty

Preface

Island (originally Bedloe's Island) in New York Harbour. It is the work of the sculptor F.A. Bartholdi and the engineer G. Eiffel, and it was made in Paris. The pedestal is the work of R.M. Hunt. The statue is 151 ft high. It was unveiled by Bartholdi on 28 October 1886 in the presence of President Grover Cleveland. Its involved and interesting history is admirably related by Trachtenberg.

There is attached to the pedestal a plaque bearing Emma Lazarus' poem 'The New Colossus'. Its most famous lines, which are presumably addressed to Europe, are these:—

'Keep, ancient lands, your storied pomp!' cries she
With silent lips. 'Give me your tired, your poor,
Your huddled masses yearning to breathe free,
The wretched refuse of your teeming shore.'

Over the past ten years the statue has been completely restored in preparation for the centenary of its unveiling.

The Lady of Justice caps the dome of the Old Bailey, the Central Criminal Court of England. It once dominated the skyline of the City of London. It is the work of the sculptor F.W. Pomeroy, who was chosen to make it for the opening of the New Old Bailey by King Edward VII in 1907. The statue is 12 ft high. It is a singularity of The Lady that she is *not* blindfolded.

The juxtaposition of the two statues on the jacket symbolically brings together the Old World and the New. This is appropriate in view of the extensive attention which is given in this book to American authors as well as to European ones.

Sources

M. Trachtenberg, *The Statue of Liberty* (Allen Lane, London, 1976). J. Morecroft, C. Coughlin, G. Glenton, E. Spring and R. Gerelli, *The Old Bailey* (the Corporation of London. London, nd).

1 ON LIBERTY AND THE REAL WILL

1. Introduction

In the chapter which he devotes to the applications of his principle of individual liberty, Mill[1] considers the question 'how far liberty may legitimately be invaded for the prevention of crime, or of accident'. On the latter topic, he writes: ' . . . it is a proper office of public authority to guard against accidents. If either a public officer or anyone else saw a person attempting to cross a bridge which had been ascertained to be unsafe, and there were no time to warn him of his danger, they might seize him and turn him back, without any real infringement of his liberty; for liberty consists in doing what one desires, and he does not desire to fall into the river.' (Q1)

Bosanquet[2] claims that here Mill admits the existence of a Real (or General) Will in Rousseau's and Hegel's sense. He writes: ' . . . as has commonly been said, "What people demand is seldom what would satisfy them if they got it". We may recall the instances in which even Mill admitted that it is legitimate to infer . . . that people do not really "will" something which they desire to do at a given moment.' (Q2)

As a preliminary to a discussion of the notion of 'the public interest', Professor Barry[3] defines 'interest' thus: 'an action or policy is in a man's interests if it increases his opportunities to get what he wants.' (Q3) But he chooses to leave 'want' and 'want-satisfaction', which are the leading concepts of his system, as primitive or undefined terms.

These three quotations (Q1-Q3) provide a convenient introduction to the theme of this essay, which is the concept of the Real Will, particularly as it figures in political arguments, and the closely related notion of Real Liberty.

2. Preliminary Analysis

The rule of the Thélémites in Rabelais'[4] novel consists in the single article, FAY CE QUE VOULDRAS. It can be englished correctly as 'Do what you *will*, or *want*, or *wish*, or *like*, or *choose*'. But although these five verbs are mutually substitutable in this context, they are not

1

so in all contexts, and so do not express the same concept. Thus, 'We really *will* not have State Socialism' does not mean the same thing as 'We do not really *want* (to have) State Socialism'. For whereas the former records our firm resolve, the latter reports either our desire or our need. (See Sec. 5.) Again, 'I *wish* that I were you' makes sense, but 'I *want* to be you' does not. I.e. the impossible is a possible object of wishing, but not a possible object of wanting.[5] Yet again, 'I *choose X*' presupposes the existence of some alternative, *Y*, which I could have chosen instead, whereas 'I *want X*' does not.[6] Finally, there is nothing illogical, or even unusual, in saying that *A wants X* although he would not *like* it if he got (i.e. were to get) it. (See Q1, Sec. 1; Sec. 4.)

Which of these five concepts, then, are we to investigate? One might well think that, since our topic is the Real Will, it must be the first one listed, viz. '*A* really will *D*' (where *D* is a deed-variable). But this would be to make the mistake of *literalism* in philosophical analysis. Here, as elsewhere, it is the first step which counts, and to select the wrong concept for treatment is to start off on the wrong foot at the foot of the wrong ladder. Actually, it is the second concept in the list which needs attention: not what a man really will do must be our theme, but what he really wants to do. However, warnings are not wanting that the ground is likely to prove slippery underfoot. Thus, Mrs Jean Austin,[7] in examining Pleasure and Happiness, unmasks as the 'real villain of the piece, the verb *to want*'.

Here, then, is an argument which might be deployed by an autocrat at the breakfast-table: 'My people do not really want democracy — they only think they do; for none of them has ever lifted a finger against my personal rule; so I am not really denying them political liberty by withholding a democratic constitution — I am only appearing to do so.' (A1) This argument brings out one of the many ambiguities in the word 'real'. For in its first appearance in A1, the function of 'really' is to contrast what actually is the case with what is mistakenly believed to be the case; whereas in its second appearance its function is to contrast what actually is the case with what misleadingly seems to be the case. (It is an error to suppose, as Idealists are prone to do, that the opposite of Reality is always and only Appearance.[8]) This in turn discloses the meaning of 'Real Liberty'. To be really free is to be not really, but only apparently restrained by another person. A1 also raises a question about the objects of wanting, namely, are these things (or persons), or events, or propositions? In fact, it does not matter which one says, since one can speak equally well of people wanting *the* vote, or *to* vote, or *that* they should vote. But it is the verb form which brings out most clearly the putative connexion between desire and freedom, since freedom is freedom *to D*.

But is A1 convincing? It relies on the truth that, if *A* wants *X*, then he will try to get *X*. Nevertheless, it is not irrefutable. For instance, the reason why the people have not lifted a finger against the autocrat's personal rule may be that he has made it very dangerous for them to do so. Moreover, there is another, more fundamental objection which applies to all the arguments A1-A6 that we shall criticise in this essay. Even if the people's outward passivity did show that they did not (really) want democracy, this would not prove that the autocrat was not (really) denying them political liberty by withholding a democratic constitution. All that it would show would be that they would not feel frustrated by his action. They would not *feel* constrained by it; but they would nevertheless *be* constrained by it.[9] The mistake lies in thinking that *A* is unfree when he is restrained from doing something *which he wants to do*; whereas in fact he is unfree when he is restrained by *B* from doing anything that it is in his power to do, regardless of whether he wants to do it or not. If I am legally prohibited from importing cannabis, my freedom is to that extent restricted; and to urge that this is not so because, as it happens, I do not want to do so (or for that matter because I want not to do so, or do want to do so, or am indifferent as to whether I do so or not) is to argue beside the point.

This error is found in Mill's definition, 'liberty consists in doing what one desires' (Q1, Sec. 1).[10] It is also found in Hobbes' definition: 'A free man is he that, in those things which . . . he is able to do, is not hindered to do what he has a will to do.'[11] The following remarks by Mr Mabbott[12] illustrate the corresponding confusion between feeling free and being free: 'It is only a genius for vicarious slavery that enables a man to develop the individualist case. I am compelled to send my children to school (not that I have any, and I should anyhow); I am unable to buy novocain (*not that I want to*) . . . in short, I suppose no session passes but Parliament adds a round dozen to these pseudo-interferences with a liberty I do not covet, and I remain in fact as free as ever.' (My italics) But the interferences in question are real interferences, not pseudo-interferences; and it is just not true that the effect of them is to leave Mabbott (and the rest of us) as free as ever. It is a point of great practical importance. Most collectivist legislation affects only relatively small sections of the population, such as importers, employers, and landowners. Consequently, the mass of the people do not feel frustrated by it, and are apt to conclude that it leaves the country as free as ever it was. But in this they are much mistaken.

It may be objected that it does not matter if people are unfree so long as they do not feel unfree. Mabbott's remarks perhaps suggest this. But the following example shows the falsity of this thesis. For political reasons, a tyranny suppresses all genetic theories except one, which it protects. Since the proportion of the population who want to propound genetic theories is minute, next to nobody will be made to feel unfree by this policy. However, the protected theory may be false and one of the suppressed theories true; and the practical application of the false, protected theory may lead to a disastrous agricultural policy which inflicts great hardship on all the citizens. The mistake inherent in the objection is the false belief that liberty is valuable only because, and insofar as, the lack of it makes people feel unfree. In this connexion, it is highly important that being free and feeling free by no means always go together. Not only can people feel free when they are unfree, as we have just seen, they can also feel unfree when they are free. E.g., I would feel unfree, but not be unfree, if I wanted to import cannabis and believed, mistakenly, that to do so was still illegal, when in fact the relevant statute had been repealed last week.

Hobbes' definition of 'freedom' (above) raises the question of the logical relation of Liberty to Ability.[13] It is that the former *presupposes* the latter. I.e. the truth of 'A can D' is a necessary condition not only of the truth, but also of the falsity of 'A is free to D'. Or, in homelier terms, if A cannot D, then the question of whether or not he is free to D does not arise. Since A cannot square the circle, he cannot be restrained from doing so by B, nor consequently be not restrained from doing so by B, i.e. be free to do so. (The relation of Liberty to Ability is also discussed in Sec. 4 of Essay 3.) I believe that it is the opinion of Hobbes, Mill, Carritt, Mabbott and others that the logical relation of Liberty to Desire is also one of presupposition. That is, they think that, unless A wants to D, the question of whether or not he is free to D does not arise. On the other hand, the main thesis of this essay is that Desire (or Will) is *irrelevant* to Freedom; meaning by this that the truth or falsity of 'A is free to D' is independent of the truth or falsity of 'A wants to D'. But it is not disputed that 'A *feels* free to D' presupposes 'A wants to D'. On the contrary, it is suggested that the erroneous view that Liberty presupposes Desire arises precisely from the failure to distinguish between feeling free and being free.

Hobbes' definition of 'freedom' also raises the question of the nature of the 'hindrance' involved in liberty.[14] Suppose that Mill's man is prevented from walking on the bridge by a tree lying horizontally across its entrance; is he unfree to do so? The answer depends on how the tree got there. If it had been blown down by the wind, it would be incorrect to say that the man's freedom had been curtailed by the wind which had caused the tree to be there. But if the tree had been placed there by another person with or without the intention of preventing him from walking on the bridge, then it would be correct to say that his freedom had been restricted by that other person.

Another argument which the autocrat might use is this one: 'My people do not really want . . . etc. (as in A1); for none of them has the faintest idea what democracy is; so I am not really denying . . . etc. (as in A1).' (A2) This argument relies on the fact that 'A wants X' entails 'A knows what X is'. But it is no more irrefutable than A1 is. Perhaps what the autocrat means by saying that none of his people know what democracy is, is that none of them can give a definition of 'democracy' which would satisfy a political scientist. Yet it is perfectly possible to know well enough what a thing is to be able to desire it without being able to give a correct definition of it. The autocrat might well say of his people in this case that they do not know what they want. However, the statement 'A does not know what he wants' is ambiguous. Here, it is an ellipsis, the sense of which can be made plain by using brackets to show what it is an ellipsis of, thus: 'A does not know what he (thinks he) wants (actually is).' But 'A does not know what he wants' can also mean 'A wants X but does not know that he wants X'. We shall touch on this use of the expression, together with yet another use, in due course. (Sec. 6)

As Bosanquet says, the Real Will is the same thing as the General Will. (Q2, Sec. 1) Nevertheless, the notion of a General Will raises problems different from those discussed so far, or to be discussed later in this essay. The principal question which arises is whether the generality of a General Will resides in its subject or in its object. Thus, suppose that A and B both want X. Have we here not only A's desire for X and B's desire for X, but also the pair's desire for X? Or again, have we here not A's desire that he should have X and B's desire that he should have X, but rather A's desire that he and B should have a 'common good', namely X, and B's desire that he and A should have the same common good? But we only mention these points in passing in the interests of a general clarification.[15]

3. Acts, Consequences and Liberty

The autocrat might also argue as follows: 'My people do not really want . . . etc.; for introducing democracy here would lead straight to anarchy, which is the last thing they want; so I am not really denying . . . etc.'

(A3)   This argument is of the same logical type as Mill's (Q1, Sec. 1), and the form of the implication corresponding to both inferences is: 'If *Y* is a consequence of *X* and *A* does not want *Y*, then *A* does not want *X*.' However, it is easy to show that the inference-pattern is invalid, and that the corresponding implication-formula is false, by the normal method of adducing an instance in which the antecedent is true but the consequent is false. Thus, it may be true that the result of Richard Roe's eating curried lobster will be a stomach-ache which he does not want, and yet be false that he does not want to eat curried lobster.

How could a thinker of Mill's distinction come to advance so plainly unsound an argument? The explanation probably lies in what Sir Isaiah Berlin[16] calls 'the natural tendency of all but a very few thinkers to believe that all the things they hold good must be intimately connected, or at least compatible, with one another'. Indeed, this tendency proceeds to the actual *identification* of the things believed to be good. Yet this is clearly wrong. *Ceteris paribus*, it is a good thing that the man should be free to walk on the bridge; and, in the circumstances which Mill describes, it is another good — and indeed better — thing that he should be prevented from walking on the bridge and so drowning. But it does not follow that the second good thing is identical with the first good thing, so that when the man is restrained from walking on the bridge he is still (really) free to do so. The correct description of the situation is that a lesser good, namely, the man's freedom of movement is properly postponed to a different and greater good, namely, the preservation of his life.

The form of Mill's argument naturally invites consideration of the implication-formula 'If *Y* is a consequence of *X* and *A* wants *Y*, then *A* wants *X*'. This is commonly rendered 'He who wills the end wills the means' and regarded as a truism. But here again it is easy to show by the same method that arguments in the corresponding inference-pattern are not in fact valid. It may be perfectly true both that if John Doe kills his father he will inherit his father's fortune, and also that John Doe wants to inherit his father's fortune, and yet be quite false that John Doe wants to kill his father.

4. Desire, Pleasure and Liberty

Alternatively, our autocrat might argue thus: 'My people do not really want . . . etc.; for they certainly would not like democracy if they got it; so I am not really denying . . . etc.'   (A4)   This is the argument which Bosanquet uses. (Q2, Sec. 1) However, it too is invalid. For it relies on the supposed fact that '*A* wants *X*' entails '*A* would like *X* if he got it'. But there is no such entailment: there is nothing illogical in '*A* wants *X*, but *X* will not make him *happy* if he gets it'. If '*A* wanted *X*' and '*A* likes *X*' are both true, that is a matter of fact, not of logic; and quite often the latter happens to be false when the former is true. As Jean Austin[17] points out: '. . . though we may very much want , . . to bring about some specific state of affairs, we may not at all like it when we have done so. This is the moral of many legends: we may have to use the last of our three wishes to wish away the sausages that landed on our nose as the result of the granting of the first.'

The second step in A4 depends on the false conditional statement 'If *A* does not (really) want to *D* (e.g. vote), then he is not (really) unfree — i.e. is (really) free — when he is *restrained from D*ing.' Now, 'restrain' and 'constrain' are symmetrical verbs, since being restrained from *D*ing is identical with being constrained to not *D*, and being constrained to *D* is identical with being restrained from not *D*ing.[18] Therefore, the preceding false conditional statement is equivalent to 'If *A* does not (really) want to *D*, then he is not (really) unfree — i.e. is (really) free — when he is *constrained to* not *D*.' Hence Rousseau's[19] contention that one can be 'forced to be free', i.e. that one can be free to *D* even when he is compelled to not *D*. It is the falsity of the conditional statement which explains the paradox.

As with A3, the cause of the mistake in A4 probably lies in the tendency to identify things which are connected but different. The connexion between Desire and Pleasure is certainly close, since, as a general rule even if not always, men both want to get what they like and also like getting what they want.[20] Moreover, although '*A* wants *X*' does not entail '*A* would like *X*', it does entail '*A* thinks he would like *X*', and it is easy to confuse the last two formulas. There is evident absurdity in saying 'I want cannabis although I believe (or know) that I shall not like it'. The philosopher's old friend, the masochist, provides no exception to this. For the masochist is not the man who wants a whipping although he believes (or thinks he knows) that he will not like it when he gets it. On the contrary, he is the man who wants a whipping because he believes (or thinks he knows) that he will like it when he gets it. The proclivity to identify wanting something with liking it is plainly revealed in common speech, since — as was noted earlier — we say indifferently 'Do as you want' and 'Do as you please.' (Sec. 2)

Finally, since '*A* wants *X*' entails '*A* thinks he would like *X*', it is natural to wonder whether the converse also holds. But the answer is clearly negative, because one can quite well say, e.g., 'I think I should like heroin if I tried it; nevertheless, I do not want to try it.' One would say this if, for instance, he feared that he would become addicted to heroin if he tried it.

5. Desire, Need and Liberty

Yet another argument which the autocrat might employ goes like this: 'My people do not really want . . . etc.; for democracy is the last thing that they want at this time; so I am not really denying . . . etc.'   (A5) It is invalid because it equivocates on two different senses of the word 'want', viz. 'desire' and 'need', which it will be convenient to distinguish as 'want(d)' and 'want(n)' respectively. For the autocrat infers from the premiss 'my people do not want(n) democracy at this time' the conclusion 'my people do not (really) want(d) democracy'.

That it is indeed 'want(n)' which appears in the premiss and 'want(d)' in the conclusion is clear from the context; and this is true generally. When it is said, e.g., that what Britain wants is another Cromwell, the chances are that the speaker is saying what, in his opinion, Britons want(n); though it is admittedly possible that he is reporting the findings of a poll on what Britons want(d) in this matter. Again, that 'War on Want' is a philanthropic slogan and not an ascetic one can be inferred from observing that those who act on it occupy themselves with distributing food etc. to those who want(n) it, and not in withholding food etc. from those who want(d) it. Yet again, when King Belshazzar was weighed in the balances and found wanting,[21] he was discovered to be, not ravenous, but impious. He was found to be, not wanting(d) food, but wanting(n) in proper reverence for the Lord.

As Professor Peters[22] points out, one main difference between 'want(d)' and 'want(n)' is that the latter is evaluative whereas the former is not. The analysis of 'want(d)' will be given later, when it will be shown to be partly descriptive and partly imperative, but not at all normative. (Sec. 6) But the normative force of 'want(n)' is easy to see. When the general of the division says of a subaltern 'That young man wants a haircut', he is most unlikely to mean that the subaltern wants(d) a haircut. In all probability he means that the subaltern wants(n) a haircut in order to reach the standard of smartness expected of an officer of the division. Another difference between 'want(d)' and 'want(n)' is that the possible subjects of the former verb are a smaller class than are the possible subjects of the latter verb. Both Jones and his car can want(n) water, but whereas Jones can also want(d) water, his car cannot. There is a third use of 'want', namely 'want(l)', in the sense of 'lacks'. 'It wants five minutes to ten' obviously does not ascribe a desire to 'it'; but neither, on the other hand, does it imply that the later time is in some way better than the earlier time.

As is often the case when one word is used for more than one concept, there are important connexions between 'want(d)' and 'want(n)'. When the normal, healthy man wants(n) X, then he also tends to want(d) X. This is obviously true of food, drink, sleep, etc. But of course the converse does not hold, because normal, healthy persons generally want(d) many more things than they want(n); though this point is complicated by the consideration that, since needs are indeterminate, a man's list of his wants(n) *can* be stretched to coincide with the list of his wants(d). The position of the abnormal, unhealthy man is, then, not that he wants(d) things that he does not want(n) to have. It is rather that he wants(d) things that he wants(n) not to have, i.e. things that are bad for him. This is the situation of the alcoholic, the chain-smoker, etc.

It would be wrong to think that the notion of 'want' can be completely elucidated simply by distinguishing between 'want(d)', 'want(l)', and 'want(n)'. For the meanings of 'want(d)' and 'want(n)' themselves need to be explained. As just said, an analysis of 'want(d)' will be advanced in the next Section. But the foregoing remarks on 'want(n)', though sufficient for present purposes, by no means exhaust the question. In fact, Peters[23] finds that 'the concept of "need" is a very dangerous and ambiguous one'. To mention only one of his points by way of illustration: it is necessary to distinguish the non-technical uses of 'need' (or 'want(n)'), such as those considered above, from its technical use in psychological theory, where the concepts of 'need' and 'need-satisfaction' provide one familiar type of all-inclusive explanations in terms of 'end-states'. But it would not be relevant to pursue the analysis of 'want(n)' any further here.

The psychologists' concepts of 'need' and 'need-satisfaction' strongly recall Barry's concepts of 'want' and 'want-satisfaction', and we must now apply the distinction between 'want(d)' and 'want(n)' to his definition of 'interest'. (Q3, Sec. 1) Is his definition true or false? The question cannot be answered unless one knows whether the 'wants' which appears in it is 'wants(d)' or 'wants(n)'. If Barry means the former, his definition is false. For it involves, e.g., that if A wants(d) opium, then the policy of allowing the unrestricted import of opium into A's country is in his interest; which is untrue. But if Barry means the latter, his definition is true, since there is indeed a close connexion of meaning between 'interest', 'want(n)' and — be it added — 'good'. For 'Guinness is good for you', 'You need Guinness' and 'It is in your interest to drink Guinness' are all equivalent in meaning, if not in advertising-power. This link between 'need' and 'good' brings out the correctness of Peters' contention that 'want(n)' is a normative notion.

Finally, the distinction between 'want(d)' and 'want(n)' throws light on Rousseau's paradox about being 'forced to be free'. (See Sec. 4) Maybe he reached the conclusion that one can be forced to be free by reasoning thus: '(1) A can be forced to do what he wants; (2) If and only if A does what he wants, then he is free; therefore, (3) A can be forced to be free.' In appraising this argument, it is first necessary to become clear whether 'wants' in (1) and (2) means 'wants(d)' or 'wants(n)'. In (2), it is 'wants(d)', for (2) is equivalent to Mill's definition of 'liberty'. (Q1, Sec. 1) But in (1), 'wants' may mean either 'wants(d)' or 'wants(n)'. If it means 'wants(n)', then (1) is true, since A can certainly be compelled to act in his own interest. But the argument nevertheless fails to prove (3) true because it is invalid through equivocation, since 'wants' has different meanings in (1) and (2). If, on the other hand, 'wants' means 'wants(d)', (1) is again true, but the argument again fails to prove (3) true because, although it is valid, (2) is false. To explain these two points: (1) is true because, as we have seen earlier, A can be forced to do what he wants(d), since 'A wants(d) to D' is irrelevant to 'A is forced to D'. E.g. I can be compelled by law not to import cannabis when I want not to do so. Similarly, (2) is false because 'A wants(d) to D' is irrelevant to 'A is free to D'. (See Sec. 2)

The point of the criticism of the argument imputed to Rousseau in the preceding paragraph can also be put as follows. Since A can, logically, be forced to do what he wants(d), but cannot, logically, be forced to be free, being free cannot consist in doing what one wants(d), as Mill avers. This Rousseau sometimes saw, as when he writes 'Liberty consists less in doing what we want than in not being subject to another's will.'[24] However, this is not his main view of liberty, which is rather that 'obedience to a law which we prescribe to ourselves is liberty'.[25] Hegel[26] is equally critical of Mill's sort of definition: '. . . if we hear it said that the definition of freedom is the ability to do what we please, such an idea can only be taken to reveal an utter immaturity of thought, for it contains not even an inkling of right, ethical life, and so forth'. Yet the distinction between 'want(d)' and 'want(n)' may shed light on the Hegelian notion of freedom too. Perhaps Hegelians interpret the specious proposition (2), above, as meaning 'A is free if and only if he does what he wants(n)'. For, on this definition, to be free is to do what is *good* for one, or to behave *reasonably*, and to be liable to be *forced* to be free by another — since, as just said, one can be constrained to act in his own interest.

6. Knowledge, Command and Liberty

We will consider now a final argument which the autocrat might use, namely this one: 'My people do not really want . . . etc.; for it is for me to say what they want, since I am the best judge of that, and I know that they do not want democracy; so I am not really denying . . . etc.' (A6) This argument is exposed to an objection which may be put in the form of the following dilemma: The 'want' in the premiss 'it is for me . . . not want democracy' is either 'want(d)' or 'want(n)'. If it is 'want(d)', then the premiss is false, so that the argument fails to prove the truth of the conclusion. If it is 'want(n)', then the argument is invalid because equivocal, and so again fails to prove the truth of the conclusion. Now to show this.

There are a number of arguments to show that, if 'want' is taken in the sense of 'want(d)', then the premiss in question is false. Firstly, there is the argument that B never knows what A wants(d) better than A does because A's wants(d) are inward occurrences which can only be discovered by the introspection of A himself. This is the Cartesian doctrine of Privileged Access, and it is criticised accordingly by Ryle,[27] who maintains that '. . . "want" and "desire" do not denote pangs, itchings or gnawings . . . desire and aversion are, then, not "internal" episodes which their owner witnesses, but his associates do not witness'.

Secondly, there is the argument that B never knows what A wants (d) better than A does, because A cannot want(d) X without knowing that he wants(d) it, so that B can at best know what A wants(d) equally as well as A knows it. The reason is that 'I know what I want(d)' is an analytic and *a priori* truth. This is McGuinness's[28] thesis. He meets the obvious objection that there are cases where B can and does claim to know what A (really) wants(d) better than A himself does by saying that his thesis is true in the 'primary' sense of 'want(d)', and that all senses in which his thesis is false are 'secondary' senses. A familiar case of such a secondary use is 'unconscious wanting(d)', where the psychiatrist may not only claim correctly to know what his patient really wants(d) better than the patient himself does, but eventually get his patient to agree with him about what he really wants(d). (See A2, Sec. 2)

Thirdly, there is the argument that it is never for B to say what A

wants(d), because this is a thing that only *A* can say. The reason is that 'I want(d) *X*' means 'I choose *X*', and only I can, logically, make my choices. On this view, to say 'I want(d) *X*' is to perform an 'executive', i.e. illocutionary,[29] speech-act. This is Toulmin's[30] position.

There is something to be learnt from all three of these theses. For, in my submission, 'I want(d) *X*' means 'I feel deprived, and I think (or I know) that *X* would satisfy me, so (please) give me *X*'. One can recognise the presence of all three constituents in the meaning by reflecting on the oddity of saying any of the following three things: (1) 'I want(d) *X*, but I do not feel in any way deprived'; (2) 'I want(d) *X*, but I think (or I know) that *X* would not satisfy me (or that I should not like *X* if I got it)'; and (3) 'I want(d) *X*, but (please) do not give it to me'. The paradoxical character of statement (2) was discussed earlier. (Sec. 4) Of these three constituents, (1) and (2) are descriptive, but (3) is not. However, (3) is not elective, as Toulmin maintains, but ràther imperative, and expresses either an order or a request. For, as we saw earlier, although 'Do as you choose' is indeed equivalent to 'Do as you want', choosing presupposes the existence of alternatives, whereas wanting(d) does not. (Sec. 2) In the debate between Toulmin on the one hand and Abelson[31] and Ezorsky on the other about whether 'I want(d) *X*' is descriptive or not, there is right on both sides. *Pace* Ryle, the Privileged Access thesis is also right in that it gives a true account of the first component of the meaning of 'I want(d) *X*'. The feelings of frustration and deprivation suffered by the man who has no voice in choosing his governors and who says 'I want(d) democracy' are genuine, private introspectibles; just as are the pangs suffered by the hungry man who says 'I want food'. Further, my analysis shows why '*A* wants(d) *X*' entails '*A* believes (or thinks he knows) that he would like *X*', but does not entail '*A* would like *X*'. (See Secs. 2, 4) For although *A* is not normally mistaken about his feeling dissatisfied, he may well be mistaken in his belief that what will allay this feeling is his getting *X*. It is quite possible that what is required in order to do that is his getting, not *X*, but *Y*. This explains in turn the third of the three senses of '*A* does not know what he wants(d)', which we distinguished earlier. (Sec. 2) In this sense, as Toulmin suggests, the man who knows what he wants(d), or who knows his own mind, is the man whose beliefs about what would relieve his feelings of deprivation tend to be right. In this sense, when *A* says of himself 'I do not know what I want(d)', he is saying that, to date, his beliefs about what would satisfy him have proved incorrect, and that he is now unable to imagine what would do so. And when *A* says of *B* 'He does not know what he wants(d)', his evidence for his assertion is likely to include his observations that B switches inexplicably from pursuing one goal to pursuing another, or pursues simultaneously goals which are in fact incompatible.

My analysis also makes it possible to decide whether it is for A or for B to say what A wants(d). It is for A to say, for the following reasons. Firstly, because A generally knows better than B whether or not he has a feeling of dissatisfaction — or, for that matter, any other feeling. Secondly, because only A can, logically, give his orders (or make his requests), such as '(Please) give me political liberty'. One may object to this that actually we do speak of B giving A's orders. The reply is that we do indeed, but that this manner of speaking must not be allowed to trip us. When the waiter gives the diner's order to the cook, the verb 'gives' means 'transmits', not 'issues'. B can give (= transmit) A's order to C, but he cannot, logically, give (= issue) A's order to C, since if B issues the order it is necessarily his order and not A's. So similarly with choice, a point which arises out of Toulmin's analysis of 'I want(d) X' as 'I choose X'. When, at A's request, B chooses between X and Y for him, B is said to make A's choice for him. But this locution must not be permitted to mislead us either. In this situation, the choice is in fact no less B's than if he had made it on his own behalf and not on A's. Finally, it is for A to say what he wants(d) because he tends to know best whether or not X would satisfy him, provided only that he is adult and sane. The last proposition is true because it is analytic, since being the best judge of whether or not he would like X if he got it forms an important part of what is *meant* by calling a person 'adult' and 'sane'. The upshot is, then, that if 'want' in the premiss of A6 means 'want(d)', then A6 fails to prove the truth of the conclusion because that premiss is false.

Taking now the other horn of the dilemma, the question is whether it can be true that it is for the autocrat to pronounce on what his people want(n), since he is the best judge of that. The question is as contentious as it is important, and the different answers to it reflect two great opposed traditions in social and political thought.

On the one hand, writers in the liberal and utilitarian tradition maintain that A tends to know best what he wants(n), and argue from this to *laisser-faire* in political economy and democracy in politics. E.g., Mill[32] contends that '*laisser-faire* . . . should be the general practice' on the ground that, on the whole, 'individuals are the best judges of their own interest'. This last proposition is now generally known as the Principle of Rational Self-interest.[33] But he admits that this non-interference rule is subject to large exceptions, the exceptions to the rule being in the main the exceptions to the Principle. Education is such an exception, since it is false that here 'the consumer is a competent judge of the commodity'. Furthermore, Mill[34] tries to prove that 'democracy is the ideally best form of government' from the premiss that 'each person is the only safe guardian . . . of his own . . . interests'.

Mill's remarks invite the following comments. Firstly, it is an important point that the Principle is proportional (or statistical), and not universal; i.e., that it is claimed to be true only as a general rule. Secondly, one should not perhaps conclude too readily that, because the Principle is approximately true in economic matters, it is also approximately true in political matters. It is quite possibly true that each tends to be the best judge of his economic interests, but false that each tends to be the best judge of his political interests. E.g., the public is more liable to be deceived by the false promises of politicians than it is by the fraudulent prospectuses of confidence-men. Thirdly, there is a great deal of difference between saying, as Mill does in the economic context, that each is the best *judge* of his interests, and saying as he does in the political context that each is the best *guardian* of his interests. For, whereas to be a good judge of one's interests requires only intelligence and knowledge, to be a good guardian of them requires not only these but also power.[35] A perfectly intelligent and completely informed pauper may be a very poor guardian of his interests when making a wage-contract with a rich employer because his bargaining-position is so weak. Mill[36] himself recognises this fact when he argues for governmental interference with freedom of contract respecting hours of labour on the ground that 'there are matters in which the interference of law is required, not to overrule the judgement of individuals respecting their own interest, but to *give effect* to that judgement'. (My italics) Finally, it is well worth recording Plamenatz's[37] conclusion on this liberal and utilitarian thesis: 'that every man is apt to be the best judge of his own needs is not enough to justify even *laisser-faire*, let alone democracy'. The reader is referred to his illuminating discussion for his reasons for this opinion. (The part played by the Principle of Rational Self-interest in Political Economy is discussed in Essay 12. The Principle is indeed about interests and not about needs, as Plamenatz claims. Interests and needs are, of course, different. If *A* needs *X*, then it is in *A*'s interest that *A* should have *X*. But it may be in *A*'s interest that *A* should have *X* although *A* does not need *X*. For example, if *A* has 1 billion pounds, it is in *A*'s interest that *A* should have another 1 billion pounds, although *A* does not need it.)

On the other hand, writers in the paternalist and collectivist tradition have contended that, in political affairs, there not only can be, but ought to be, Another who always knows better what the citizens want(n) than they do themselves. This Other manifests himself in various guises. Now he appears as the Philosopher-King, who is the best judge of what his subjects want(n) just as, in one of Plato's[38] favourite tropes, the physician knows best what is best for his patients. Then he appears as the Legislator, the desirability of whose existence Rousseau[39] establishes as follows: 'How can a blind multitude, which often does not know what it wants, because it rarely knows what is good for it, carry out for itself so great and difficult an enterprise as a system of legislation? . . . This makes a legislator necessary'. Yet again he appears as the Hero, of whom Hegel[40] is reported to have said: 'The great man of the age is the one who can . . . tell his age what its will is, and accomplish it.' Not least, he figures as the Leader of the 'Party of the Proletariat', whose infallible knowledge, and perfect devotion to the provision, of what the people want(n), is a truth by definition.[41]

In fact, of course, whether rulers know better what the ruled want(n) than do the ruled themselves, depends on which rulers and which ruled one is speaking of. Enlightened despots over barbaric nations have certainly done so; but there have been many governors with a less sure grasp of their subjects' interests than their subjects have had. In Britain today, it is still probably true that the gentleman in Whitehall knows better what the citizens want(n) than do the majority of the citizens themselves; but this is likely to become progressively less true if the general level of education rises.

We may therefore grant our autocrat, for the sake of argument, that he knows better what his people want(n) than they themselves do. But the concession avails him nothing, since although the premiss in his argument A6 is allowed to be true, the argument is invalid. For the first step in it is the move from 'My people do not want(n) democracy' to 'My people do not (really) want(d) democracy', which is clearly equivocal. In conclusion, it must be remembered that, even if this first step in A6 were valid, the argument would still fail, because the second step is also invalid. This is the step from 'My people do not (really) want(d) democracy' to 'I am not (really) denying them political liberty by withholding a democratic constitution', which commits the fallacy of *ignoratio elenchi*. As was said earlier, arguments A1-A5 are also exposed to this basic criticism. (Sec. 2) (The relation of Liberty to Desire is also discussed in Sec. 2 of Essay 3.)

7. Conclusion

It is submitted that A1-A6 comprise all the important 'Real Will' arguments on liberty. We have found each of them to be defective on more than one count, the chief count being the fallacy of *ignoratio elenchi* just referred to, which is common to them all. So much for what Hobhouse[42] correctly calls 'the most penetrating and subtle of all the intellectual influences which have sapped the rational humanitarianism of the eighteenth and nineteenth centuries'. For although Popper[43] is undoubtedly right in finding one main putative justification of the tyrannies of our era in their supposed 'inevitability', I am sure that an at least equally important one is the doctrine that these *régimes* do not really diminish liberty, because they do not really prevent people from doing anything that they really want to do.

We have also found that this same fundamental fallacy vitiates the definitions of 'liberty' given by Hobbes, Mill and others. (Sec. 2) Nor is it a coincidence that the same fault occurs both in these definitions and also in arguments A1-A6. For the Empiricist and Positivist thesis, that *A cannot be free to D unless (among other things) he wants(d) to D*, has generated the Rationalist and Idealist antithesis, that *A cannot (really) be unfree to D if he does not (really) want(d) to D*. Perhaps the dialectical movement has now reached the point where this 'contradiction' is resolved in a higher synthesis, which consists in recognition of the fact that whether or not *A* wants(d) to *D* is irrelevant to whether or not he is free to *D*; i.e., that *there is no connexion between Freedom and the Will*.

APPENDIX

The preceding essay was completed before the publication of Berlin's[44] *Four Essays on Liberty*. But since he raises in the Introduction an interesting point which bears directly on my main thesis, a short Appendix may be excused. Berlin there corrects an error in his 'Two Concepts of Liberty' to which a critic has drawn attention. Namely, that he begins this essay by expounding '*A* is free' as '*A* is not restrained from doing what he wants by *B*', notwithstanding that in the rest of the essay he criticises this notion of liberty. One criticism to which it is exposed is that 'if degrees of freedom were a function of the satisfaction of desires, I could increase freedom as effectively by eliminating desires as by satisfying them'.

It is of more than historical interest that one famous theory of liberty, the Stoic, amounts to precisely this. In the words of Epictetus[45]: '. . . freedom is secured not by the fulfilling of men's desires, but by the removal of desire'. Apparently Epictetus, like Hobbes, Mill and others, believes mistakenly that Liberty presupposes Desire.(See Sec. 2) For it is indeed true that, if 'A is free to D' presupposes 'A wants to D', then A cannot be unfree to D if he suppresses his desire to D; which seems to present the unfree with a solution to their problem.

However, this 'solution' is so unsatisfactory as to constitute no solution at all. For firstly, although it follows from the presupposition thesis that A cannot be *unfree* to D if he suppresses his desire to D, it also follows that, if he does this, he cannot be *free* to D either. Secondly, it is absurd to claim that the difficulty of A's unfreedom to D can be surmounted by bringing about a state of affairs in which the question of his being free, or unfree, to D just does not arise. Common sense recognises that it is not only morally repulsive, but also logically outrageous, to tell the autocrat's subjects that the way out of their difficulty in being politically unfree is to suppress their desire to have the vote. One might as well argue that, since Liberty presupposes Ability, the way to dispose of the problem of a prisoner's unfreedom of movement is to amputate his limbs. (See Sec. 2) Thirdly, the Stoic doctrine is in any case simply false, because if the people did suppress their desire to have the vote they would nevertheless still *be* just as politically unfree as they were before they did so, since Desire is irrelevant to Liberty. But they would indisputably no longer *feel* politically unfree if they suppressed this desire; for it is as true that 'A feels free to D' presupposes 'A wants to D' as it is false that 'A is free to D' presupposes 'A wants to D'. Presumably Epictetus too was misled into his paradoxical position through confusing being free with feeling free. However, it is also plausible to suppose that what he was really concerned to do was to abolish or mitigate the sense of unfreedom and not unfreedom itself. Indeed, his teaching probably provides the best anodyne available to despairing slaves. But he has nothing to say to those who hope to become, or to remain, freemen.

Notes

1. J.S. Mill, *On Liberty*, Ch. V.
2. B. Bosanquet, *The Philosophical Theory of the State* (London, 1899), p. 110.
3. B. Barry, *Political Argument* (London, 1965), pp. 176ff.

4. F. Rabelais, *La Vie très Horrifique du Grand Gargantua*, Ch. LVII.

5. G. Ezorsky, 'Wishing Won't — but Wanting Will' in S. Hook (ed.), *Dimensions of Mind* (New York, 1960).

6. B.F. Skinner, 'Concept-formation in Philosophy and Psychology' in Hook, *Dimensions of Mind*.

7. Jean Austin, 'Pleasure and Happiness', repr. in J.B. Schneewind (ed.), *Mill* (New York, 1968), p. 235.

8. J.L. Austin, *Sense and Sensibilia* (Oxford, 1962), Ch. VII. Cf: '. . . for us anything, which comes short when compared with Reality, gets the name of appearance.' (F.H. Bradley, *Appearance and Reality* (London, 1899), p. 485.)

9. M. Cranston, *Freedom: a New Analysis* (London, 1953), p. 15; W.L. Weinstein, 'The Concept of Liberty in 19th Century English Political Thought', *Political Studies*, Vol. XIII, Oxford, 1965.

10. J.P. Plamenatz, *Consent, Freedom and Political Obligation* (Oxford, 1938), pp. 109ff.

11. T. Hobbes, *Leviathan*, Pt. II, Ch. XXI; E.F. Carritt, 'Liberty and Equality', *Law Quarterly Review*, Vol. LVI, 1940.

12. J.D. Mabbott, *The State and the Citizen* (London, 1947), p. 70.

13. I. Berlin, 'Two Concepts of Liberty', repr. in A. Quinton (ed.), *Political Philosophy* (Oxford, 1967), p. 142. Plamenatz, *Political Obligation*, pp. 110ff.

14. Berlin, 'Two Concepts'; Plamenatz, *Political Obligation*.

15. Plamenatz, *Political Obligation*, Chs. II, III. B. Mayo, 'Is there a case for the General Will?' in P. Laslett (ed.), *Philosophy, Politics and Society* (Oxford, 1956).

16. Berlin, 'Two Concepts', p. 197, note 1.

17. Jean Austin, *'Pleasure and Happiness'*, p. 238.

18. S.I. Benn and R.S. Peters, *Social Principles and the Democratic State* (London, 1959), p. 213, note.

19. J.J. Rousseau, *Social Contract*, Bk. I, Ch. VII.

20. A. Kenny, *Action, Emotion and Will* (London, 1963), p. 127.

21. *Daniel*, V, 27.

22. R.S. Peters, *The Concept of Motivation* (London, 1958), pp. 17f. Benn and Peters, *Social Principles*, pp. 142ff.

23. Peters, *Motivation*, p. 128. H.B. Acton, *The Illusion of the Epoch* (London, 1955), pp. 112ff.

24. *Letters from the Mountain*, No. VIII.

25. *Social Contract*, Bk. I, Ch. VIII.

26. G.W.F. Hegel, *Philosophy of Right*, tr. T.M. Knox (Oxford, 1942), p. 27. Plamenatz, *Political Obligation*, pp. 109f.

27. G. Ryle, *The Concept of Mind* (London, 1949), p. 109.

28. B.F. McGuinness, 'I Know What I Want', *Aristotelian Society Proceedings*, Vol. LVII, London, 1957.

29. J.L. Austin, *How to Do Things with Words* (Oxford, 1962), pp. 99ff.

30. S.E. Toulmin, 'Concept-Formation in Philosophy and Psychology' in Hook, *Dimensions of Mind*.

31. R. Abelson, 'A Spade is a Spade, so Mind your Language' in Hook, *Dimensions of Mind*.

32. *Principles of Political Economy*, 7th edn., Bk. V, Ch. XI, secs. 7-12.

33. H. Clay, *Economics* (London, 1916), Chs. XXI, XXII.

34. *Representative Government*, Ch. III.

35. Weinstein, 'The Concept of Liberty', pp. 148f.

36. *Political Economy*, Bk. V, Ch. XI, sec. 12.

37. Plamenatz, *Man and Society*, Vol. II (London, 1963), p. 30.

38. R. Bambrough, 'Plato's Political Analogies' in Laslett, *Philosophy, Politics and Society*. He refers in particular to the *Gorgias* and *Politicus*.

39. *Social Contract*, Bk. II, Ch. VI.

40. Hegel, *Philosophy of Right*, p. 295. Cf.: 'It was not an abstract greatness (Hegel) admired in Napoleon, but the quality of expressing the historical need of the time.' (H. Marcuse, *Reason and Revolution* (London, 1941), pp. 169f.)

41. Cf.: 'Since the proletarian dictatorship *is* the dispossession and the suppression of the capitalists, it *is* also the end of exploitation. We might almost say that exploitation is *defined* out of the social order through the dictatorship of the proletariat.' (Acton, *The Illusion of the Epoch*, p. 244.) T.D. Weldon, *The Vocabulary of Politics* (London, 1953), pp. 130f.

42. L.T. Hobhouse, *The Metaphysical Theory of the State* (London, 1918), p. 6.

43. K.R. Popper, *The Poverty of Historicism* (London, 1957).

44. *Four Essays on Liberty* (Oxford, 1969), pp. xxxviiff. Cf. pp. 135ff.

45. Epictetus, *Discourses*, tr. P.E. Matheson (Oxford, 1916), Bk. IV, Ch. I.

2

FAIRNESS AND FORTUNE

1. Introduction

We call many different sorts of things and persons fair or unfair. However, in this essay I am concerned with fairness only as it relates to chance; and here the notions which need to be examined seem to be those of a fair sample, a fair device, and a fair competition. I aim to expose three important mistakes, two errors of the vulgar and one error of the philosophers, as Berkeley would have called them. But I hope that the discussion has constructive as well as critical value. For, although much has been said about justice and probability severally, not much has been said about the relationship between them.

2. Fair Samples: Probability and Randomness

The expression 'fair sample' has long been current in ordinary, as con-trasted with technical use, and its meaning is generally familiar. The word 'sample' means much the same as 'specimen', and saying that X is a fair sample of Y is like saying that, for example, a certain man is a fair specimen of a Norman or a typical Norman. The term 'fair' in 'fair sample' has evaluative as well as descriptive meaning, and is plainly commendatory. Indeed, fair samples might just as well be called good samples. The sense of 'good' involved here is straightforwardly instrumental, and the descriptive meaning of 'fair sample' is revealed by considering what a sample is for. Its purpose is, of course, to convey information about that which it is a sample of; and it will do this if it resembles the latter exactly in respect of properties deemed relevant. So a piece of cloth in a tailor's pattern-book, for instance, is a fair sample of the roll of cloth from which it is taken if it matches the latter exactly in respect of, say, weight, texture and colour.

In the popular view, then, the defining relation between a fair sample and the thing sampled is exact resemblance in respect of some relevant properties. Another relation between them is random selection, meaning 'unbiased selection', such as might be effected by pricking names in a list with a pin with one's eyes shut. This second relation is thought to be linked with the first one by the fact that a sample is unlikely to be fair (as defined) if it is biased. Thirdly, any sample, fair or unfair, is related to the thing sampled as part to whole. This is so not only in the case of the relation of pattern to roll, but also in cases where the relation could be regarded differently, namely, as that of sub-set to set; as when a sample of applies is taken from a barrelful in order to discover what proportion of the latter is rotten.

Finally, the popular notion about the size of samples is as follows. It has more than one measure; for example the size of the sample of apples (above) could be determined by measuring either its volume or its weight. Moreover, size is important because the larger a random sample is, the more likely it is to be fair in the sense defined. This idea is linked with that of the relation of sample to thing sampled as part to whole. For plainly, in the limiting case where the sample is so big that it coincides with the thing sampled, what is true of the former must also be true of the latter. So similarly, it is thought, when the sample is big enough to be a considerable proportion of the thing sampled, then what is true of the former is probably also true of the latter.

With the rise of statistical theory, however, the expression 'fair sample' acquired new and technical descriptive meanings while keeping its old evaluative meaning. In the scientific conception, 'fair sample' means descriptively, firstly, 'random sample'; and a sample is defined to be randomly selected when every possible sample of its size, n (i.e. having n individual members), has an equal chance of being chosen. The difficulty about a random sample is not how to define it, but how to obtain it; and this practical problem is met by employing a reliable random sampling device, such as Tippett's random sampling numbers or a chance-machine like Ernie (abbr. E) which selects the winning Premium Bond numbers.

Random sampling is the best technique to use with homogeneous populations (i.e. things sampled), such as a well-mixed bagful of marbles of the same shape, size, weight and hardness. But with non-homogeneous populations, such as the British electorate, a better technique is stratified sampling, which is used in, for example, the Gallup polls. In this method, the population is stratified in respect of properties (for example age) which are relevant to the one under investigation (for example voting Liberal); individuals are selected at random from each stratum; and the sample is made up by including in it individuals from each stratum in the proportion in which the strata exist in the population. Stratified samples, which statisticians also call 'representative samples', are therefore weighted combinations of random sub-samples. Stratified samples cannot be less reliable than pure random samples and may be more so. For suppose that the colour-composition of the marbles in a bag is one-half white, but that the population is spatially non-homogeneous in respect of colour, three-quarters of the marbles in the right half of the bag being white and one-quarter of the marbles in the left half of the bag being white. Then a simple random sample from the bag may misrepresent the colour-composition of the population by including more (or less) than one-half the marbles from the right (or left) half of the bag; whereas with a sample which is appropriately stratified this source of error is eliminated. In the scientific conception, therefore, the descriptive meaning of 'fair sample' is, secondly, 'stratified sample'.[1]

Stratified samples must be distinguished from quota samples, which are also much used in social investigations. The latter resemble the former in being composed by including in them individuals from relevant strata of the population, but differ in that the selection from the strata is made not randomly but purposively by the investigator. For this reason, quota samples are regarded by many as unreliable because biased.[2]

A comparison of the scientific conception with the popular conception of a fair sample, then, reveals the following essential differences. First, in the popular conception, fairness is defined in terms of resemblance between sample and population, whereas in the scientific conception it is defined in terms of how the sample is selected from the population. Interestingly, the everyday expression 'a fair selection of X' is ambiguous in this respect. Thus, to say that the candidates admitted were a fair selection of those who applied is to say that the former were an unbiased or random selection, not a typical selection, of the latter. But to say that an exhibition of an artist's paintings is a fair selection of his works is to say that the former is a typical selection, not a random selection, of the latter. Secondly, the scientific definition of 'random sample' in terms of equiprobability is a considerable refinement on the popular notion of a random sample; just as the devices for obtaining random samples which are judged reliable by statisticians are much more sophisticated than the devices which the common man regards as good enough. Thirdly, to the common man 'representative sample' means the same as what he understands by 'fair sample', namely, an exactly matching sample. But to the statistician 'representative sample' means 'stratified sample'. Fourthly and vitally, in the statistical view, the relation of sample to population is that of sub-set to set (i.e. class-inclusion), not that of part to whole, as in the popular view.[3] Finally, in the statistical conception, there is one unique measure of the size of sample, namely, the number (n) of individual members of the sub-set; not more than one measure, as in the popular conception. As for the importance of size of sample, the scientific view is that what is true of a large random sample is probably *approximately* true of the population, not probably *exactly* true, as in the popular view. For example if one-half of the marbles in a large random sample are white, one may infer that *about*, not *exactly* one-half of the marbles in the bag are probably white.[4]

An important mistake arises from these facts. Namely, that the common man tends to overestimate the reliability of what *statisticians* call fair samples (i.e. either random samples or stratified samples) and representative samples (i.e. stratified samples), because he wrongly identifies these with what *he* calls fair samples or representative samples (i.e. in both cases, exactly matching samples). In particular, he fails to appreciate that the statistician's fair sample is at best a probable near-match of the population and may be at worst a complete mis-match of it.

The cause of the mistake is retaining the same old name, 'fair sample', of the popular conception for the new scientific conception; a practice which is natural, if confusing, since the evaluative meaning is the same in both cases although the descriptive meaning is quite different. It is the sort of situation which often arises in the history of science. Thus, men had an intuitive idea, 'force', long before Newton defined it as 'product of mass and acceleration'. But a time of conceptual confusion ensued when the new notion was first superimposed upon the original one under the same old name. So similarly here; for statistical theory is still quite a young science — only about as old as this century, in fact — and its concepts have not yet been generally assimilated.

This is an error of the vulgar and not (one trusts) of the philosophers. Ideally, the situation could be rectified by the common man coming to grasp the basic facts about sampling set out in the preceding paragraphs. But that cure would be long and complicated. Meanwhile, the statisticians could apply a remedy which would be short, simple and effective. They could strike from their vocabulary the expressions 'fair sample' and 'representative sample', and retain instead only 'random sample' and 'stratified sample' respectively.

3. Fair Devices: Probability and Propensity

By 'a fair device' I mean, for example, a fair die (for dicing with), a fair bowl (for bowling with), or a fair sampling-device. Fair sampling devices reveal the connection between fair devices and fair samples. For we have seen (Sec. 2, above) that the way to obtain a fair (or random) sample is to use a reliable fair (or random) sampling-device. But a fair die is just such a device. Thus, one acceptable way of selecting one of six men at random is to put the men into one-one correspondence with the faces of a fair die, and to choose the man who corresponds to the face which lands uppermost when the die is fairly thrown.

The notion of a fair die, or equivalent fair device, is central to the propensity theory of probability, which I shall now discuss. Originally outlined by Peirce and Popper, this theory has recently received a first-rate elaboration by Mellor,[5] whose version of it I shall consider accordingly.

The gist of Mellor's theory is as follows (p. 122) (I) (1) 'This die (abbr. D) is fair' is a propensity statement which *means* (2) 'If D were to be thrown fairly many times, then it would show each face uppermost an approximately equal number of times'. (II) (3) 'D has been thrown fairly many times and has shown each face uppermost an approximately equal number of times' *displays* the truth of (1). (III) The truth of (1) is the justification of the corresponding chance statement (4) 'The probability (*p*) of D landing with an odd number uppermost when thrown with a fair throwing-device is one-half.' (1) *justifies* (4) because (4) not only expresses the degree of belief of its maker, but also asserts that this degree of belief is reasonable. (IV) The subjunctive conditional statement (2) is an *induction* which is therefore inductively probable (or improbable, or certain, or contracertain). It is an induction from the evidence of the indicative conjunctive statement (3) (p. 77).

Now it follows from (I), (III) and (IV) that statistical probability (or chance, abbr. SP) presupposes inductive probability (or degree of confirmation, abbr. IP), since any chance statement needs a corresponding induction to justify it. But this misrepresents the relation of SP to IP by greatly exaggerating the dependence of the former on the latter. This is a philosophical error rather than a vulgar one, but is nevertheless serious. For the relation of SP to IP is a major problem in the philosophy of probability, and indeed its ability to give an acceptable account of it is a good test of the worth of any philosophical theory of probability. What, then, is wrong with the propensity theory?

As to the relation of (1) to (2), there are four objections to the thesis that (1) means (2).

First, (1) is a categorical statement whereas (2) is a conditional one, and no statement about what is the case means the same as any statement about what would be the case if certain conditions were realised. This is Berlin's[6] basic and correct objection to Phenomenalism, and the contention that (1) means (2) is wrong for the same reason as is the contention that 'D is hard' means 'If anyone were to have first the sort of visual sensation that one has on seeing a die, and then the sort of sensation of movement that one has on extending his hand, then he would have the sort of tactual sensation that one has on touching something hard.' For, as will be shown shortly, fairness is an occurrent property like hardness, and not a dispositional one like solubility.

Secondly, (1) is an evaluative statement (or judgement) whereas (2) is a descriptive statement. For 'fair' is evaluative when predicated of devices just as it is when predicated of samples.

Thirdly, (1) can be given as a non-trivial reason for (2). I.e., to say '(2) because (1)' is not to advance an argument in the valid but unhelpful form 'q because q'. Similarly, an objection to the thesis that 'X is good' means 'X is pleasant', is that the latter can be given as a non-trivial reason for the former. Furthermore, (2) provides a non-trivial reason for (1).

Fourthly, (2) can be false when (1) is true, and (2) can be true when (1) is false. This can happen by chance, i.e. for some unknown reason. For example, unconscious psycho-kinesis (abbr. UPK) may be a fact, and (2) may be false when (1) is true because A unconsciously wills D to fall with a preponderance of odd-numbered faces uppermost. Similarly, (2) may be true when (1) is false because A wills as just described and this psychic force exactly counteracts the gravitational force of D's bias in favour of even-numbered faces falling uppermost.

Although it is not the case that when (1) is true then (2) is true and conversely, it is the case that when either is true then the other is probably true. I.e. either is a good, though not a conclusive reason for the other, because the relationship between them is mutual inductive probabilification. It is like that between, for example, 'A is healthy' and 'A is active'.

The evaluative meaning of 'fair' in 'fair device' is 'good' in the instrumental sense, as in 'fair sample'. Similarly, the descriptive meaning of 'fair device' depends on the purpose which the device is intended to serve. Thus, (1) means descriptively (5) 'D is unbiased', because dice are for playing games of chance with, and these games require the probabilities of the six possible outcomes of a throw with a die to be equal. The fairness of D is one means to this end, and the fairness of the throwing of D is another. Similarly, 'E is fair' means descriptively 'E is unbiased', because E is intended to give every bond number an equal chance of being chosen. But 'This bowl (abbr. B) is fair' means descriptively 'B is biased', because bowls are for playing a game of skill with which requires them to move in a curved line rather than a straight one when bowled.

The conditions under which it is true to say that a device is fair depend on the purpose and nature of the device. Thus, the simple mechanical chance-device D is fair if its centre of gravity (abbr. CG) lies at its geometrical centre. But the simple mechanical skill-device B is fair if its CG is eccentric, which is achieved by turning it on a lathe. The complex electronic chance-device E will be fair if it is operationally faultless; i.e. if it lacks any occurrent property (such as wires not properly attached to terminals, fractures in switches, etc.) which would prevent it from operating as it is intended to operate.

Of course, *A* need not know these truth-conditions in order to be able to assert meaningfully that a device is fair or unfair. He may be quite ignorant of mechanics in general and of CGs in particular, and yet say meaningfully that D is fair; and he may be quite ignorant of electronics in general and of electric currents in particular, and yet say meaningfully that E is fair. The meaning of his assertion is that the device lacks any occurrent property — he knows not what — which would prevent it from operating as it is intended to operate.

The upshot is, then, that the meaning of (1) can be explained and understood without reference to (2).

Passing now to the relation of (1) to (3), (II) is false because (3) does not display the truth of (1) but evidences it. The difference is that 'to display' is what Ryle[7] calls 'an achievement verb' whereas 'to evidence' is not. To illustrate by an example of Austin's:[8] it is illogical to say that *A*'s outburst displayed (or manifested) anger although he was not angry really; but it is not illogical to say that the tremor in *A*'s voice evidenced (or was a symptom, or sign) of anger although he was not angry really. So (3) does not display the truth of (1) because (1) can chance to be false when (3) is true. This can happen in the same way as (1) can be false when (2) is true, namely, by UPK (see above).

The false belief, (II), lands the propensity theorists in the verificationist fallacy, i.e. the fallacy of thinking that, because (3) evidences (1), therefore (1) means (3). This is the same mistake as that which Mellor, following Kneale (*op. cit.*, pp. 193 f.), rightly attributes to the frequency theorists. For they suppose that (4) means (6) 'The relative frequency (*f*) of throws with an odd number uppermost among a large number of fair throws with this die is one-half', because (6) evidences (4). In fact, the propensity theory is actually inconsistent. Whereas (II) says that (3) displays the truth of (1), (IV) says that (3) evidences (2) which (according to (I)) is equivalent to (1). But I think that the inconsistency is concealed from the propensity theorists precisely because they fail to distinguish evidence from display.

In fact, (3), like (2), inductively probabilifies (1), and so is good but not conclusive evidence for it. Conversely, (1) explains (3). As Mellor points out, the approximately equal frequency of odd-numbered and even-numbered faces falling uppermost is not even good evidence for (1) unless we also know that the throws were fair. In the case of B, we need to know more. The fact that it described a curved path when bowled is not even good evidence for its fairness (i.e. bias) unless we know not only that it was delivered fairly (e.g. not overarm) but also that the green is a level green and not a crown green.

But it is not necessary to know (3) at all in order to establish (1). For, as is explained in introductory texts on mechanics, the way to find a body's CG is to perform a simple experiment on it, namely, to suspend it. So (1) is a *description* which is true or false, not a prediction (i.e. induction) which is probable or improbable. And it can be established to be true or false by observation. Consequently, the fact that (III) is true does not entail that SP presupposes IP. This is my thesis.

An analogy will clarify the point. There is an exact correspondence between the concept of fairness as predicated of chance-devices and the concept of road-worthiness as predicated of motor-vehicles. There could be a propensity theory of road-worthiness, according to which (1—) 'This car (abbr. C) is road-worthy' means (2—) 'If C were to be driven carefully many miles, then C would not break down'; and (3—) 'C has been driven carefully many miles and C has not broken down' displays the truth of (1—). But in fact (1—) means descriptively (5—) 'C is operationally faultless'. The conditions under which it is true to assert (1—) are that C lacks any occurrent property (such as leads not properly attached to sparking-plugs, a loose fan-belt, etc.) which would prevent it from operating as it is intended to operate, namely, so as to convey its occupants safely, comfortably and swiftly from point to point. However, *A* need not know any of these truth-conditions in order to be able to assert meaningfully that C is road-worthy; he can do so if he is quite ignorant of how cars work. So the meaning of (1—) can be explained without reference to (2—).

Finally, it is not necessary to know (3—) in order to establish (1—). For (1—) can be, and is established by checking C systematically for possible faults in a testing-station. However, the test in the station can be, and is cross-checked by a subsequent test on the road. Naturally, the results of the two tests are expected to agree. If the test in the station reveals no faults, then the mechanic is surprised when C breaks down during the subsequent test on the road. And when he then takes C back to the station for further testing, he expects this second test to disclose some fault which caused the breakdown and which the first test in the station had failed to reveal. Similarly, if *A*'s suspension experiment shows D to be unbiased, then he is surprised when D does not show each face uppermost an approximately equal number of times in a large number of fair throws. And when he then repeats the suspension experiment, he expects it to reveal that D's CG is eccentric after all.

4. Fair Competitions: Chance and Skill

When is a competition which involves chance unfair (or fair) for a competitor, and when is it unfortunate (or fortunate) for him? As first step towards answering this interesting and neglected question, let us inspect the ideas 'competition', 'game of chance' and 'game of skill'.

Some contests are not competitions. These are unregulated contests, for example a free fight. The difference between a boxing-match, which is a competition, and a free fight is that the former is governed by the Queensberry Rules whereas the latter is governed by no rules at all. Competitions are either 'for real' or for diversion, for example respectively commercial competitions and athletic competitions or games. But some games are not competitions, for example most children's games. All competitive contests, whether games or not, are either contests of chance or contests of skill. It will be convenient to consider first games of chance and games of skill, and then real-life competitions.

Although games of chance and games of skill are jointly exhaustive, they are not mutually exclusive. For, although what are called 'games of chance' involve no real skill, what are called 'games of skill' usually do involve chance. Chance enters into the latter in two different ways. First, by design. For example, in cricket, which team bats first is decided by tossing a coin. Secondly, by accident. In golf, for example, this is called a 'rub of the green', which is defined thus: 'A "rub of the green" occurs when a ball in motion is stopped or deflected by any outside agency'.[9]

Games of chance and games of skill are not exclusive in the further and special sense that either can be treated as if it were the other. Thus, football is a game of skill, not of chance. But many who 'do the Pools' know nothing of the game or the teams, and fill in their coupons at random. It is a possible procedure, but inept; like playing chess by choosing between moves permitted by the rules by means of a chance-device. Conversely, games of chance can be treated as games of skill. This is the case with those who play the former according to systems or strategies. It is a possible procedure, but pointless. For suppose that it is a question of deciding at what betting quotient (abbr. BQ) to offer to bet on throwing an odd number with a fair throw of this fair die (q). The theorem of Bernoulli referred to earlier (Note 4) tells us that, in a large number of such throws, the relative frequency, f, of throws of an odd number will approximately equal the probability, p, of a throw of an odd number. Consequently, he who bets on q at any BQ $\neq$ p will lose in the long run. (BQs are defined in terms of betting odds thus: if the odds on q are $n:m$, then the BQ on q is $n/(n + m)$. Thus BQs, like SPs, are measured by real numbers in the interval [0,1].)

So when is a contest (un)fair for a contestant and when is it (un)fortunate for him? Consider first a free fight between two contestants, *C1* and *C2*. This can only be fortunate for *C1* (if he wins), or unfortunate for him (if he does not win). It cannot be fair or unfair. For unfairness arises only when there is either foul play (that is, breach of the rules of the contest), or inequality in the arrangement of the contest. But since in unregulated contests there are no rules and no arrangement, the question of fairness does not arise.

Consider next, then, games of chance. Take a simple dicing-game, G, governed by certain rules, called 'Odds and Evens'. *C2* throws a die and *C1* calls 'Odd' or 'Evens'. When *C1* calls right, *C2* pays him 1p; and when he calls wrong he pays *C2* 1p. *C1* wins G if, after 1 hour, he has received from *C2* more than he has paid him; and similarly, *mutatis mutandis*, for losing and drawing. It may be said that G, like a free fight, can only be unfortunate for *C1* if he does not win and not unfair, because if there is foul play by *C2* or some inequality in the arrangement, then G is not (truly called) a game of chance. This is true, but trivial; as usual, it is unprofitable to employ the definitional stop. What matters is that *in fact* what are called games of chance usually are such; for example the games of chance played in any respectable household or well-ordered gaming establishment. This is because it is practically possible to eliminate the sources of unfairness, namely, foul play and inequality in the arrangement. The former arises when, say, contrary to the rules of G, the die is biased against odd numbers, and either (1) *C2* knows this but *C1* does not (which is deliberate foul play, or cheating, by *C2*); or (2) neither *C1* nor *C2* knows it (which is accidental foul play by *C2*). The latter arises when, say, *C2*'s throwing is biased against odd numbers. Factually and importantly, therefore, as well as 'logically' and trivially, games of chance are normally (un)fortunate for competitors but not (un)fair. (Games of chance are interesting in that with them fairness is identical with Equality, which is exceptional. See Subsec. 2.3 of Essay 8.

We pass, then, to games of skill. Take the example where *G* is a running-race, governed by certain rules, between *C1* and *C2*; and where there are also a referee, *R*, to enforce the rules, and an organiser, *0*, to make the arrangements for *G*. There are three sorts of case involving chance to be considered.

Case (1)

C1 does not win (i.e. he loses or draws) because he falls, and he falls because he slips on wet leaves which the wind has blown on to his lane but not on to *C2*'s lane. Here *G* is unfortunate, not unfair for *C1*. The case corresponds to a rub of the green in golf; the 'outside agency' is the leaves. It may be objected that *G* is unfair, not unfortunate for *C1*, because there is an inequality in the arrangement, since there are wet leaves on his lane but not on *C2*'s. But the reply is that the objection is false, because there is no *arrangement* in this case at all; in this respect, Case (1) differs crucially from Case (3) (below). There is rather inequality in the *conditions*. But this inequality is not brought about by any action or inaction by any of the persons involved in *G*, namely *C1*, *C2*, *R* and *0*. It just happens; and, as Acton [10] points out, 'something that merely *happens* can be neither just or unjust'. (For the purposes of this essay, it is not necessary to distinguish between fairness and justice. The distinction is elucidated in Subsec. 2.1 of Essay 8). This brings out the important point that when we call a *competition* unfair for *C1*, there is always an ulterior reference to some fault of commission or omission by some other *person* involved in *G*, be it *C2*, or *R*, or *0*. (This is because the root idea of Justice is that of just *action*. See Subsec. 2.1 of Essay 8.)

Naturally, the outside agency may be a person. Thus, *G* is unfortunate, not unfair for *C1* if a bystander, *B*, throws a bottle and, either accidentally or not, knocks him out. But what if *B* does this deliberately at the instigation of *C2*? In that case, *G* is unfair, not unfortunate for *C1*. However, that which makes it unfair is not the action of the agent *outside G*, namely *B*, but the action of the agent *inside G*, namely *C2*. It is highly plausible to suppose that *C2*'s action here is not foul play, because there is no rule of *G* covering this contingency. Nevertheless, *G* is judged unfair for *C1* because *C2* breaks a rule of law, morality or custom (see below).

Case (2)

C1 does not win because he falls, and he falls because *C2* trips him accidentally. Here, *G* is unfair, not unfortunate for *C1*, because (we take it) tripping a competitor is a foul, i.e. a breach of a rule of *G*. It may be objected that *G* is unfortunate, not unfair for *C1*, since the foul was accidental. But the reply is that the objection is false, because fouls can be either deliberate or accidental. No-balls at cricket are rarely intended. The reason for the objection is probably the existence of transferred uses of 'foul play' which do indeed connote intention. For example, the foul play that the police suspect is dirty work at the crossroads. In this case, the persons at fault are *C2* and perhaps *R*.

Case (3)

C1 does not win because there is an inequality in the arrangement of *G*. For *O* organises *G* thus: the course is a circuit; *C1* and *C2* run in concentric and adjacent lanes; the starting line is also the finishing line; and the choice of lane is decided by a fair toss of a fair coin. *C2* wins the toss and chooses the inner lane, and he and *C1* reach the finishing line simultaneously. Here, *G* is of course unfair, not unfortunate for *C1*. The person at fault is *O*, who ought not to have started the competitors level, but to have given *C1* such a start over *C2* as would have equalised the distances that both had to run. Just as *G* is unfair for *C1* whether *C2*'s foul play is accidental or not (Case (2)); so *G* is unfair for *C1* whether *O*'s unequal arrangement of it is accidental or not. It would be accidental if, say, *O* had simply failed to appreciate that his arrangement involved an inequality. It may be objected that *G* is unfortunate, not unfair for *C1*, since the reason why he did not win is that he lost the toss, which is a matter of chance. But the reply is that the objection is false, because the reason why *C1* did not win is *not only* that he lost the toss *but also* that the arrangement was unequal. But for the inequality, his loss of the toss would not have mattered.

Like a game of chance which really is a pure game of chance, a game of skill which really is a pure game of skill cannot be unfair. Unlike the former, however, the latter cannot be unfortunate either. If *C2* wins solely because he is more skilful than *C1*, then the latter has no right to complain of bad luck. But the crucial point is that, whereas so-called games of chance in fact usually are pure games of chance, what are called games of skill usually are not pure games of skill. Chance will break in in the form either of accidental fouls (Case (2)) or of accidental inequalities (Case (1)). The latter are much the more serious because they are practically uncompensatable. If *C1* is tripped accidentally by *C2*, he can be compensated, say by *R* disqualifying *C2* in accordance with a rule of *G*, so that *C1* wins. However, he cannot be similarly compensated for the wet leaves on his lane. It may be objected that he can, and that a certain number of seconds should be deducted from his time for the race. But the reply is to ask exactly, or even approximately how many seconds should be so deducted. Practically speaking, the question is unanswerable.

So, finally, to the contests of real life. In some moods, we see life as a free fight in which anything goes. In others, it strikes us as a game of Snakes and Ladders, in which the ups and downs of the players are decided by the fall of a die. In yet others, it seems to be a race, a race indeed of rats rather than of men. Speaking strictly, of course, it is as false that life is a free-for-all, or a toss-up, or a rat-race, as that all the world is a stage. Yet all four metaphors have their point, and are appropriate to different spheres of life. That of the free fight is believed to apply to love and war, in which proverbially all is fair. (However, the belief is false — at any rate of war. For instance, most States subscribe to the Geneva Conventions which regulate the treatment of prisoners of war by belligerents.) That of dicing applies, perhaps, to physical life; to be stricken by multiple sclerosis is like landing on some fearful snake. That of the rat-race applies — if only in the folk-lore of Socialism — to the business world. I shall explore briefly this last analogy, the analogy between an athletic competition, G, and a commercial competition, C; between the concept of fair play and the concept of fair dealing.

Let C be a competition for a business appointment. We find exact analogies with the three cases of a game of skill involving chance, discussed above, as follows. *Case (1—)*. $C1$ does not win because his application is accidentally destroyed by a fire. Here, C is unfortunate, not unfair, for $C1$, just as in Case (1). *Case (2—)*. $C1$ does not win because the post goes to $C2$ who, however, is over 35, contrary to a rule of C. But $C2$ breaks the rule unintentionally because, unknown to him, his birth-certificate misrepresents his age. Here, C is unfair, not unfortunate for $C1$, just as in Case (2). $C2$'s unintentional unfair dealing in Case (2—) corresponds precisely to $C2$'s accidental unfair play in Case (2). *Case (3—)*. $C1$ does not win because of an inequality in the arrangement of C. For O organises C thus. The six candidates are interviewed individually by a selector, S, for 1 hour each. The interviews are successive, and their order is determined by a fair throw of a fair die. $C1$'s interview chances to come last. But this puts him at a disadvantage, because by the time his turn comes S is tired and hungry; a fact which O ought to have foreseen. Here, C is unfair, not unfortunate for $C1$, just as in Case (3).

We have seen that the essential difference between games of skill and real-life competitions of skill is precisely that play is for fun but work is for real. However, the distinction tends to wear thin. In what sense — it may well be asked — is a match between professional golfers for a large prize a game or diversion, or any less for real than a competition between salesmen for a valuable order? We have also seen from the six cases which we have considered that there is identity in the conditions of (un)fairness in both sorts of competitions. There is also identity in the conditions thereof not only in cases where there is breach of the rules of, say, golf matches or business appointments, but also in cases where there are breaches of rules of law, morality or custom. Thus, *Case (4)*, *G* is unfair for *C1* if, contrary to a legal rule, *C2* deliberately wounds him; and *Case (4—)*, *C* is unfair for *C1* if, contrary to a legal rule, *C2* deliberately falsifies his birth-certificate. Further, even if assault and fraud were not illegal, *G* and *C* would be judged unfair for *C1* in these cases because *C2* breaks a moral rule. Finally, even if assault and fraud were neither illegal nor immoral, *G* and *C* would probably still be judged unfair for *C1* in these cases because what *C2* does is 'not the done thing', i.e. is a breach of a rule of custom. The moral and customary ingredients in the concept of fair dealing are particularly clear in notions such as 'fair price', 'fair rent' and 'fair wage'.[11]

So since, on the one hand, the conditions of fair play and fair dealing are identical; whereas, on the other hand, the essential difference between competitive games and real-life competitions is often thin; it is not surprising that the two concepts are effectively identified, and that the former is transferred to contexts where the notion which is strictly in place is the latter. We have already discerned this tendency in the police practice of referring to dirty work as foul play. We find it again when, say, in Case (4—), *C2*'s conduct in deliberately falsifying his birth-certificate is deprecated as 'not cricket'. Finally, it is to be found in philosophy when Rawls[12] gives to a principle which he lays down concerning 'schemes of social cooperation' the name of 'the Principle of Fair Play'.

There result from these considerations two complementary vulgar errors which are unfortunately as common as they are bad. I shall typify them as that of the Grumbler and that of the Tychist (from the Greek τυχη, meaning 'chance'). The Grumbler is a literalist who believes that what are called competitions of skill really are just that and involve no chance at all. Consequently, when *C1* does not win although his skill is greater than *C2*'s, the Grumbler alleges injustice in the form either of breach or faulty enforcement of the rules, or of inequality in the arrangement — especially when *C1* is himself. The words which are all too often on his lips are 'It was not fair'. The Tychist, on the other hand, is a sceptic who believes that what are called competitions of skill are really no such thing and involve nothing but chance. Since he believes that Chance governs all, the words which are all too often on his lips are 'It was bad luck'. He is the man who, when *C1* is the victim of injustice, adds insult to his injury by condoling with him on his misfortune — especially when *C1* is someone else.

The remedy is to face the facts. Namely that, whereas what are called games of chance are usually pure games of chance, what are called competitions of skill are usually not pure competitions of skill but contain an element of ineluctable mischance. So that, when one encounters such misadventures, he should not complain, but should rather take them and suffer them nobly as what they truly are, the slings and arrows of outrageous Fortune.[13]

APPENDIX

In Section 4 of the text, the following variant on Case (2) is mentioned: *C1* reaches the finishing line after *C2*, because he is accidentally tripped by *C2*; but *C1* nevertheless wins, because *C2* is disqualified by *R* for foul play in accordance with a rule of *G*.

Here, *G* may well be judged disadvantageously unfair, not unfortunate for *C2*, because the rule is unfair. Disqualification, it may be urged, is too severe a penalty for an accidental foul; and the rule covering this contingency ought rather to be, say, that the race should be run again. *G* may well be judged unfair, not unfortunate for *C1* too. However, the meaning of this is not that *G* was disadvantageously unfair for him, because he was fouled; but rather that *G* was advantageously unfair for him, because he was over-compensated for the foul by the enforcement of the unfair rule. Again, Case (2—), the rule requiring competitors to be under 35 may be judged unfair because it is discriminatory.

In these cases too the principle referred to in Case (1) is satisfied, namely, that when a competition is judged to be unfair, there is an ulterior reference to some fault by some person involved in it. Here, the persons deemed to be at fault are the makers of the rules of *G* and *C* respectively.

To sum up. Of the following four conditions, each is sufficient to make a competition which involves chance, *C*, unfair for some competitor in it, *C1*. (1) Some other competitor in *C*, *C2*, breaks a rule of *C*, or of law, or of morality, or of custom, in such a way as either to disadvantage or advantage *C1*. (2) Some referee in *C*, *R*, fails to enforce these rules. (For example a competitive game which involves chance,

G, is unfair for *C1* (*a*) if *R* either penalises *C1* for a foul which he did not commit, or fails to penalise *C2* for a foul which he did commit; or (*b*) if *R* fails to penalise *C2* for, for example, wounding *C1*, even though *C2*'s action breaks no rule of *G*.) (3) Some rule-maker in *C* makes some rule which is unfair for *C1*. (4) Some organiser in *C* makes some arrangement which is unfair for *C1*.[14] On the other hand, the following one condition is both sufficient and necessary to make *C* unfortunate for *C1*. (5) Some agency outside *C* causes some inequality in the conditions of *C* which disadvantages *C1*. However, the occurrence of (5) is not exceptional, but normal.[15]

Correction

In the fourth paragraph of Section 4, I infer invalidly from the true premiss that *football* is not a game of chance the false conclusion that *football pools* are not matters of chance. In fact, the finding of those who have studied them is that they are. (See J. Cohen, *Chance, Skill and Luck* (London, 1960), p. 85.) What is possible, but inept, is to treat football matches as if they were games of chance.

Notes

1. See J.P. Day, *Inductive Probability* (London and New York, 1961), pp. 172ff.; I. Hacking, *Logic of Statistical Inference* (Cambridge, 1965), Ch. viii; L.H.C. Tippett, *The Methods of Statistics* (London, 4th edn, 1952), Sec. 12.2; *Statistics* (London, 1943), Ch. vi; G.U. Yule and M.G. Kendall, *An Introduction to the Theory of Statistics* (London, 14th edn, 1950), Ch. xvi.

2. See J. Madge, *The Tools of Social Science* (London, 1953), p. 212; W.E. Deming and A. Stuart, 'Sample Surveys', *International Encyclopedia of the Social Sciences*, Vol. XIII (New York, 1968), p. 613.

3. See D. Williams, *The Ground of Induction* (Cambridge, Mass., 1947), pp. 97, 101.

4. See the discussions of Jacques Bernoulli's Central Limit Theorem in J.M. Keynes, *A Treatise on Probability* (London, 1921), Chs. xxix, xxxi; W. Kneale, *Probability and Induction* (Oxford, 1949), Sec. 29; J.R. Lucas, *The Concept of Probability* (Oxford, 1970), Ch. v. Statisticians also have special methods for making inferences from *small* samples to populations, but this refinement need not concern us here.

5. D.H. Mellor, *The Matter of Chance* (Cambridge, 1971). For earlier versions of the theory, see C.S. Peirce, 'Notes on the Doctrine of Chances', *Collected Papers of C.S. Peirce*, ed. C. Hartshorne and P. Weiss, Vol. II (Cambridge, Mass., 1960), pp. 404ff.; K.R. Popper, 'The Propensity Interpretation of Probability', *The British Journal for the Philosophy of Science*, Vol. X (Edinburgh, 1960), pp. 25ff. See also A.R. White, 'The Propensity Theory of Probability', *The British Journal for the Philosophy of Science*, Vol. 23, 1972.

6. I. Berlin, 'Empirical Propositions and Hypothetical Statements', *Mind*, Vol. LIX (Edinburgh, 1950), p. 302.

7. G. Ryle, *The Concept of Mind* (London, 1949), pp. 149ff.

8. J.L. Austin, 'Other Minds', *Philosophical Papers*, ed. J.O. Urmson and G.J.

36 Fairness and Fortune

Warnock (Oxford, 1961), pp. 75f.

9. *Rules of Golf*, as approved by the Royal and Ancient Golf Club of St Andrews and the United States Golf Association, effective 1 January 1972, Sec. 11, No. 27.

10. H.B. Acton, *The Morals of Markets* (London, 1971), p. 63.

11. See the remarks on 'just price' and 'just wage' in Acton, pp. 27ff., 60ff.; and the entries 'fair price', 'fair rent' and 'fair wage' in *Palgrave's Dictionary of Political Economy*, Vol. II, ed. H. Higgs (London, 1926). The concepts 'fair dealing', 'fair price' and 'fair rent' figure also in the law: see the entries in *Words and Phrases Judicially Defined*, Vol. II, ed. R. Burrows (London, 1943); *Stroud's Judicial Dictionary*, Vol. II (London, 1972).

12. J. Rawls, 'Legal Obligation and the Duty of Fair Play', *Law and Philosophy*, ed. S. Hook (New York, 1964), pp. 9f.

13. Chance has long been regarded as a sort of cause, not only by the vulgar, but also by the philosophers, for example Aristotle. The former think of Fortune (τυχη, *Fortuna*) as a divine agent; and Fairness (δικη, *Justitia*) has been similarly deified. See, for example, the statue of Justice which surmounts the Old Bailey (the Central Criminal Court of England), and the painting of Fortune which is reproduced in F.N. David, *Games, Gods and Gambling: The Origins and History of Probability and Statistical Ideas from the Earliest Times to the Newtonian Era* (London, 1962), p. 24. See also Kneale, *Probability and Induction*, pp. 116f.; W.D. Ross, *Aristotle*, 5th edn (London, 1949), pp. 75ff. Both Fairness and Fortune are usually depicted blindfolded. But the symbolism is quite different in the two cases, since the bandaged eyes represent the impartiality of Justice but the indiscriminateness of Chance. It is her indiscriminateness and her inconstancy, symbolised by her wheel, that make Fortune outrageous. As Machiavelli truly said of her, she is a bitch-goddess. Cf. *The Prince*, ch. 25.

14. To be exact, conditions (1)—(4) specify the different ways in which *C* is *normally* unfair for *C1*. However, the other persons involved in *C* can also cause injustice for him in unusual ways. For example, *O* may make *G* advantageously unfair for *C1* by bribing *C2* to lose *G*. Here, not only is *O* at fault for offering the bribe, but *C2* is also at fault for accepting it. This case therefore illustrates the point that *G* can be unfair for *C1* in more than one way at the same time. Or again, in a professional football match, *R* may assault *C1*; which would not only make the match disadvantageously unfair for *C1*'s team, but would also make news as certainly as would Man Bites Dog.

15. I am grateful to Prof. J.O. Urmson for his comments on an earlier version of this essay.

3 THREATS, OFFERS, LAW, OPINION AND LIBERTY

1. Introduction

Do threats and offers curtail liberty? The doctors disagree over this question, which is a sure sign of a philosophical problem in need of treatment. The following summary shows the nature and extent of the disagreement. (1) Both do. (Aristotle, *Nic. Ethics*, tr. Ross, 1110a; Bay (1958), p. 93; Cassinelli (1966); Frankfurt (1973).) (2) Threats do, but offers do not. (Benn and Weinstein (1971), p. 201; Hart and Honoré (1959); Nozick (1972).) (3) Neither do. (Parent (1974 (2)); Steiner (1975).) (See also Pennock (1972), pp. 5f.) Unsurprisingly, no one maintains that (4) offers do, but threats do not.

Unsurprisingly, too, this crude categorisation needs qualification and amplification. Thus, as to (1), it is usually maintained that both *sometimes* do, namely, when the threat is strong or the offer is large. As to (1) and (2), it is usually contended that, when the threat is strong, the threatenee is not *fully* free, or has no *real* choice. As to (3), the position of Parent, e.g., is that threats do not diminish *social freedom*, though they do sometimes diminish *freedom of choice*, which he takes to be a different concept from social freedom (Parent (1974 (2)), p. 156).

The doctors disagree not only in what they say, but also in why they say it. For they are predominantly either (i) arguers or (ii) reporters. Thus, (i) Frankfurt, Nozick and Steiner offer argument in support of their positions. But, (ii) Aristotle follows his usual procedure of considering what we ordinarily say (for a start, at any rate); and so do Benn and Weinstein, Hart and Honoré, and Parent. However, this crude categorisation, too, needs qualification and amplification. For, firstly, in conceptual analysis, the distinction between reporting and arguing is in any case not clear cut. Secondly, whereas Aristotle and Parent claim to report truly what is ordinarily (or correctly) said in common speech, Hart and Honoré and Benn and Weinstein claim to report not only this, but also what is ordinarily said in the semi-technical discourse of *politics and law*. E.g., on politics, Hart writes '(coercion) into obedience by the threat of legal punishment . . . rather than physical restrictions is what is normally meant in the discussion of political arrangements by restrictions on liberty' (Hart (1961), p. 21). While on the law, he points out, e.g., the following fact. Suppose that a highwayman (H) points a pistol at a traveller (T) and says to him 'Your money or your life'; and that T hands over the money which he is carrying, which, however, happens to be not his own but his employer's. The common man would say that T's action was 'not wholly voluntary', whereas the Anglo-American lawyer would say that it was done 'without *mens rea*'; but both would say that it was 'excusable' (Hart (1962), pp. 169f.).

I consider position (2) (above) to be the correct one, and my primary objective is to provide argument to show why it is so. My argument is different from Nozick's, however, and so will be found, I hope, to complement his valuable discussion. Finally, it may well be thought that this question forms only a small part of the general philosophical question, or questions, about liberty. We shall find, however, that this is not the case, and that answering it involves providing an elucidation of the idea of liberty in general; which is, indeed, my secondary and main objective in this essay.

2. Desire and Liberty

Steiner argues as follows to prove that neither threats nor offers, which he calls collectively 'interventions', diminish liberty (Steiner (1975), p. 43). The effect of H's threat to T (above). 'Either you will not have your money, or you will not have your life', is normally to change T's desire. Before the threat, T wants to keep his money, but after the threat he wants not to do so. Likewise with offers. H's conditional offer to T, 'If you will give me your money, then I will give you my life', normally implies (in the popular, not in any logician's sense of 'implies') 'Either you will not have your money, or you will not have my life.' The effect of this, again, may be to change T's desire to keep his money into a desire not to do so. However, whether T desires to have his money or not is irrelevant to whether T is unfree to have his money or not. So the argument goes thus. (1) The effect of any intervention is normally to change the desire of A (the intervenee) to D into a desire to $-D$. (2) 'A desires to D' and 'A desires to $-D$' are both irrelevant to 'A is unfree to D.' Therefore, (3) No intervention curtails liberty.

I shall argue now, not that (3) is false (though I shall do this later (Sec. 3)), but rather that Steiner's argument fails to prove (3) true because one of its premisses is false. The false premiss is not, however, (2). For it is now generally agreed that, although the truth or falsity of 'A desires to D' is relevant to the truth or falsity of 'A *feels* unfree to D', it is not relevant to the truth or falsity of '*A is* unfree to *D*.' This is what is wrong with, e.g., Mill's definition of liberty, 'liberty consists in doing what one desires' (*On Liberty*, v). (See Friedman (1966); Berlin (1969), pp. xxxviiff.; Cassinelli (1966), p. 22; Day (1970), pp. 190ff.; Oppenheim (1961), pp. 143ff.; Steiner (1975), pp. 33ff.) It is premiss (1) which is false. For, logically, there are four possibilities. T can (i) both have his money and have his life; (ii) not have his money but have his life; (iii) have his money but not have his life; (iv) both not have his money and not have his life. Happily for T, however, (iv) can be eliminated. This is because H's threat, 'If you will not give me your money, then I will take your life' normally implies (in the popular, not any logician's sense of 'implies') 'If you will give me your money, then I will not take your life.' Now, in fact, H's threat does not affect T's desire at all, since what T would like to do, both after the threat as well as before it, is (i). The effect of H's threat is rather to bring T to realise that, after the 'dead-line' has been passed, he will be unable to do as he wants to do, namely, (i); and so to reflect whether he is less averse to doing (ii) than to doing (iii), or conversely; and to choose accordingly. Normally, he will choose alternative (ii). However, because the first conjunct of (ii) is 'not to have his money', it *looks as though*, after and because of the threat, T wants not to have his money. This is what makes Steiner's argument seem plausible.

A possible obstacle to the realisation that desire is irrelevant to liberty is the existence of the locution '*A* is free to *D* if he wants to.' As Benn and Weinstein point out, the force of this is ironic, as in 'Of course you are perfectly free to cut off your ears, if that is what you really want to do' (Benn and Weinstein (1971), p. 195). Similarly, Hare notes the irony in 'If you want to break your springs, go on driving as you are doing' (Hare (1952), p. 36). This locution brings out an important point about the relation of liberty to desire, which is that we do not normally speak of *A* being (un)free to *D* unless to *D* is the sort of thing that the average, reasonable man might want to do. However, a literalist might be misled by the locution into believing that the truth of '*A* desires to *D*' is a sufficient condition of the truth of '*A* is free to *D*'. In fact, of course, 'You are free to cut off your ears if you want to' no more entails 'If you are not free to cut off your ears, then you do not want to' than 'There is beer if you want it' entails 'If there is no beer, then you do not want any.'

A more serious cause of the false belief that the concept of liberty is linked to that of desire is the confusion of 'voluntarily (or freely)' with 'willingly (or gladly)'. Hobbes, e.g., writes as follows respecting a case discussed by Aristotle (*Nic. Ethics*, tr. Ross, 1110a), from whom he doubtless took it. '. . . when a man throweth his goods into the Sea for fear the ship should sink, he doth it nevertheless very *willingly* . . . It is therefore the action, of one that was *free* . . .' (*Leviathan*, II, xxi, first emphasis added). This sounds plausible; yet, on consideration, it is plainly false. For, in the circumstances which Hobbes describes, the average man does not jettison his goods willingly (or gladly). On the contrary, he jettisons them very unwillingly (or reluctantly). On the other hand, he does jettison them voluntarily (or freely), since no one compels him to do so. Locke makes the same mistake as Hobbes. He considers the case where A is locked in a room where there is B, whom A wants very much to see. Consequently, A remains in the room very willingly; from which Locke infers, wrongly, that he does so voluntarily (*Essay*, II, xxi, 10; cf. Melden (1961), p. 219; O'Connor (1971), p. 77). Hobbes' example shows how A can D voluntarily but unwillingly. For another illustration of how A can D willingly but not voluntarily, consider the good soldier who dies executing an order to hold his position at all costs. He does not act voluntarily, because he cannot leave his position, since if he tries to do so, his superior will shoot him. Yet he acts willingly, for he believes that his cause is just, and that the execution of the order is necessary for the victory of his cause. However, 'A Ds willingly' entails 'A wants to D'. So he who confuses 'willingly (or gladly)' with 'voluntarily (or freely)' will believe, falsely, that the truth of 'A desires to D' is a necessary condition of the truth of 'A is free to D'.

The latest type of desire (or will) theories of liberty is based on the concept of a second-order desire. According to Plamenatz and Dworkin, A Ds unfreely if and only if he Ds from a motive from which he desires not to act (Dworkin (1970); Plamenatz (1938), p. 122; cf. Locke (1975), pp. 104ff.). However, if H kills T because he desires to have T's money, although he desires not to have that base desire; it does not follow that H acts unfreely in killing T. 'I did not want to want to do it' is no more an excuse than is 'I did not want to do it.' This sort of theory too breaks down on the fact that desire (or will) is irrelevant to liberty. (The special case in which A Ds unfreely because B arouses in A an irresistible desire to D, will be considered later (Subsec. 5.2).)

3. Threats, Offers and Liberty

H's threat to T, 'Either you will not have your money, or you will not have your life', curtails T's liberty because it makes T (about to be) unable to do something which he can now do, namely, (i) both have his money and also have his life (Sec. 2). (It is assumed that the threat is a normal, i.e. genuine one; i.e., that H sincerely intends to execute his threat and is not bluffing; that he is able to execute his threat and has not forgotten to load his pistol, and so forth.) It is necessary to say that H's threat makes T 'about to be' unable to do (i), because he will not actually be unable to do it until the time-limit has expired. With a normal threat like this one, the threatener always allows an interval between making it and executing it, so that the threatenee can reflect before deciding between (ii) and (iii). Similarly, with normal offers, the offerer allows the offeree time to think it over before deciding whether to accept it or to reject it.

The failure to understand why and how threats curtail liberty proceeds from concentrating attention on T's *simple* action, keeping his money, rather than on the *complex* (i.e., conjunctive) action (i). The difficulty is that it is rightly recognised, on the one hand, that H's threat curtails T's liberty *somehow*; and yet, on the other hand, that it does not make him unfree to keep his money. The first step towards understanding why and how threats curtail liberty is to recognise that a threat (unlike an offer (Subsec. (6.1)) must be complex, and is best expressed by an alternation; and that any alternation negates some conjunction. In the Calculus of Propositions, the formula $(-P \wedge -Q)/(P \ \& \ Q)$ is a tautology. (Cf. Pollock (1973), p. 235.) I think that this point may have been overlooked because philosophers of action tend to neglect the important subject of complex actions.

In the light of these considerations, it is possible to reply to an objection by Cassinelli to the view that threats diminish freedom (Cassinelli (1966), pp. 33f.). He considers the case where A murders B in a state in which there is a law against murder which is backed by a threat of punishment by death. The fact that A nevertheless did murder B, says Cassinelli, shows that the threat did not make him unfree to do so; for it is illogical to say that A was unfree to do something which he in fact did. The reply to this objection is that it is quite true, but that it commits the fallacy of *ignoratio elenchi*. For it does not show that A was not unable both to take B's life and also to keep his own life; which is how this threat in fact curtails A's liberty (Subsec. 6.2).

But does not H's complex (i.e., conditional or alternative) offer to T, 'Either you will not have your money, or you will not have my life', similarly diminish T's liberty by making him (about to be) unable to do something which he can now do, namely, both have his money and also have H's life? It does not do so. For the crucial distinction between threats and offers is as follows. Before H's threat, T does and therefore *can unconditionally* both have his money and also have his life; whereas after H's threat T cannot do both these things. But before H's offer, T *cannot unconditionally* both have his money and also have H's life. For, in this context, 'have H's life' means 'receive H's life from H'. And T cannot do this *unless and until H gives his life to T.* Consequently, H's offer does not make T (about to be) unable to do something which he can unconditionally now do. H's threat *deprives* T by making him (about to be) unable to do something which he can unconditionally now do; whereas H's offer does not do this. This is the vital difference between threats and conditional offers, on which hinges the fact that threats curtail liberty whereas conditional offers do not, and to recognise it is to take the second step to understanding the relation of threats and offers to freedom. Furthermore, we shall see shortly that offers not only never decrease the liberty of the offeree, but also sometimes (though not always) increase it (Sec. 4). Threats, on the other hand, never increase the liberty of the threatenee. What has been said is true of any threat, regardless of its strength. H's very weak threat, 'Either you will give me your money, or I will give you the rough edge of my tongue', also diminishes T's freedom, because it makes him (about to be) unable to do something which he is now doing and therefore can unconditionally now do, namely, both have his money and also have his ears secure from verbal assault. (Cf. Austin (1961); Locke (1975); Moore (1912); Nowell-Smith (1954); O'Connor (1971), pp. 26ff.)

4. Ability and Liberty

B decreases A's liberty by decreasing the number of alternative actions which A can perform. The effect of H's threat to T, 'Your money or your life', is to eliminate (in the near future) the alternative of T's both keeping his money and also keeping his life. Similarly, T now has the alternatives of either going from London (L) to York (Y), or staying in L. If H imprisons T, he eliminates the former alternative, and thereby decreases T's freedom. So may not B increase A's freedom by increasing the number of alternative actions which A can perform? Some certainly think so. MacMurray, e.g., maintains this position as part of the following general thesis on liberty. Freedom is the *summum bonum*, and there are two main roads to it, the philosophical-religious high road and the scientific-technological low road. The former, Platonic-Stoic-Christian way is the way of diminishing our desires, and the latter, modern Western way is the way of increasing our powers. MacMurray thinks that the low road has turned out to be no road, and that we should do better to return to the high road (MacMurray (1949), I).

We have in effect already rejected MacMurray's thesis about the high road as resting on a misconception of the relation of liberty to desire (Sec. 2). If H makes T unable to go to Y by imprisoning him, then T will not cease to *be* unfree to go if he suppresses his desire to go; though he will admittedly cease to *feel* unfree to go if he does this. So T will not increase his freedom by decreasing his desires. But we must also reject MacMurray's thesis respecting the low road.

Two centuries ago, when T wanted to go from L to Y, he had no alternative but to go by road. One century ago, he had the alternatives of going either by road or not by road, but the latter alternative took the single form of going by rail. Today, however, the alternative of going not by road includes the two sub-alternatives of going by rail or going by air. The question is whether the inventors of railways and aircraft have made T more free. It may be argued that they have, as follows.

When H releases T from prison, he adds to T's alternative of staying in L the alternative of going to Y, and thereby augments T's freedom. Similarly, when the inventor of aircraft adds to T's options of going to Y by road or by rail the further option of going by air, he too increases T's liberty. But the objection is that there is a crucial difference between the two cases. Before H released T from prison, T was *unfree* to go to Y; and this is why H's giving T the additional alternative of going to Y increases T's *freedom*. But before their inventor invented aircraft, T was not unfree, but *unable* to fly to Y; and this is why their inventor's giving T the additional alternative of going to Y by air increases T's *power*. Now liberty, so far from being identical with ability (or power) presupposes it. I.e., the truth of '*A* is able to *D*' is a necessary condition both of the truth and also of the falsity of '*A* is free to *D*' (Day (1970), p. 180). Consequently, it is neither true nor false that, one century ago, T was unfree to fly from L to Y. Rather, the question, whether he was unfree to do so or not, does not arise.

The case is similar with offers; for these, like inventions, often increase the number of alternative things that *A* can do (Benn and Weinstein (1971), p. 201). So do such offers augment liberty? The answer is implicit in what has just been said. If H first imprisons T in L, and then says to him 'If you will give me your money, then you may go to Y', he increases T's liberty by giving him the alternative of going to Y; because before the offer T was *unfree* to go to Y. But if H says to T, as T is setting out for Y on foot, 'If you will give me your money, then you may have my horse', then H does not increase T's liberty by giving him the extra option of going to Y on horseback; because before the offer T was not unfree, but unable to go to Y on horseback. In this case, the effect of H's offer is to increase T's power, not his liberty.

So the answer to the question posed at the beginning of this Section is that only sometimes does *B* increase *A*'s freedom by increasing the number of alternative actions which *A* can perform. At the other times *B* thereby increases, not *A*'s freedom, but his power.

One likely cause of the confusion of liberty with ability is the fact that the same word, 'can', is used for both concepts. The point of the statement 'Today, T can fly from L to Y', may be either (1) that today we have aircraft, whereas one century ago we had not (ability); or (2) that today there is no governmental prohibition on civil aviation, whereas yesterday there was (liberty).

Moore's theory fails through not distinguishing unfreedom from inability. According to Moore, *A Ds* unfreely when and only when he cannot -*D* if he chooses (Moore (1912); Austin (1961)). Yet when *A* is so sick that he cannot leave his bed if he chooses, he does not stay in his bed unfreely. His illness diminishes his power, not his liberty. (Cf. Hobbes, *Leviathan*, II, xxi.)

5. Conditions of Unfreedom

Generally speaking, it is not disputed that the truth of '*B* makes *A* unable to *D*' is a sufficient condition of the truth of '*A* is unfree to *D*'. (However, we shall have to notice an important qualification of this statement shortly (Subsec. 5.5).) Consequently, in saying that H's threat to T, 'Your money or your life', curtails T's liberty because it makes T (about to be) unable both to have his money and also to have his life, I am saying nothing controversial. I am saying that the way in which this threat curtails T's liberty is not essentially different from the way in which H curtails T's liberty to go from L to Y when he imprisons him. However, some maintain that threats and offers diminish freedom in ways that are different from this way.

5.1 Ineligible Alternatives

We have seen that Benn and Weinstein hold that threats curtail liberty but that offers do not (Sec. 1.). They contend that threats do this by making some alternative action ineligible. 'Ineligible' is an evaluative term, and the concept of an ineligible alternative is relative to the average man, so that 'an ineligible alternative' means 'an alternative which it is unreasonable for the average man to choose'. Only a strong threat, such as 'Your money or your life', confronts T with an alternative that it is unreasonable for the average man to choose, namely, to keep his money but to lose his life. A weak threat, such as 'Either you will give me your money, or I will give you the rough edge of my tongue', does not diminish freedom, because it would not be unreasonable for the average man to choose to keep his money but to forfeit the security of his ears from verbal assault. On this account, therefore, H's strong threat curtails T's liberty not (or at any rate, not only) by making it (about to be) *impossible* for him both to keep his money and also to keep his life, but (or at any rate, but also) by making it *unreasonable* for him to keep his money. H does this by attaching to T's keeping his money the very high price of losing his life; for in this situation, to choose to keep his money is in effect to choose both to keep his money and also to lose his life. On this view, therefore, there are two ways in which B can make A unfree, namely, (1) by making some alternative impossible for A, and (2) by making some alternative ineligible for A.

This theory seems to me to be open to the following objections. Firstly, it involves Cassinelli's paradox (Sec. 3). For suppose that T *is* unreasonable; i.e., that he keeps his money and loses his life. Then, on this theory, T does a thing which he is unfree to do. But this is illogical.

Secondly, suppose that H holds out to a female T a large sack full of money and says to her 'You may have all this money.' Then H presents T with two alternatives, namely, either to accept his offer or to reject it, the latter of which is very ineligible. On this theory, therefore, T is unfree to decline the money. But this contradicts its authors' thesis that offers do not diminish freedom.

Thirdly, suppose that the sum of money which T is carrying is very large and furthermore all that he possesses; and that H, without showing a gun, says to him imploringly 'Please give me your money.' Then H presents T with two alternatives, namely, either to grant H's request or to refuse it, the former of which is very ineligible. On this theory, therefore, T is unfree to hand over his money. But this conflicts with the received view that requests do not diminish freedom.

By attaching to T's keeping his money the price of losing his life, H *deters* (or attempts to deter) T from keeping his money. But B does not make A unfree to D by deterring him from Ding. To do this, B must *prevent* A from Ding. The ineligible alternatives theory is so plausible precisely because men tend not to distinguish between deterrence and prevention. However, we shall see later that this distinction is crucial for the analysis of the concept of liberty (Subsecs. 6.2, 6.3).

5.2 Irresistible Motives

We have also seen that Frankfurt maintains that both threats and offers diminish freedom (Sec. 1). He argues that, in the case of strong threats, B makes A unfree to D by arousing in him a motive 'so powerful that he cannot prevent it from leading him to submit to the threat' (Frankfurt (1973), p. 77). Similarly, in the case of attractive offers, B makes A unfree to D by arousing in him an irresistible desire to gain the offered benefit.

This theory seems to me to be open to the following objection. Suppose that, when H says to T 'Your money or your life', H's mien is so terrifying and T's disposition is so timid that H's action arouses in T an intense fear amounting to panic, in consequence of which T hands over his money 'automatically'. This is perfectly possible; but it is not a case of pure threatening. For, although H *menaces* T, he also *intimidates* him; and T does not *comply with H's threat* at all, but is cowed into doing as he does. Although threatening and intimidating are usually not distinguished, they are, I think, quite different concepts. In the field of labour-relations, e.g., it is surely no less important (and difficult) to distinguish threatening from intimidating than it is to distinguish threatening from warning (see Nozick (1972), pp. 120ff.). Paradoxical as it may seem, the paradigm threat situation is one from which emotion is wholly absent; i.e., one in which H is quite unalarming and/or T is quite fearless, and in which T chooses to keep his life and lose his money, rather than conversely, from as dispassionate a consideration of his *interest* as when he decides to spend a legacy on a new car rather than on new furniture. The failure to distinguish between threatening and intimidating is explained by an obvious overlap between the concepts. Very often, when B threatens A, he also (not necessarily intentionally) intimidates him; and when A complies with B's threat, he is very often moved by fear as well as by interest.

Similarly with offers. Suppose that H holds out to a female T a large sack full of money and says to her 'You may have all this money if you will give me your hand in marriage', and that T is both avaricious and destitute. Then H's action may arouse in T a desire so intense that she 'instinctively' snatches the sack with one hand and gives her other hand to H. However, this is not a case of pure offering. For, although H *makes T an offer*, he also *tempts* her; and T does not *accept H's offer* at all, but is lured into doing as she does. Here again, the paradigm offer situation is one from which emotion is wholly absent, and in which A decides to accept or to decline B's offer by a purely rational calculation of his interests. But here, too, there is an obvious overlap between offering and tempting. Very often, when B makes A an offer, he also (not necessarily intentionally) tempts him; and when A accepts B's offer, he is very often moved by desire as well as by interest. Moreover, although not all offering involves tempting, all tempting does involve offering.

I agree with Frankfurt, then, that B can make A unfree to D by making him unable to D through arousing in him either an irresistible fear of Ding, or an irresistible desire of -Ding. But I do not agree that this shows that and how threats and offers curtail liberty, because what have just been described are extreme intimidation and extreme temptation; and intimidating is not identical with threatening, nor is tempting identical with offering. However, the fact that B can simultaneously both threaten A and intimidate him, or both make A an offer and tempt him, brings out again the importance of complex (conjunctive) actions (Sec. 3.6). We describe these complex actions by such locutions as 'B made A a very tempting offer.'

5.3 Psychological Unfreedom

Some say that, in the cases of extreme intimidation and extreme temptation just discussed (Subsec. 5.2), H coerces T psychologically. But why 'psychologically'? If T, moved by extreme fear, hands over his money 'automatically', or, moved by extreme desire, snatches H's money 'instinctively', then we describe what T does as 'purely *physical* reactions'. Moreover, it is precisely and only in these extreme cases where there are purely physical reactions that T is coerced. When T is only moderately frightened or tempted, he is not unfree. In any case, the 'physically/psychologically' distinction is not clear cut. If H uses post-hypnotic suggestion to make T unable to walk from L to Y, does H coerce T psychologically or physically? The important point is that, for the purposes of this inquiry, it does not matter. All that matters is that H *makes* T *unable* to walk from L to Y; whether 'physically' or 'psychologically' is immaterial.

Cassinelli says that the kleptomaniac (K) is psychologically unfree to refrain from stealing because his irresistible desire to steal makes him incapable of not stealing (Cassinelli (1966), pp. 39f.). But this is incorrect, for an important reason. Unfreedom is essentially an *interpersonal* affair, in which B *makes* A *unable* to D. But K is not *made* unable to refrain from stealing by another person; he just *is* unable to do so. Or, if he is made unable to do so, it is not by another *person*, but by his own irresistible *desire*. This is the conception of freedom as an *intraper-sonal* relation between one part of one man's mind and another part of it. This vital distinction is clearly revealed in the language of the psychologists, who call K's thefts not *compulsory*, but *compulsive*. 'Compulsory', or 'compelled', are ellipses of 'compelled by *B*'; whereas 'compulsive' does not thus implicitly connote the existence of a compeller. This, again, is why K's case is quite different from that discussed above (Subsec. 5.2) in which T is tempted to take H's money; for in that case T is tempted *by H*.

Bay makes extensive use of the concept of psychological unfreedom. He derives it from Green's and Bosanquet's notion of 'positive' freedom as self-realisation, and brings it up to date with the findings of modern psychologists, especially those of Fromm. 'Positive freedom . . . is . . . the full realisation of the individual's potentialities. . . .' For Bay, the unfree man is the psychotic or severe neurotic, and Bay's model of him is the authoritarian personality (A), whose defensiveness is caused by fear.

But the case of A is on all fours with that of K, just discussed. A is not unfree, because he is not made unable to realise his potentialities by *B*; he simply is unable to do so. (Cf. Pennock (1972), p. 6.) Or, if he is made unable to do so, it is not by another person, but by his own fears.

Bay recognises the intrapersonal character of his 'psychological unfreedom,' and contrasts it with two interpersonal concepts, 'social unfreedom' and 'potential unfreedom', the latter of which I shall consider shortly (Subsec. 5.4). He also recognises that the Idealists' intrapersonal conception of liberty originates with Plato, in whose terms A is 'a slave to his fears' because 'the better part (of his soul) is overwhelmed by the worse' (*Republic*, 430-1, tr. Cornford). But then, as Green and Bosanquet stress, this notion of Plato's rests on nothing more substantial than the most famous of all his political *analogies*, namely, that which he draws between the good man and the good society — 'a man is just in the same way that a state (is) just' (*Republic*, 441; Green (1937), pp. 3f., 9f.; Bosanquet (1923), pp. 128ff.). We must resist the lure of Plato's master/slave trope, and insist that liberty is necessarily interpersonal. Speaking strictly and correctly, '*A* is unfree to *D*' entails '*B* makes *A* unable to *D*', where the variables *A* and *B* range over agents and the variable *D* ranges over simple or complex actions.

Plato's notion of intrapersonal freedom is the main source of the thesis that liberty is virtue. For in his view the unfree man, who is a slave to his passions, is also the bad (or 'unjust') man; whereas the free man, who is master of himself (i.e., of his passions), is the good (or 'just') man. (The importance of Plato's identification of the free man with the virtuous man is also discussed in Appendix I to Essay 10.)

5.4 Potential Unfreedom

Bay's potentially unfree man is the manipulated man (M), who is so called because the open or hidden persuaders who manipulate him 'hamper (his) potential behaviour, not his actual behaviour'. Bay finds the source of this notion of unfreedom in Rousseau: 'If it is good to know how to deal with men as they are, it is much better to make them what there is need that they should be. The most absolute authority is that which penetrates into a man's inmost being, and concerns itself no less with his *will* than with his *actions*' (*A Discourse on Political Economy*, tr. Cole, emphases added). Skinner gives a contemporary expression to the same thought: '. . . a system of slavery so well designed that it does not breed revolt is the real threat (to freedom)' (Skinner (1971), p. 40). (It is explained in Sec. 1 of Essay 6 why Rousseau and Skinner are right in thinking coercion by manipulation to be the most effective form of coercion.)

Most misunderstandings about liberty proceed from a misconception of the relations of liberty to desire (or will) (Sec. 2) and/or to ability (or power) (Sec. 4). Bay's concepts 'potential freedom' and 'psychological freedom' illustrate this truth. What he calls 'social freedom' is in fact freedom *sans phrase*, and we are now ready to elucidate this potent idea.

5.5 Final Analysis of Unfreedom

Our inquiry into the conditions of unfreedom has reached the following position. Critically, we have rejected the theses that A is unfree to D when he is incapable of Ding (Sec. 4); or when he acts unreasonably by Ding (Subsec. 5.1); or when he acts immorally in Ding (Subsec. 5.3); or when he does not feel unfree in Ding (Subsec. 5.4).

There is one further thesis to be dismissed. This is the position that A is unfree to D if he acts predictably in Ding. For I accept what O'Connor (1971) calls 'the consistency hypothesis', i.e., Hobbes' contention that '*Liberty* and *Necessity* are consistent' (*Leviathan* II, xxi.; cf. Hume, *An Enquiry concerning Human Understanding*, VIII; Mill, *A System of Logic*, VI, ii). When H points his pistol at T and says 'Your money or your life', we can predict that T will almost certainly hand over his money, because we know that this is what almost everybody does in such a case. But it neither follows nor is true that T is unfree to keep his money in this situation; as he would be if H forced him to hand it over, or cowed him into handing it over. In the threat situation, T's action in handing over his money is both predictable and also free. (Cf. Ayer (1959); Fain (1958).)

Constructively, we have found that A is unfree to D when B makes it impossible for him to D. E.g., T is unfree to keep his money (1) when H forces him to hand it over, or (2) when H cows T into handing it over. Again, (3) T is (about to be) unfree both to keep his money and also to keep his life when H makes T (about to be) unable to do these two things (the threat situation). Consequently, it looks very much as if B's making A unable to D is the unique sufficient condition of A's being unfree to D. I shall claim accordingly that, subject to a qualification to be made shortly, the truth of 'B makes A unable to D' is the sufficient *and necessary* condition of the truth of 'A is unfree to D'. So we arrive, in the end, at the formulation of Bentham: '. . . coercion, which (liberty) is the absence of . . .' (*Of Laws in General*; cf. Friedman (1966)). Or, in a contemporary version, 'An individual is unfree if, and only if, his doing of any action is rendered impossible by the action of another individual' (Steiner (1975), p. 33).

However, two further clarifications are called for, both of which concern the relations of liberty to ability. Firstly, I pointed out earlier that liberty presupposes ability; i.e., that the truth of 'A is able to D' is a necessary condition both of the truth and also of the falsity of 'A is unfree to D' (Sec. 4). But since 'A is unfree to D' is materially equivalent to 'B makes A unable to D', it follows that the last formula also presupposes 'A is able to D'. And this is indeed so. H can make T unable to walk from L to Y, because that is a thing which T is able to do. But H cannot *make T unable* to walk from L to New York, because that is a thing which T *is unable* to do anyway. If A is unable to D, the question of his being made unable to D cannot arise.

Secondly, although the truth of 'B makes A unable to D' is a necessary condition of the truth of 'A is unfree to D', the truth of the former is not strictly a sufficient condition of the truth of the latter, for an interesting reason. Consider the following three ways in which H can make T unable to walk from L to Y: (1) by imprisoning him; (2) by cutting off his legs; (3) by breaking his left ankle. In case (1), we have no hesitation in saying that T is unfree to walk from L to Y; it is a paradigm case of unfreedom. In case (2), which is also a paradigm, we have no hesitation in saying that T is unable, not unfree, to walk from L to Y. In case (3), we perhaps hesitate but are prepared to allow that T is unfree, not merely unable, to walk from L to Y. Plainly, the difference resides in whether the inability is irretrievable or not. We do not talk of A being unfree to D

unless *B* has made *A* unable to *D* in such a way that it is possible for *A* to be again able to *D*. T will again be able to walk to Y if he is released from prison, or when his ankle mends; but he will never be able to do so if his legs have been cut off. This is why, even when H imprisons T for the term of his natural life, we still call T 'unfree'. For we think that there is always a chance that he will escape or be rescued, or that H will relent. Let us therefore speak of *B* making *A* '(ir)retrievably' unable to *D*. (Cf. White (1970).)

We have seen that not all increases in the number of alternative actions open to *A* augment his liberty, since some such increases augment, not *A*'s liberty, but his power (Sec. 4). Similarly, we now see that not all decreases in the number of alternative actions open to *A* curtail his liberty. For when *B* inflicts an irretrievable disability on *A*, he curtails, not *A*'s liberty, but his power.

Finally, then, the sufficient and necessary condition of the truth of '*A* is unfree to *D*' is the truth of '*B* makes *A* retrievably unable to *D* by *E*ing *A*.' E.g., 'H makes T retrievably unable to walk from L to Y by imprisoning T.' The presence of the first agent-variable, *B*, brings out the essentially interpersonal character of freedom. The presence of the second action-variable, *E*, stresses the important truth pointed out by Bay, that 'it is the *means* and not the *ends* of power exercise that determine the extent to which . . . freedom is interfered with' (Bay (1958), p. 91, emphases added). The presence of the modifier 'retrievably' meets the point made in the preceding paragraph, and illustrates again the truth of Bay's contention that it makes a difference *how B* renders *A* unable to *D*. So, whenever any assertion is made about liberty, it is always possible to discover exactly what (if anything) is being asserted by seeking values for the four variables in the above formula, in order to obtain a clear statement which is either true or false. (Cf. MacCallum (1972).)

6. The Logic of the Will and the Philosophy of Law

The position which I have maintained thus far is essentially Hobbist. It will be fruitful to introduce now some leading ideas of Bentham's. Bentham is the creator of the imperative theory of law, according to which a law is a command to a subject that is declarative of his sovereign's will (*Of Laws in General*, i. 1). But more, he is the creator of the philosophy of law itself, since, as Mill says, 'he found the philosophy of law a chaos, he left it a science' ('Bentham', *Dissertations and Discussions*, I). More yet, he is the creator of what he calls 'the logic of the will', which is called today 'deontic logic'. (See Hart (1971), pp. 60ff.; McLaughlin (1973), pp. 215f.) So far, I have analysed the concept of liberty (or freedom) by exhibiting its relations to the four concepts of ability (or power), desire (or will), threat and offer. I shall now complete my analysis of it by showing its connexions with Bentham's three cardinal concepts, order (or command), permission, and law (or mandate). (Sec. 1, end.)

6.1 Influence and Liberty

I use 'to influence' in a wide sense, such that 'B either induces, or tries to induce A to D.' For the purposes of this inquiry, the most important distinction between the different ways in which B can impose his will on A is that between coercive influence and non-coercive influence. B compels (or coerces) A to D if and only if B makes A retrievably unable to -D by Eing A. E.g., H compels T to remain in L by making him retrievably unable to leave L through imprisoning him. Hence, A is unfree to D if and only if B compels A to -D. In other words, as Bentham says, freedom is the absence of compulsion (Subsec. 5.5).

(A) Coercive modes of influence are: (1) forcing, (2) threatening, (3) extreme intimidation, (4) extreme temptation, (5) extreme domination, and (6) extreme provocation. (B) Non-coercive modes of influence are: (7) ordering, (8) requesting, (9) offering, (10) persuading, (11) advising, (12) warning, (13) praising, (14) blaming, (15) rewarding, (16) punishing, (17) deterring. In (A), but not in (B), B is said in the language of the law to 'cause' (or 'make') A to D (Hart and Honoré (1959), pp. 71, 173). (I now think that the key concept involved here is not *influence*, but *control*. See Sec. 5 of Essay 10.)

As to (2), the main difference between threatening and the other five coercive modes of influence is that, whereas in the latter B makes A unable to D, in the former B makes A unable both to D and also to E.

(5) and (6) resemble (3) and (4). In (5), B bullies A into Ding, since B's ascendancy over A is so great that A is unable to -D. (6) includes extreme incitement, instigation and exhortation. E.g., B taunts A so grossly that A strikes B in purely reflex retaliation.

In the law, (4) and (6) are treated as calling for *mitigation* of penalty, but not for *excuse* from penalty (Hart (1962), pp. 168ff.). Yet it is hard to see any justification for this. It seems to me that (3), (4), (5) and (6) render A unfree, so that he ought to be excused punishment. Naturally, this is not to deny the difficulty of establishing in any particular case whether B's temptation, or provocation, or etc. of A was in truth so strong as to make A unable to -D. Since we usually lack the relevant information about the individual A, we fall back on the concept of the average man. Aristotle, e.g., speaks of pardoning (i.e., excusing) A 'when (A) does what he ought not under pressure which overstrains human nature' (*Nic. Ethics*, tr. Ross, 1110a). Aristotle's 'human nature' is plainly the statistical concept, 'the average man'. But this difficulty arises whenever B is alleged to make A unable to D. Thus, does the locked door make the imprisoned T unable to go to Y? If T is a man of average strength, yes; but if he is exceptionally strong, no. So, unless we know that T *is* exceptionally strong, we deem him unable to go to Y (cf: Benn (1967), pp. 267f.).

As to (9), all offers (or invitations) are permissions, but not conversely. E.g.respectively (i) H says to T 'You may have all this money if you will give me your hand in marriage', and (ii) an employer says to his secretary 'You may go if you have finished your work.' Permissions of class (i) are influences. We have seen that the two main differences between (9) and (2) are first, that threats coerce whereas offers do not coerce; and secondly, that offers can be either simple or complex, but threats can only be complex (Sec. 3). Examples of simple and complex offers are respectively 'You may have all this money' ('no strings attached'), and (i), above.

(1), (10) and (17) differ from the other 14 verbs under consideration in being, like 'induce', what Ryle calls 'achievement verbs' (Ryle (1949), pp. 149ff.). I.e:, it is illogical to say 'B forced A to D, but A did not D.' The fact that, if B persuades A to D, then A cannot -D, tends to create the illusion that persuasion is a compulsive type of influence; and similarly with deterrence. Again, most of these verbs fall naturally into groups. Thus, dominating, intimidating, provoking and tempting are members of the same family. And requesting goes naturally with ordering, as does offering with persuading, and warning with advising. Also praising goes with rewarding, as blaming does with punishing.

Just as there are complex (conjunctive) actions which involve both threatening and intimidating, and both offering and tempting; so there are other sorts of complex actions which involve others of the 17 sorts of actions that we are talking about (Subsec. 5.2). E.g., B can both order A to D and bully A into Ding; and B can both persuade A to D and provoke A into Ding. We describe these types of complex actions by such locutions as 'B roared at A an order to D', and 'B needled A into Ding.' Consequently, just as it may be hard to distinguish offering from tempting, threatening from intimidating, and threatening from warning; so it may also be difficult to discriminate between ordering and bullying, persuading and provoking.

Again, one can combine an offer with a threat, as in 'Either you will take my money, or I shall take your life.' For these combinations, I shall borrow from Steiner the name 'throffer.' (Steiner himself, however, gives this name to more complex combinations, typified by 'Either you will take A's life and take my money, or I will take your life.') Throffers coerce, not *qua* offers (which are non-coercive), but *qua* threats (which are coercive). An important type of hybrid is exemplified by 'Give me your money'! or I shall take your life', the obvious name for which is 'throrder'. Steiner, indeed, gives this as an example of a threat; but this is not so, since the corresponding pure threat is, as we have seen, 'Either you will give me your money, or I shall take your life' (Sec. 3). Throrders too coerce *qua* threats, not *qua* orders. For H's pure order to T, 'Give me your money!', does not make T unable to keep his money, or indeed unable to do anything else. The request, 'Please give me your money', is similarly non-coercive (Subsec. 5.1). But compare with this pure request the coercive and ironic threquest (for the use of gentlemanly Hs), 'Pray give me your money, or I shall take your life.'

The fact that pure orders do not compel raises a doubt about whether there are such things, since they seem to be pointless. So may not what seem to be pure orders always be really either orders *implicitly* backed by threats, or *implicit* throrders? The answer to this question is, No. Speaking strictly, Bradley is right in saying that 'threat is not of the essence of command; command need not imply the holding forth . . . of consequences' (Bradley (1927), p. 207). But Bradley's thesis is contradicted by the antithesis that all imperatives are 'hypothetical' (in Kant's sense) and reducible to indicatives. According to this antithesis, 'Let A D!' is always an ellipsis of 'If A will not D, then it will be the worse for A' (or of 'Either A will D, or it will be the worse for A') (Hare (1952), pp. 7ff., 33ff.). However, this antithesis differs importantly from the view that all orders are either (a) orders explicitly or implicitly backed by threats, or (b) explicit or implicit throrders. (a) is illustrated by 'Give me your money! For either you will give me your money, or I will take your life.' For, on this last view, orders are certainly not reducible to *indicatives*. This is because the second alternant in the alternation (α) 'Give me your money! or I shall take your life', and the consequent in the conditional (β) 'If you will not give me your money, then I shall take your life' is not *descriptive*. It is rather a declaration of intention, and so what J.L. Austin calls *commissive*, because it commits him who says it to a certain course of action (Austin (1962), pp. 40ff., 156ff.). (β) is not a conditional prediction like (γ) 'If you will not give me your money, then I shall be less rich than my brother.' Hence the impossibility of a truth-functional treatment of threats, since commissives are neither true nor false. I mentioned earlier the difficulty and importance of distinguishing warnings from threats (Subsec. 5.2). Thus, if H says to T (δ) 'If you will not give me your money, then I shall take my life', is that a threat or a warning? Without further information, there is no telling. E.g., if H knows that T desires H to take H's life, then (δ) is neither a threat nor a warning.

Economists sometimes distinguish 'demand' from 'effective demand', and a parallel distinction between 'command' and 'effective command' is helpful here. Nevertheless, it is false that all effective commands are either (a) orders explicitly or implicitly backed by threats, or (b) explicit or implicit orders. For a religious leader might order his disciples to give all their possessions to the poor, and the order might prove effective, neither because of any threat made or implied by the leader, nor because of his power, but because of his authority over his disciples. (Cf. Broadie (1972), p. 190.) But such cases are infrequent, and we must conclude, firstly, that effective orders are generally either of type (a) or of type (b); and secondly, that effective orders are coercive, not because they are orders, but because they involve threats. Finally, orders, like offers, can be either simple or complex, and complex in either the conjunctive or alternative modes. Examples of the two types of complex orders are respectively, 'Give me your money or give me your life!' and 'Give me your money or give me your life!' An example of a conjunctive offer is 'You may have my money and you may have my life.'

As for (13)—(16), praise and blame, reward and punishment are of course the modes of influence to which moral philosophers have given most attention. I shall consider shortly the relations of the last two to threats, offers, law, opinion and liberty (Subsecs. 6.2, 6.3).

The 17 modes of influence which I have discussed are the common ones. But there are others. One unusual one is post-hypnotic suggestion, which, as we have seen, is coercive (Subsec. 5.3). Ordinary suggestion, on the other hand, is often not a mode of influence at all; but when it is, it is non-coercive, and merges in persuasion. There are other such mergers. Thus, I take forcing to cover compelling and constraining, preventing and restraining; approving and encouraging to be covered by praising, and disapproving and discouraging by blaming; provoking to cover instigating, protesting, exhorting and urging; offering to cover inviting and bribing; advising to cover guiding and instructing; requesting to cover demanding and petitioning; persuading to cover coaxing and cajoling; and deterring to cover hindering and impeding.

6.2 Law and Liberty

According to Bentham, 'a law by which nobody is bound, a law by which nobody is coerced, a law by which nobody's liberty is curtailed, all these phrases which come to the same thing (are) so many contradictions in terms.' (*Of Laws in General*, vi, 3). This is thought to follow from his imperative theory of law (Sec. 6). According to Hart's improved model of the imperative theory, which is substantially Austinian rather than Benthamite, the form of any law is (really) (1) 'Let S D! For either S will D, or R will punish S', where R (*Rex*) is any sovereign and S is any subject of R (Hart (1961), pp. 18ff., 234ff.). Four points in this account of a law call for comment. Firstly, on the relation of law to desire (or will). In laws, the modes in which R's will is declared are (I) command and (II) prohibition (command to forbear) (Sec. 6). Secondly, one must speak of a general order 'explicitly' backed by a threat, because the sanction which backs a penal law needs to be stated, not implied, else the law will not deter as it is intended to do (see Bentham, *Of Laws in General*, xi, 3-4). Thirdly, one may speak of R 'punishing' S for non-compliance; but not of, e.g., H 'punishing' T for non-compliance. The reason for this is that in the former case the threat is executed by an *authority*, whereas in the latter case this is not so (Hart (1962), pp. 161f.). Fourthly, it seems to me that the imperative theory could equally well represent any law as an explicit general throrder of the form (2) 'Let S D! or R will punish S' (Subsec. 6.1). This version of the theory has the advantage of being shorter and simpler than (1) (above).

However, it is false that *all* laws are of this type. Bentham's insistence that, despite appearances to the contrary, all laws are ('really', or 'reducible to') imperatives, contrasts instructively with the view, mentioned above, that all imperatives are ('really', or 'reducible to') indicatives (Subsec. 6.1). For instance, the Wills Act of 1837 does not *order S* to make a valid will on pain of punishment if he does not comply; rather, it *permits* and *enables* him to do so (Hart (1961), pp. 27f.). Again, general orders may be backed by offers, instead of by threats. Such laws are non-coercive, since offers, being a species of permissions, do not compel (Subsec. 6.1). Bentham calls them 'praemiary laws' (from the Latin *praemium*, meaning 'a reward'). E.g., a law providing that any S who reports a robbery to R shall receive from R a reward of £10. Bentham also notes that there can be 'a law with alternative sanctions'. E.g., a law providing that S shall be given a reward of £10 if he reports a robbery to R, but that he shall be fined £10 if he fails to do so. Manifestly, these alternative sanctions are throffers, and are of the same type as 'Either I will give you my money if you will give me your hand in marriage, or I will take your money if you will not give me your hand in marriage' (Subsec. 6.1). Bentham points out, however, that orders backed by offers are much less effective than orders backed by threats. He gives several cogent and characteristic reasons why the legislator must rely far more on the stick than on the carrot, such as that 'the sources of pleasure are few and soon exhausted; the sources of pain are innumerable and inexhaustible' (*Of Laws in General*, xi, 1-10).

But even if the imperative theory does not apply to all laws, it holds approximately true of some laws. The sort of law that it fits best is a criminal statute enacted by the British Queen in Parliament. So let us take as paradigm of a law such a statute, which prohibits $S1$ from murdering $S2$ on pain of punishment by death (L). Then how, and why, does L restrict $S1$'s liberty? Firstly, it does not do so *qua* order, because orders do not coerce; but it does so *qua* threat, because threats do coerce (Subsec. 6.1). (Cf. the quotation from Hart on the usual meaning of 'unfree' in political contexts (Sec. 1)). Secondly, L does not diminish $S1$'s liberty by making $S1$ unable to murder $S2$, but by making $S1$ unable both to murder $S2$ and to remain alive. (It is assumed that L is effectively enforced.) We have seen that Cassinelli shares the popular misconception on this point (Sec. 3). For, thirdly, the purpose of L is not to prevent $S1$ from murdering $S2$, but to *deter* him from doing so.

6.3 Opinion and Liberty

Mill emphasises that his 'principle of individual liberty', which asserts that C's only justification for coercing A is to prevent him from harming B, defines the proper bounds not only of governmental compulsion but also of the 'coercion of public opinion'. This raises the question whether public opinion does in fact coerce and, if so, how. The answer is that it does so because, as Mill puts it, 'society can and does execute its own mandates' (*On Liberty*, i). E.g., a community (C) makes a mandate (M) that any fellow (F) of C who does not attend church at least once on Sundays shall be ostracised. M resembles L in the following important respects. Firstly, M curtails F's liberty by making him unable both to absent himself from church on Sundays and also to be socially accepted. For, secondly, the purpose of M is not to prevent F from absenting himself from church on Sundays, but to deter him from doing so. On the other hand, M differs from L in the following important respects. Firstly, if C ostracises F for non-compliance with M, then C is not rightly said to 'punish' F, because C is not an authority. In this respect, C's position is the same as H's and different from R's. Secondly, whereas the threat which backs L is always explicit, the threat which backs M is normally tacit (Subsec. 6.2). The evidence for the existence of the threat is C's actions. If C regularly does ostracise recusants, then F must infer that C is tacitly threatening to ostracise him if he does not comply with M. H, too, can threaten T tacitly, i.e. by deed rather than by word. Instead of saying to T 'Either you will give me your money, or I will take your life', H could silently point a pistol at T's heart with one hand and extend his other hand to T with the palm upwards and open.

There are also praemiary social mandates corresponding to praemiary state laws. E.g., C makes a mandate that any F who attends church more than once on Sundays shall be honoured. Here, the order is backed by an offer. But, like praemiary state laws, praemiary social mandates are non-coercive because offers are non-coercive. On the other hand, my principal contention here is precisely that the concept of a *tacit threat* is a very important one, because tacit ('veiled') threats are the means whereby society normally coerces its members. With some reason, Mill considers 'the tyranny of the prevailing opinion' to be a danger at least as great as 'the tyranny of the magistrate' (*On Liberty*, i).

In formulating his famous principle, Mill speaks sometimes of 'preventing' A from harming B, but at other times of 'deterring' him from doing so. It is, of course, the latter which is correct, since it is deterrence and not prevention which is the object both of minatory state laws and also of minatory social mandates; which are what Mill is discussing. To repeat: the purpose of L is not to *prevent S1* from murdering *S2*, but to *deter S1* from murdering *S2* by *preventing S1* from both taking *S2*'s life and also keeping his own life. If *R*'s purpose were to prevent *S1* from murdering *S2*, he could achieve it, not by making L, but by e.g. locking up *S1* and/or by locking up *S2* ('protective custody'). However, the superiority of deterrence over prevention is obvious. It would be both immoral and impractical for *R* to lock up every potential murderer, or every potential murderee, in his realm.

6.4 Concluding Elucidations

Some points remain in need of clarification.

The notion of a complex (conjunctive) action has figured largely in the argument of this study. However, this notion must not be confused with the more familiar idea, with which Bentham was acquainted, of alternative descriptions of an action (*Of Laws in General*, v. 1-10). Nevertheless, the two concepts are sometimes associated. For if it is true that, e.g., B made A a tempting offer, then it is also true that '*B* made *A* an offer' and '*B* tempted *A*' are alternative (or rather, disjunctive) descriptions of what *B* did to *A*.

I say that a threat, such as H's to T, 'Either you will give me your money, or I will take your life', curtails T's liberty by making T about to be unable both to keep his money and also to keep his life (Sec. 3, beginning). Dr Steiner objects that this is not so, because H may relent between uttering the threat and executing it; so that, generally, it is the implementing of a threat and not the making of it which diminishes freedom. I reply, firstly, that this is paradoxical, since the received view is that it is the making of threats which restricts liberty. This is particularly clear in the case of L, which is generally held to make *S* less free from the time of its enactment. Moreover, if L were to fulfil its deterrent purpose with complete success, the threat which backs it would never be executed. Consequently, on Steiner's view, L would never curtail liberty; which seems highly paradoxical. Secondly, I confine the discussion to normal or genuine threats, i.e. threats which the threatener both sincerely intends and is able to execute. I think that our view that the making of genuine threats abridges freedom rests on the fact that, *as a general rule*, threateners do execute genuine threats upon non-compliant threatenees. It is exceptional for H to change his mind between the utterance of his threat and the attainment of the deadline, or to forget to load his pistol. However, in a society where, as a general rule, threateners did not execute genuine threats upon non-compliant threatenees, Steiner's view would be the received view.

Since the generalisation 'Almost all genuine threats are executed upon non-compliant threatenees' is statistical and not universal, one must say in strictness of speech that H's utterance of his threat *very probably* makes T about to be unable both to keep his money and also to keep his life. It will not do so if, e.g., H relents. But it is important to recognise that there is no difference in this respect between the way in which threats curtail liberty and the way in which attempted compulsion or restraint do so. For, as we have seen already, the generalisation 'Almost all persons who are locked in a room in L are unable to go from L to Y' is also statistical and not universal (Subsec. 6.1). Consequently, one must say similarly that H's imprisoning T in L *very probably* makes T unable to go from L to Y. It will not do so if, e.g., T is exceptionally strong. Our concept of unfreedom, like so many others of our concepts, is relative to our idea of the average man or of human nature. Thus, we deem *A* to be unfree if he is threatened by *B*, and *B* is a normal threatener; or if *B* does to *A* the sort of thing that makes the average man retrievably unable to *D* (e.g., imprisons him, or binds him). The concepts of the average agent and of the average patient are central to the philosophy of action in the same sort of way as the notions, 'the normal observer' and 'normal conditions', are central to the philosophy of perception.

This fact is connected with another important point about our concept of unfreedom, namely, that it is the concept of *some person* being made unable to perform *some sort* of action by *some other person's* performing *some other sort* of action on him. E.g., we think of *A's freedom of movement* being curtailed by *B's imprisoning* him. This has a significant bearing on what Mill, Hampshire, and Steiner, e.g., call 'individual liberty' (Subsec. 6.3; Hampshire (1965); Steiner (1975)). For when we think of some *individual*, H, making some other *individual*, T, unable to perform the *particular action* of walking now from L to Y by performing the *particular action* of locking him in his bedroom now; then we think of this particular transaction as an individual instance of the general formula just stated about persons, freedom of movement and imprisonment. The concept of individual liberty is the concept of the liberty of the *individual variable, A*, and not the concept of the liberty of the *particular individual*, T. Hence, we deem H's action to abridge T's liberty, unless we know that T is strong enough to be able to break down his bedroom door.

I also say that *B*'s threat to *A* diminishes *A*'s liberty, because it makes *A* about to be unable to perform some conjunctive action which he can unconditionally now perform (Sec. 3, end). In the case of H's threat to T, it is indisputable that, before the threat, T can unconditionally both have his money and also have his life; for he is now doing so. In the case of L, however, Professor Hart objects that it is false that, before *R* makes L, *S1* can unconditionally both take *S2*'s life and also keep his own life (Subsec. 6.2). For, firstly, *S1* is not now killing *S2*. And secondly, *S1* cannot kill *S2* unless *S1* does not die first, and unless *S2* does not kill *S1* first, and unless *S1* and *S2* are not simultaneously struck dead by lightning first, and unless . . . etc. I think that the reply to this objection is as follows. We deem *A* to be unconditionally able to *D* unless we know or believe that some preventing condition is not merely possible, but either actual or probable. Thus, it is true that *S1* cannot kill *S2* if both are simultaneously struck dead by lightning first. But since we know that this compound (conjunctive) event is *very improbable*, we do not cease to consider *S1* as unconditionally able to kill *S2* merely because we know that this compound event is possible. Consider, by contrast, the statement 'Before H offers his life to T in exchange for T's money, T cannot have H's life unless H gives it to T.' Here, we deem T to be only conditionally able to have H's life, because we know it is a *fact* that, unless H gives his life to T, T cannot have H's life in the relevant sense of 'have H's life,' namely 'receive H's life from H'. (See O'Connor (1971), pp. 26ff.)

Next, the subjects of liberty. It is implicit in what precedes that *what* is free is a person, and I have answered the question *when* a person is free in detail above (Sec. 5). However, we call many other sorts of things free, the most important of which are actions and wills. But I agree with Hobbes that all these uses must be explained in terms of the freedom of persons. Thus, (1) as to free action, *A* *D*s freely if and only if *A* *D*s and it is not the case that *A* is unfree to -*D*. (2) as to free will, *A* *D*s of his own free will (or choice) if and only if *A* *D*s freely; the analysis of this last formula being (1). As Hobbes says, 'from the use of the word *Free-will*, no Liberty can be inferred of the will . . ., but the Liberty of the man . . . ' (*Leviathan*, II, xxi).

It is an important fact about liberty that there are degrees of it, as there are also degrees of potency (see Oppenheim (1961), pp. 179-210). Suppose, then, that H chains to T's left ankle an iron ball, which is not so heavy as to immobilise T completely, but is heavy enough to slow him down considerably. Does H thereby make T more unfree to walk from L to Y? No; because, firstly, the last expression is illogical. For although we speak of *A* as more (or less) unfree, we do not speak of him as more (or less) unfree *to D*. The reason for this is, secondly, that *B* makes *A* unfree to *D* if and only if *B* makes *A* retrievably unable to *D*, and that there are no degrees of ability or possibility (Subsec. 5.5). However, this last fact is liable to be obscured by improper manners of speaking. E.g., a sufferer from arthritis is apt to say 'I am not so able to move about as I was' instead of 'I am not able to move about so much as I was.' Nor is this error exclusive to the vulgar. Philosophers of probability, for instance, are prone to speak of 'equally possible' alternatives. Consequently, *A* becomes more (or less) free, or more (or less) powerful, by becoming able to do more (or less) things; not by becoming more (or less) able to do any given number of things (Sec. 4, Subsec. 5.5). What H achieves by means of the ball and chain is to *impede* T's walking from L to Y. Hobbes' definition of freedom is open to criticism on this score, since he speaks of *A* being free to *D* if he is not 'hindered' from *D*ing by *B* (*Leviathan*, II, xxi). But 'hindered' means the same as 'impeded', and Hobbes needs for his definition a stronger verb, such as 'prevented' or (as he himself says elsewhere) 'stopped' (cf. Subsec. 5.1, end).

Finally, a word on the importance of freedom. Oppenheim remarks that '. . . "liberty" is perhaps the word which occurs most frequently in political life and in political theory' (Oppenheim (1961), p. 109).

Why is this? Part of the answer, without doubt, is the high value that men set on liberty. In this essay, however, I have virtually ignored the evaluative aspect of the philosophical problem of liberty. For instance, we have considered whether laws do curtail liberty; and if so, how exactly, and why. But nothing has been said about the great and complex question of whether laws ought to be used to curtail certain sorts of liberties; and if so, to what extent, and how exactly, and why. I deliberately say nothing here about the *right* to liberty, because it is quite task enough for one study to explain the *meaning* of 'free'. Nevertheless, it is relevant to add that the very fact that liberty is a right throws into relief what we have seen to be an essential feature of freedom, namely, its interpersonal character. For a right is always held or claimed by some person, *A*, against some other person *B*. Or, to put the same point differently, it is a telling objection against Plato's intrapersonal, master/slave conception of unfreedom that it carries with it the absurd consequence that one can speak meaningfully of one part of *A*'s soul invading the right to liberty of another part of it (Subsec. 5.3).

We have seen that Plato's view rests on metaphor, and there is another common metaphor which deserves notice. *A* may tell *B* that he is unfree to dine with him tomorrow because he has engaged himself to dine with *C*. This is literally false, because *A can* break his engagement to *C* and dine with *B* instead. Suppose, however, that *R* makes a law which provides that, if *S1* breaks his engagement to marry *S2*, then he must pay *S2* damages. Then *S1*'s liberty is curtailed, because he cannot both break his engagement and also keep (all of) his money. But what curtails *S1*'s liberty is not his promise, but *R*'s law. Talk of 'binding promises' and 'moral laws' is as-if talk, like talk of 'slavery to the passions' and 'irresistible offers'.

References

References are given in the text between brackets either (*a*) in the case of classic works, by part, chapter, section etc.; or (*b*) in the case of other works, by page number to the works listed below. No works published after 1975 are included in this list.

Austin, J.L., 'Ifs and Cans', *British Academy Proceedings*, vol. 42 (1956), pp. 109-32.
—— *How to do Things with Words* (Oxford, 1962).
Ayer, A.J., 'Freedom and Necessity'. *Polemic*, no. 5 (1946), pp. 36-44.
Bay, Christian, *The Structure of Freedom* (Stanford, 1958).
Benn, S.I, 'Freedom and Persuasion'. *The Australasian Journal of Philosophy*, Vol. 45 (1967), pp. 259-75.
Benn, S.I. and Peters, R.S., *Social Principles and the Democratic State* (London,

1959), Chs. 9, 10.
Benn, S.I. and Weinstein, W.L., 'Being Free to Act, and Being a Free Man', *Mind*, Vol. 80 (1971), pp. 194-211.
—— 'Freedom as the Non-Restriction of Options', *Mind*, Vol. 83 (1974), pp. 435-8.
Berlin, Isaiah, 'From Hope and Fear Set Free', *Aristotelian Society Proceedings*, Vol. 64 (1964), pp. 1-30.
—— *Four Essays on Liberty* (Oxford, 1969).
Bosanquet, Bernard, *The Philosophical Theory of the State* (London, 1923).
Bradley, F.H., 'My Station and its Duties' in *Ethical Studies* (Oxford, 1927).
Broadie, Alexander, 'Imperatives', *Mind*, Vol. 81 (1972), pp. 179-90.
Cassinelli, C.W., *Free Activities and Interpersonal Relations* (The Hague, 1966).
Cranston, Maurice, *Freedom: A New Analysis* (London, 1953).
Crick, Bernard, 'Freedom as Politics' in *Philosophy, Politics and Society*, series 3, ed. by Peter Laslett and W.G. Runciman (Oxford, 1967).
Day J.P., 'Unconscious Perception', *Aristotelian Society Supplement*, Vol. 34 (1960), pp. 47-66.
—— 'On Liberty and the Real Will', *Philosophy*, Vol. 45 (1970), pp. 177-92.
Duncan-Jones, Austin, 'Freedom to Do Otherwise', *The Cambridge Journal*, Vol. 3 (1950), p. 750.
Dworkin, Gerald, 'Acting Freely', *Nous*, Vol. 4 (1970), pp. 367-83.
Fain, Haskell, 'Prediction and Constraint', *Mind*, Vol. 67 (1958), pp. 366-78.
Feinberg, Joel, *Social Philosophy* (Englewood Cliffs, 1973), Chs. 1-3.
Frankfurt, H.G., 'Coercion and Moral Responsibility' in *Essays on Freedom of Action*, ed. by Ted Honderich (London, 1973).
—— 'Three Concepts of Free Action', *Aristotelian Society Supplement*, Vol. 49 (1975), pp. 113-25.
Friedman, R.B. 'A New Exploration of Mill's Essay *On Liberty*', *Political Studies*, Vol. 14 (1966), pp. 281-304.
Green, T.H., 'On the Different Senses of "Freedom" . . . etc.' in *Lectures on the Principles of Political Obligation* (London, 1937)
Hampshire, S.N., *Freedom of the Individual* (London, 1965).
Hare, R.M. *The Language of Morals* (Oxford, 1952).
Hart, H.L.A., 'Prolegomenon to the Principles of Punishment', *Aristotelian Society Proceedings*, Vol. 60 (1960), pp. 1-26.
—— *The Concept of Law* (Oxford, 1961).
—— *Law, Liberty and Morality* (London, 1963).
—— 'Bentham's *Of Laws in General*', *Rechtstheorie*, Vol. 2 (1971), pp. 55-66.
Hart, H.L.A. and Honoré, A.M., *Causation in the Law* (Oxford, 1959).
Locke, Don, 'Three Concepts of Free Action', *Aristotelian Society Supplement*, Vol. 49 (1975), pp. 95-112.
Lyons, Daniel, 'Welcome Threats and Coercive Offers', *Philosophy*, Vol. 50 (1975), pp. 425-36.
Mabbott, J.D., *The State and the Citizen* (London, 1947) Pt. B.
MacCallum, G.C., 'Negative and Positive Freedom', *The Philosophical Review*, Vol. 76 (1967), pp. 312-34.
MacMurray, John, *Conditions of Freedom* (Toronto, 1949).
McCloskey, H.J., 'A Critique of the Ideals of Liberty', *Mind*, Vol. 74 (1965), pp. 483-508.
McLaughlin, R.N., 'Deontic Logic and Conditional Obligation', *Mind*, Vol. 82 (1973), pp. 207-17.
Melden, A.I., *Free Action* (New York, 1961).
Moore, G.E., *Ethics* (London, 1912), Ch. 6.
Nowell-Smith, P.H., *Ethics* (London, 1954), Chs. 19, 20.
Nozick, Robert, 'Coercion' in *Philosophy, Science and Method: Essays in Honor of Ernest Nagel*, ed. by S. Morgenbesser *et al.* (New York, 1959).

O'Connor, D.J., *Free Will* (London, 1971).

Oppenheim, F.E., *Dimensions of Freedom* (New York, 1961).

Parent, W.A., 'Freedom as the Non-Restriction of Options', *Mind*, Vol. 83 (1974), pp. 432-4.

—— 'Some Recent Work on the Concept of Liberty', *American Philosophical Quarterly*, Vol. 11 (1974), pp. 149-67.

Pennock, J.R., 'Coercion: An Overview', *Nomos*, Vol. 14 (1972), pp. 1-15.

Plamenatz, J.P., *Consent, Freedom and Political Obligation* (Oxford, 1938), Chs. 5, 6.

Pollock, Lansing, 'Freedom and Universalizability', *Mind*, Vol. 82 (1973), pp. 234-48.

Ryle, Gilbert, *The Concept of Mind* (London, 1949), Ch. 3.

Skinner, B.F., *Beyond Freedom and Dignity* (New York, 1971).

Steiner, Hillel, 'Individual Liberty', *Aristotelian Society Proceedings*, Vol. 75 (1975), pp. 33-50.

Weinstein, W.L., 'The Concept of Liberty in Nineteenth Century English Political Thought', *Political Studies*, Vol. 13 (1965), pp. 145-62.

White, D.M., 'Negative Liberty', *Ethics*, Vol. 80 (1970), pp. 185-204.

Wilson, John, 'Freedom and Compulsion', *Mind*, Vol. 67 (1958), pp. 60-9.

4 RETRIBUTIVE PUNISHMENT

1. The Problems of Retributive Punishment

The present position regarding the philosophical problems of what Bentham calls 'political punishment' is as follows. The central problem is taken to be one of justification; namely, what moral right has any state to deprive any offending citizen of any goods, e.g. of his property by fining him, or of his liberty by imprisoning him? Two main types of solution are offered, the teleological or utilitarian, and the retributivist. According to the former, a punishment can only be justified by its good consequences; whereas according to the latter a punishment may be justified regardless of its consequences. However, these types are not mutually exclusive, and there are compromise solutions, such as Hart's, which belong to what Ezorsky calls the teleological-retributivist type. For more than 50 years before 1939, the teleologists had things pretty much their own way; but the publication of Mabbott's essay in that year initiated what may be called 'the retributivist reaction'.

I agree that the problem of justification is central, yet I do not think that it is the most important philosophical problem involved here (see below). Further, the utilitarian/retributivist dichotomy seems to me misleading, because the theory which is called 'utilitarian' is not so in fact. Accordingly, I shall propose an alternative dichotomy later (Sec. 5). Again, whereas Benn and others see Kant as the classic exponent of the retributivist theory, it seems to me that Hegel plays that part.

The teleological theory is on the whole clear. Its adherents hold that any state has a duty to protect its citizens by, above all, deterring potential offenders by means of threats of punishment; and, to a much less extent, by means of preventing actual offenders from offending again, e.g. by imprisoning them. The only point in the theory which needs clarification concerns how punishment curtails liberty, to which I shall offer an answer later (Sec. 5).

Very different, however, is the situation of the retributivist theory, where we find a striking paradox, which I shall call 'the retributivist paradox'. Namely that, although the retributivist reaction shows that many philosophers are now disposed to regard retributive punishment as justified or *good*, there is no general agreement about what retributive punishment *is* — or better, about what the words 'retributive punishment' *mean*. I believe that this basic conceptual confusion has prevented the retributivist reaction from exerting its full effect. Here are two illustrations. Some philosophers (e.g. Mabbott) seem to define 'a retributive punishment' as 'a non-teleological punishment', i.e., a punishment imposed without regard to its consequences. But, first, it is a general rule of definition that a word should be defined in positive terms rather than in negative ones. Secondly, since by this definition any punishment which is at all teleological is non-retributive, it excludes the useful compromise category of teleological-retributive punishments. Again, Rashdall defines 'a retributive punishment' as 'a punishment which does no one any good'. However, Rashdall surely mistakes his *definiendum*. For the latter expression defines 'a pointless punishment', not 'a retributive punishment'.

I aim to solve the problem of justification by defending Hegel's thesis that the justification of retributive punishment resides in the fact that, when the state punishes an offender retributively, it 'annuls the crime, which otherwise would have been held valid, and restores the right'. However, this thesis is not exclusively Hegelian, since it is maintained not only by the idealists Green, Bradley and Bosanquet, but also by the utilitarian Mill and the intuitionist Ross. Again, a recent advocate of it, Doyle, explicitly disavows Hegel's philosophical principles. But despite this distinguished support, I suspect that most philosophers would endorse Honderich's appraisal of it as 'a retribution theory of very secondary interest'.

I follow Hart and Armstrong in distinguishing the problem of definition (Sec. 2), the problem of justification (Sec. 3), and the problem of distribution (Sec. 4). My treatment has two main emphases. First, the indispensability of a close attention to law and criminology; to the laws of contract and of tort, but above all to a certain striking tendency in the development of the law of crimes during the last quarter-century (Sec. 5). Secondly, as might be expected from the above remarks about 'the retributivist paradox', the primacy of the problem of definition, even over the problem of justification. The problems of retributive punishment seem to me pre-eminently philosophical, in that they are essentially conceptual. After the problem of definition has been solved, it becomes comparatively easy to solve the other two problems and to present a coherent theory of political punishment as a whole (Sec. 5). But not before. For, as Hegel says, 'so long as the concepts here at issue are not clearly apprehended, confusion must continue to reign in the theory of punishment'.

2. The Problem of Definition

The initial task, then, is in Hart's words 'to dispel the mist from the idea of retribution'. For elucidating the idea, *retribution* is the necessary first step towards elucidating the idea, *retributive punishment*. The following concepts are needed in order to construct a simple model. There is a Sovereign, *Rex* (R), who is legislature, executive and judiciary all in one, and who has some subjects (S). There is a law (L) which provides that, if S1 steals X from S2, then S1 must give back either X or an equivalent of X, (EX), to S2 on pain of punishment by R in the event of non-compliance. L is construed in the Benthamite manner as an order addressed by R to all S which is backed by a threat of punishment. Finally, there is one S who is an offender (SOR), whom R has convicted of breaking L, and another S who is the corresponding offendee (SOE).

The English verb 'to retribute' derives from the Latin verb *retribuere* and means the same as it does, viz. 'to give back'. So the basic formula is 'B gives back an X to A in return for the X which A gave to B'. Retribution is therefore a reciprocal interpersonal transaction. It is a relation which has three terms or four accordingly as the X which is given back is numerically identical with the X which was given (restitution), or is an EX (compensation). Retribution is one member of a family of similar reciprocative concepts which differ in evaluative rather than in descriptive meaning. Thus, the meaning of 'to retribute', 'to retaliate', etc., is 'B gives back an evil to A in return for the evil which A gave to B'. But the meaning of 'to restitute', 'to recompense', etc., is 'B gives back a good to A in return for the evil which B gave to A'. For 'B gives back a good to A in return for the good which A gave to B' the name is, in personal relationships, 'gratitude'; and in economic relationships, 'exchange' (i.e., barter, sale, hire, etc.). 'Ingratitude' means 'B gives back an evil to A in return for the good which A gave to B'. But 'to return', 'to render', etc., are non-evaluative words which can therefore be used in any of the foregoing contexts.

Restitution and compensation are either unimposed or imposed. An unimposed restitution occurs when SOR, who has stolen X from SOE, repents and returns X to SOE voluntarily. Again, an important type of unimposed compensation occurs when R gives back EX to SOE in return for the X of which SOR deprived SOE. E.g., the Criminal Injuries Compensation Board makes an *ex gratia* payment out of public funds to SOE for the left eye of which SOR deprived SOE when SOR robbed SOE with violence.

Imposed restitutions and compensations are either unauthoritatively imposed or authoritatively imposed. An unauthoritatively imposed restitution or compensation occurs when (1) SOE makes SOR give back to SOE a good (X or EX) in return for the good (X) of which SOR deprived SOE, and (2) SOE thereby also gives back to SOR an evil (deprivation of X or EX) in return for the evil (deprivation of X) which SOR gave to SOE. Here, SOE *revenges* himself on SOR. A synonym of 'to revenge oneself' is 'to get one's own back', an expression which brings out clearly the Janus nature of the word under consideration. For, in the example, SOE both gets his own good back *from* SOR (restitution), and also gets his own evil back *on* SOR (retribution). An unauthoritatively imposed restitution or compensation also occurs when some S other than SOE — SOE's brother, say, or some knight-errant — makes SOR give back to SOE a good (X or EX) in return for the good (X) of which SOR deprived SOE. Here, S *avenges* SOE on SOR.

Retributive punishment is *one sort* of authoritatively imposed restitution or compensation, the formula for which is: (1) R makes SOR give back a good (X or EX) to SOE in return for the good (X) which SOR intentionally made SOE give to SOR; and (2) R thereby gives back an evil (deprivation of X or EX) to SOR in return for the evil (deprivation of X) which SOR intentionally gave to SOE. This is what happens when, e.g., R orders SOR, whom he has convicted of stealing SOE's car, to return it to SOE, as provided by section 28 of the Theft Act, 1968 (referred to in this essay as 'L'). There are a number of points in and about this formula which require comment.

First, I call deprivation of X or EX 'an evil'. For I do not agree with Mabbott that deprivation of a good is no evil. Secondly, the verb 'makes' in the formula means 'causes', in that sense of 'causes' which figures in the law and in interpersonal transactions generally. Its meaning is importantly different from that which it has in the natural sciences. R *indirectly causes* the deprivation of SOR, (2), by *directly causing* the compensation of SOE, (1).

Above all, it is necessary to guard against two common and important misunderstandings of retributive punishment. For, thirdly, the stock objection to it is that it cannot be morally justified, because two evils do not make a good. Doyle calls this objection 'simplistic', and his criticism is exact. The simplemindedness consists in seeing in retributive punishment only the *simple* transaction, (2), instead of the *complex* (conjunctive) transaction, (1) and (2). The very name, 'retributive punishment', reveals this mistake; it would be less misleading to speak of 'restitutive-retributive punishment'. Nevertheless, I shall adhere to the established usage. Plainly, 'retributive punishment', like 'revenge', is a

Janus-word.[1] The concentration on the retribution, (2), is the more surprising because it is the restitution, (1), which is the important transaction. (2) is only the necessary consequence, the inevitable by-product of (1). For R cannot, logically, make SOR give back X or EX to SOE without depriving SOR of X or EX. On my analysis, there is no need to have recourse to the desperate expedient of trying to make out that the two evils in (2) are severally bad but conjunctly good. Nor is it necessary to argue, as Moore does, that the conjunction of (a) SOE's being deprived of X with (b) SOR's being deprived of X or EX, is *less bad* than is (a) alone. The significant conjunction is that of (2) with (1); not that of (b) with (a), as Moore believes. For, in my theory, the complex transaction, (1) and (2), is morally justified if and only if the good in the restitution, (1), outweighs the bad in the retribution, (2) (Sec. 3). This is so in the above example of the stolen car, but it is not always so, as will be shown later (Sec. 4).

Fourthly, we must consider Benn's contention that 'punishment is . . . not the exaction of compensation or restitution', and Hart's reference to 'a primitive confusion of the principles of punishment with those that should govern the different matter of compensation to be made to the victim of wrong-doing'. I am sure that what Benn and Hart have in mind here are restitutions or compensations imposed by R *in civil proceedings*; e.g. for a breach of contract, or for a tort, such as a libel. In which case, of course, they are perfectly right. For a punishment is necessarily for an offence against some legal rule — a crime — and torts and breaches of contract are not crimes. But restitutions or compensations imposed by R *in criminal proceedings*, e.g. for theft, *are* punishments; not only because this necessary condition of *punishment* is satisfied, but because all its other necessary conditions are satisfied too. These are generally agreed to be: (i) It must deprive the punishee of some good; (ii) It must be of an actual or believed offender for his offence; (iii) It must be intentionally administered by some person other than the offender; and (iv) It must be imposed and administered by an authority constituted by a legal system against which the offence is committed.[2] So I submit the following definition: 'a retributive political punishment' means 'a restitution or a compensation to SOE imposed by R on SOR for an offence against SOE'.

Three elucidations of this definition are needed. First, a generally necessary condition for a crime (*actus reus*) is a criminal intention (*mens rea*). This is why, in the above formula for retributive punishment, I speak of 'the evil (deprivation of X) which SOR *intentionally* gave to SOE'. Secondly, it is necessary to explain the connection between authoritatively imposed restitutions or compensations, crimes and rights (cf. Hegel's 'restoring the right by annulling the crime'). The sort of crime for which SOR is retributively punished by R is a violation of some human right of SOE, e.g. his rights to life, or to immunity from bodily harm, or to property. Such violations are the crimes of, e.g., murder, rape and larceny. (However, not all crimes are of this type. Treason, e.g., is an offence against R, not against some SOE.) Finally, it is the existence of restitution and compensation in civil proceedings as well as in criminal proceedings which explains why I said that retributive punishment is *one sort* (i.e., not the only sort) of authoritatively imposed restitution or compensation.

3. The Problem of Justification

I have suggested that R has a moral right to punish SOR retributively if and only if the good in the restitution outweighs the bad in the retribution. As Hegel says, this happens when the restitution restores some human right of SOE. Thus SOE, being the owner of the car, has a human right to property in it, which SOR invades by stealing it. Similarly, if SOR puts out SOE's left eye, monetary compensation by SOR (partly) restores SOE's human right to immunity from bodily injury.

In truth, however, it is not a question of R's *right* to punish retributively under the condition specified, but of his *duty* to do so. Why is this? Benn claims that Hegel's theory is covertly utilitarian. I.e., that it is R's duty to punish SOR retributively because it is his duty to maximise pleasure. But this is not so. For suppose that SOE owns 5 cars and SOR owns 0 cars. Then SOR will increase pleasure by stealing 1 car from SOE, because of the diminishing marginal utility of cars. Conversely, R will decrease pleasure by making SOR give it back. So the reason for R's duty to do this cannot be his duty to maximise pleasure.

The reason is rather that it is R's duty to maintain the human rights of all S. As Ross says, 'the essential duty of the state is to protect the most fundamental rights of individuals'. There follow three derivative duties of R *after* some SOR has invaded some human right of some SOE. (We shall see later what derivative duties of R follow *before* any SOR has invaded any human right of any SOE (Sec. 5).) (1) R's duty to make SOR restitute to or compensate SOE as nearly completely as SOR can. The difficulty is that very often SOR cannot do so. In which case, there follows (2) R's duty to make an *ex gratia* payment to SOE out of public funds. (See the reference in Sec. 2 to the work of the

Criminal Injuries Compensation Board.) There is further (3) R's duty to induce and enable SOR to discharge his *moral* obligation to make as full voluntary restitution or compensation to SOE as he can. This is a significant part of R's duty to *reform* SOR. Important as they are, however, (2) and (3) are unimposed restitution or compensation — i.e., are not penal and coercive — and so do not concern us here.

What, then, are the reasons for R's derivative duty (1)? There are two, one of which is pointed out by Ross. He observes that L has a dual aspect accordingly as it is seen from the standpoint of SOR or of SOE. To any potential SOR, L is (an order backed by) a threat of punishment. But to any potential SOE, L is a conditional promise of redress if some right of his is invaded and if R catches and convicts SOR. So if R fails to punish SOR retributively, he breaks his promise to SOE. R's duty to punish retributively is therefore grounded partly in his obligation to fidelity. The contract in question is tacit, and is of the type which is inferred from conduct; as when A is deemed to promise to pay the fare by his action in boarding a bus. The corresponding conduct by R is his enactment of L, which implies that he will enforce it. Equally important, R makes a similar tacit promise *not* to 'punish' any S who does *not* break any law. As Ewing points out, this is why R ought not to 'punish' (i.e. deprive) the innocent. For there is a tacit understanding by all S that R permits what he does not prohibit legally.

The other reason for R's duty (1) is pointed out by Hegel when he observes that 'otherwise (sc., if R had not annulled it) the crime would have been held valid'. I.e., if R does not make SOR give SOE his car back, he in effect condones the theft. But if R does that, he is unfair to SOE. For he treats him as if his title to the car were no better than SOR's; which, however, is by no means so, since SOE acquired it by honest toil, whereas SOR acquired it by theft. Hence, R breaks part of the moral Rule of Justice, viz., 'to treat unalike (unequally) those who are unalike (unequal) in relevant respects' (Feinberg, p. 100). A retributive punishment is called an act of *retributive justice* because R is unfair to SOE if he fails to administer it. Distributive justice and retributive justice are both species of justice because they are both applications of the above Rule of Justice. The specific difference is that distributive justice is about the application of the rule to the *distribution* of goods, whereas retributive justice is about its application to the *re-redistribution* of goods after some initial distribution of them has been redistributed by a crime. E.g., there is an initial distribution whereby SOE has 1 X and SOR has 0 X. It may be asked whether this is fair when judged by some such criterion as need, which is a question of distributive justice. SOR then steals X from SOE, so that there is a criminal redistribution whereby SOE has 0 X and SOR has 1 X. Finally, R restores the *status quo* by making SOR restitute X to SOE, so that there is a penal re-redistribution whereby again SOE has 1 X and SOR has 0 X. This penal re-redistribution is an act of retributive justice. In other words (Hegel's), when R punishes this crime retributively, 'justice reasserts itself by negating this negation of itself'.[3] Both the Rule of Justice and the distributive/retributive dichotomy are due to Aristotle. Hence, R's duty to punish retributively is grounded in his obligation to justice as well as to fidelity. So, finally, the answer to the question about R's moral right to deprive SOR of some good when punishing him retributively, is that R cannot discharge his duty to maintain SOE's human rights without doing so (Sec. 1).

Three elucidations are needed. First, the person who has the right which is correlative to R's duty is of course SOE. Secondly, R's duty is defeasible, not unconditional. He is not obliged to punish SOR when some condition of SOR's exculpation is satisfied (see Hart, 1968, pp. 28 ff.). Finally on terminology. It is usual to call R's obligation to make SOR restitute to or compensate SOE as nearly completely as SOR can the Rule of Retributive Justice (see, e.g., Carritt, pp. 97 ff.). Aristotle calls this sort of justice 'diorthotic justice', which Ross translates as 'rectificatory justice'. It is also called 'corrective justice' (Lamont), or 'commutative justice' (Feinberg, 116). These names are better than 'retributive justice', for the same reason that 'restitutive punishment' is better than 'retributive punishment'. Here too, however, I adhere to the prevailing convention, and speak of 'retributive justice' as well as of 'retributive punishment'. (The several Rules or Principles of Justice are discussed in Subsec. 2.2 of Essay 8.)

4. The Problem of Distribution

The problem of penal distribution is that of determining the right kind and amount of punishment to be administered. In retributive punishment, this is the question of assessing EX. Philosophers tend to be skeptical about the very existence of EX. They seem bemused by the adage 'what is done cannot be undone' (*quod factum est infectum fieri nequit*). But this is wrong, since R regularly compensates very many deprivations. Nevertheless, questions certainly arise about the adequacy of some of his compensations, and about whether all deprivations can be compensated. E.g., is it possible to compensate a person who has been rendered permanently unconscious by an injury? Civil law is a mine of information on such matters. But this information is relevant here too, because the same principles of compensation apply in criminal proceedings (which do concern us) as in civil proceedings (which do not).

In the laws both of tort and of contract, the relevant primary rule is the Rule of Complete Compensation (*restitutio in integrum*). According to this, R ought to make the unsuccessful defendant compensate the successful plaintiff as nearly completely as the former can. Evidently, this rule is the civil counterpart of the criminal Rule of Retributive Justice (Sec. 3). The law of tort then proceeds to lay down secondary rules which apply the primary rule to different sorts of cases. Two illustrations must suffice. First, damage to a chattel, such as a car. Predictably, the simple secondary rule here is to take as measure of the damage the amount by which the car's value has been diminished, and to equate this with the cost of repair. Secondly, loss of prospective earnings through personal injury. Here, the secondary rule is more complex. R must estimate the period of future disability and the rate of earning during this period, and so arrive at a lump sum. This must then be discounted to allow for the fact that it is not paid over a period of time, and for 'the normal vicissitudes of life'.

The Rules of Retributive Justice and of Complete Compensation, that the offender/defendant ought ideally to compensate the offendee/plaintiff completely, reveal an important connection between justice and equality. The Rule of Retributive Justice also gives a clear meaning to the otherwise obscure notion of R's duty to make the punishment (his depriving SOR of X or EX) fit (i.e. equal) the crime (SOR's depriving SOE of X). Further, it follows from this equality requirement that, as R can wrong SOE by making SOR under-compensate him; so R can wrong SOR by making him over-compensate SOE. This is the idea which is symbolised by the scales of the goddess, Justice. The equipoised arms of her balance represent the equality just described. (See Eckhoff, pp. 29 ff.; and F.J. Pomeroy's statue, The Lady of Justice, which surmounts the Central Criminal Court of England.) (The Rule of Complete Compensation is discussed in Subsec. 2.2 of Essay 8, and the relationship of Justice to Equality is treated of in Subsec. 2.3 of that Essay.)

The rule of distribution to which philosophers have devoted most attention in their discussions of retributive punishment is that which I shall call, after Aristotle, the Rule of Reciprocity. According to this, R ought to retribute to SOR the same kind and amount of evil as SOR gave to SOE. E.g., if SOR puts out SOE's left eye, then R ought to exact SOR's left eye in return. Aristotle remarks that in many cases the Rule of Reciprocity and the Rule of Retributive Justice are not in accord. This case is certainly one of them, since R does not make SOR compensate SOE as nearly completely as SOR can. For here, since the eye which R exacts from SOR is no good to SOE, the only thing which R makes SOR restitute to SOE is a feeling of vindictive satisfaction at seeing his hurter hurt. But this is no equivalent of SOE's eye. Consequently, by my principle, this retributive punishment is unjustified, since the great evil in the retribution (depriving SOR of an eye) far outweighs the exiguous good in the restitution (giving SOE a feeling of vindictive satisfaction) (Sec. 2). R ought rather to make SOR restitute to SOE as large a monetary compensation as he can. Again, suppose that R imprisons SOR for six months for having imprisoned SOE for six months, as the Rule of Reciprocity requires. This retributive punishment too is similarly unjustified by my principle; SOE's feeling of vindictive satisfaction, which is all that SOR gives back to him, is no equivalent of six months' liberty. R ought rather to make SOR compensate SOE monetarily for his six months' loss of earnings. Nevertheless, as Aristotle allows, the Rule of Reciprocity and the Rule of Retributive Justice are sometimes in accord. Consider, e.g., the following contrafactual case: SOR puts out SOE's left eye and destroys it; SOR's left eye is qualitatively identical with SOE's left eye; and eye-transplants are completely reliable and completely easy. In this case, for R to exact SOR's left eye and give it to SOE would be an act of perfect retributive justice. For he would thereby make SOR compensate SOE completely, and the admittedly great evil in the retribution would nevertheless be outweighed by the greater good in the restitution.

When I said that R's exaction of SOR's eye in the non-contrafactual case was unjustified, I meant of course unjustified *qua retributive* punishment. It might conceivably be justified *qua deterrent* punishment; but that is another matter (Sec. 5). My reason for discussing the Rule of Reciprocity is that exhibiting its relations to the Rule of Retributive Justice elucidates the latter, and also that revealing its deficiencies clarifies my own thesis. The reason is certainly not that I support Kant's advocacy of it. On the contrary, I agree with Aristotle, Hegel and modern philosophers in rejecting it, except when it is in accord with the Rule of Retributive Justice, as in the above contrafactual case. Indeed, I think that *ius talionis* ('retribute like for like!') belongs with other aberrations of primitive thought on the subject of likeness, such as homoeopathic medicine ('treat like with like!') and homoeopathic magic ('act on X by acting on a likeness of X!').[4] Finally, it will be noticed that my thesis answers two questions about justification and not only one (Sec. 3). Namely, not only (1) *why* R is sometimes justified in punishing SOR retributively (viz., because he cannot uphold SOE's human right without doing so); but also (2) *when* R is justified in doing so (viz., when and only when the good in the restitution outweighs the bad in the retribution).

Naturally, this thesis covers partial as well as complete compensation. Thus, suppose that SOR can only compensate SOE in half the value of SOE's car, because that is all the money that SOR has. If SOR pays that sum to SOE, the requisite conditions are nevertheless satisfied: (1) that SOR compensates SOE as nearly completely as SOR can; and (2) that the good in the restitution is greater than the evil in the retribution. Again, in determining what SOR *can* pay in compensation to SOE, consideration must of course be given to other and possibly stronger claims on SOR, e.g., those of his dependants.

Lastly, 'a life for a life' fares as badly on my principle as does 'an eye for an eye' (in the non-contrafactual case). The stock objection here is that, if SOR murders SOE, then the question of compensation does not arise, since there is no SOE to compensate. But the obvious reply is that, on SOE's death, his right to compensation passes to some other person, say, his son and heir. R's execution of SOR is unjustified, because the only compensation that SOR is thereby made to give to SOE's son and heir is the negligible one of a feeling of vindictive satisfaction; so that the evil in the retribution far outweighs the good in the restitution. R ought rather to make SOR pay compensation to SOE's son and heir; or, if SOR has no money, R ought to make SOR render some service to him. So, since *capital punishment* (for murder) is unjustifiable *qua* retributive punishment, it can only be justified (if at all) *qua* protective punishment. To a brief consideration of this last sort of punishment we must now turn.

5. Retributive Punishment and Protective Punishment

Since this essay is about retributive punishment, it is necessary to discuss *protective punishment* only schematically, so as to show the place of retributive punishment in political punishment as a whole.

We have seen that R's secondary duty to punish retributively derives from his primary duty to uphold the human rights of all S *after* some SOR has invaded some human right of some SOE (Sec. 3). R's secondary duty to punish protectively derives from the same primary duty *before* any SOR has invaded any human right of any SOE. This derivative duty is twofold. First, R is obliged to deter any potential SOR. He does this by addressing to all S orders to refrain from crimes, which are backed by threats of punishment. Such orders (e.g. L) are called 'penal (or criminal) statutes'. Secondly, R is sometimes obliged to prevent some actual SOR from offending again, e.g. by imprisoning him. So there are two species of protective punishment, *deterrent punishment* and *preventive punishment*, of which the former is much the more important.

Protective punishment and retributive punishment are alike in the following respects. In both species, it is not so much a question of R's right to punish as of his duty to do so. In both species, too, this secondary duty derives from the same primary duty (above). This is why I objected earlier to calling theories which stress the deterrent aspect of punishment 'utilitarian' (Sec. 1). In my opinion, neither retributive punishment nor protective punishment is justifiable on utilitarian grounds (Sec. 3). I do not agree with Bentham's thesis that 'the end of (criminal) law is to augment happiness'. Again, both in retributive punishment and in protective punishment R's duty is defeasible. Thus, if he considers that potential SORs will be deterred more effectively by offers of reward than by threats of punishment, then it is his duty to enact what Bentham calls 'praemiary laws' and not 'comminatory' ones. Further, both in retributive punishment and in protective punishment, there are answers both to the question *why* R is sometimes justified in punishing, and also to the question *when* he is justified in doing so. The answers to the former question are, again, the same in both cases; viz. that R cannot discharge his primary duty without doing so.

But the answers to the latter question are quite different in the two cases (Sec. 4, end). The conditions in which R is justified in punishing protectively are complex, and can only be sketched here. As to deterrent punishment: R is *not* justified in threatening punishment when it is what Bentham calls 'inefficacious', or 'unprofitable', or 'needless'. As to preventive punishment: R is *not* justified in punishing more severely than the offence warrants, e.g. in imprisoning for life a young first offender in petty theft.

Another difference between retributive punishment and protective punishment is that, in the former, the holder of the right which is correlative to R's secondary duty is SOE; whereas, in the latter, the holders are all S.

Again, retributive punishment is retrospective, since its purpose is to right some actual wrong that has been inflicted on some actual SOE.[5] But deterrent punishment is prospective, since its purpose is to avert some possible wrong that may be inflicted on some potential SOE. Retributive punishment therefore necessarily involves actual punishment; i.e. not only *enacting* (e.g.) L, but also *enforcing* it. But deterrent punishment does not necessarily involve actual punishment. For if the threat which backs (e.g.) L is completely effective, no offence will be committed; so that no punishment can, logically, occur. Deterrence requires only the enactment of (e.g.) L, not its enforcement; indeed, the essence of deterrent punishment is not so much the threat of *punishment* as the *threat* of punishment. Some say that deterrent punishment requires *some* actual punishment in order to make R's threats credible. But this is not so, since R can easily prove himself to be completely a man of his word otherwise than by executing his threats of punishment.

Preventive punishment (e.g. imprisonment for theft) is retrospective, since SOR is inside for an offence which he has committed. But it is also prospective in two ways. First, so long as SOR is inside, thefts by him from outsiders will certainly be averted. Secondly, SOR will (one hopes) be deterred from stealing again after his release (the individual deterrent); and any other potential offender will (one hopes) be deterred from stealing by the example that R has made of SOR (the general deterrent). So preventive punishment is really preventive-deterrent punishment. Of course, if R locks up some S not for having stolen but purely in order to prevent him from stealing, that is not *preventive punishment* at all, since there is no offence (Sec. 2). It is rather *preventive detention*.

Retributive punishments and deterrent punishments are appraised differently, since the former are called justified or unjustified (Sec. 3), whereas the latter are called efficient or inefficient. However, the same punishment can be appraised in both ways. Thus, suppose that L provides merely that if SOR steals X from SOE, then SOR must return X or EX to SOE. In this case, L is an insufficient and therefore inefficient deterrent, but the enforcement of L is a justified retributive punishment. Suppose, on the other hand, that L provides that if SOR steals X from SOE and destroys it, then SOR must pay both EX to SOE ('compensation') and also a substantial sum to R (a 'fine'). In this case, L is an efficient deterrent, and the enforcement of L is again a justified retributive punishment. Similarly, R can punish the same offence both retributively and protectively. E.g., SOR steals SOE's car and smashes it up, and R both makes SOR compensate SOE and also imprisons him.

A final important difference is that between the way in which preventive punishment curtails liberty and the way in which both deterrent punishment and retributive punishment curtail liberty (Sec. 1). If R imprisons some actual SOR for six months for theft, then he curtails that SOR's liberty by making him unable to perform the *simple* action of stealing from any SOE outside the prison for six months. But if R threatens any potential SOR with six months' imprisonment should he

steal, then R curtails the liberty of any potential SOR by making him
unable to perform the *complex* (conjunctive) action of both stealing and
also remaining unimprisoned. Retributive punishment curtails liberty in
the same way as deterrent punishment does. For L, which provides that
if SOR steals X from SOE, then SOR must return X or EX to SOE,
is backed by a threat that, if SOR does not comply, then he will be (say)
imprisoned for six months. So here R curtails the liberty of any potential SOR by making him unable both not to compensate SOE and also
to remain unimprisoned. (See Sec. 3 and Subsec. 6.2 of Essay 3.)[6]
However, although different sorts of punishment thus curtail liberty in
different ways, all punishment is coercive and deprives the punishee of
liberty in *some* way. But this evil is justified provided that it is outweighed
by a greater good. In preventive punishment, this occurs when SOR's
incarceration averts his stealing from any SOE outside the prison. In
deterrent punishment, this occurs when the threat induces potential SORs
to refrain from theft. And in retributive punishment, this occurs when
the threat induces SOR to compensate SOE.

Finally, a few words on the senses in which the retributivist reaction
is, and is not 'reactionary'. It is, first, a reaction against the sharp division between criminal law and civil law (especially the law of tort), and
a proposal, in Del Vecchio's words, 'in effect to reduce penal justice
to civil justice'. Although this division has now existed for a considerable
time, in the earlier history of law the concept of imposed reparation by
the offender to his victim had an established position for many centuries.
It figures in the Code of Hammurabi, the Law of Moses, and the laws
of the ancient Greeks, Romans and Germans. More recently it has been
advocated by Sir Thomas More, Herbert Spencer, R. Garofalo and E.
Ferri. But the most extensive development of the idea has occurred in
a number of countries in the past quarter-century, beginning with the
work of Margery Fry in Great Britain and continuing with that of A.
Eglash, B.R. Jacob and S. Schafer in the U.S.A. The motive has been
compassion for the victims of crime, especially of crimes of violence.
This movement of public opinion has had its effect on the criminal law.
E.g., Section 1 of the Criminal Justice Act, 1972 makes extensive provision for imposed compensations for personal injuries and for loss of
or damage to property.

A natural consequence of the separation of the law of crimes from
the law of torts was the view of political punishment as an interpersonal
transaction which (1) involves only R and SOR, and (2) has as its sole
aim to deter any potential SOR from breaking the law. This view is
already fully explicit in Hobbes' definition of 'punishment'.[7] But the

retributivist reaction is directed, secondly, against both (1) and (2). As to (2), it sees punishment as primarily retributive and only secondarily protective. The most striking manifestation of (1) is precisely the belief that the central question in the philosophy of political punishment is, what right has R to deprive any SOR of any good? (Sec. 1). It is Hobbes, again, and Beccaria who give primacy to this question. The retributivist reaction, however, puts this question in its place by showing it to be a mere corollary of the true basic question, viz., why is it R's duty to right the wrongs of SOE? (Sec. 2). In this way, retributivists bring back into the penal picture the forgotten third man, namely, SOE.

All of which shows that the retributivist reaction is anything but 'reactionary' in the obnoxious sense of that word. One need not be a L.C. Jeffreys or a L.C. Eldon in order to insist on R's duty to make restitution and compensation orders, so as to maintain the human rights of the all-too-numerous casualties of crime.[8]

Notes

1. This useful term is borrowed from P.H. Nowell-Smith's *Ethics* (Penguin, London, 1954).

2. This list is a slightly revised version of the criteria originally proposed by Flew.

3. McTaggart interprets Hegel as maintaining that R has a duty to punish SOR since SOR has a right to be punished. This is because punishment reforms SOR by making him repent of his crime. I agree that this is a part of Hegel's theory, but I do not think that it is the main part, which turns on the right of SOE and not on the right of SOR. Cooper does not think so either. See also Honderich, 49 ff.

4. The principle, *similia similibus curantur,* was laid down by Samuel Hahnemann (1755-1843); but the general idea of 'a hair of the dog that bit you' was already familiar to Hippocrates. On homoeopathic magic, see J.G. Frazer, *The Golden Bough* (abr. edn, Macmillan, London, 1922), Chs. 3, 51. Interestingly, the Rule of Reciprocity is advocated in some or all cases by some leading teleologists. Thus, Beccaria supports it in all cases (Ch. 19), and Bentham recommends, e.g., branding for arsonists. See also Westermarck.

5. 'A wrong' means 'a violation of a right'. It is as necessary to distinguish 'a wrong' from 'wrong' as it is to distinguish 'a right' from 'right'. See Hart (1955).

6. Restitution and compensation orders in civil proceedings, which are not penal, nevertheless also curtail liberty in the same way as retributive punishments do. For they are backed by a threat of punishment for contempt of court in the event of non-compliance.

7. It is a paradox, such as Hegel himself relished, that he, who is the greatest philosophical champion of the state after Hobbes, is yet also the classic exponent of the theory of political punishment which is generally regarded as the antithesis of that professed by Hobbes, Beccaria and Bentham.

8. I am obliged to Miss Elizabeth Barnard for guiding me to relevant criminological literature.

80   *Retributive Punishment*

References

What follows is not a bibliography of the extensive literature on the philosophy of punishment, but simply a list of works which I have found helpful in composing this essay, and which may therefore prove useful to other students of this complex of problems. No works published after October 1977 are included.

Aristotle, *Ethica Nichomachea*, tr. and ed. W.D. Ross (Clarendon Press, Oxford 1915), Bk. 5.
—— *Politica*, tr. B. Jowett, ed. W.D. Ross (Clarendon Press, Oxford, 1921), Bk. 3, Ch. 9.
Armstrong, K.G., 'The Retributivist Hits Back', *Mind*, Vol. 70 (1961), pp. 471-90.
Barnett, R.E., 'Restitution: A New Paradigm of Criminal Justice', *Ethics*, Vol. 87 (1977), pp. 279-301.
Beccaria, Cesare, *On Crimes and Punishments*, tr. Henry Paolucci (Bobbs-Merrill, Indianapolis, 1963).
Benn, S.I. and Peters, R.S., *Social Principles and the Democratic State* (Allen and Unwin, London, 1959), Chs. 5, 6, 8.
Bentham, Jeremy, *An Introduction to the Principles of Morals and Legislation*, ed. J.H. Burns and H.L.A. Hart (Athlone Press, London, 1970), Chs. 13-15.
—— *Of Laws in General*, ed. H.L.A. Hart (Athlone Press, London, 1970), Ch. 11.
Bosanquet, Bernard, *Some Suggestions in Ethics* (Macmillan, London, 1918), Ch. 8.
—— *The Philosophical Theory of the State*, 4th edn (Macmillan, London, 1923), Ch. 8.
Bradley, F.H., *Ethical Studies*, 2nd edn (Clarendon Press, Oxford, 1927),essay 1.
Carritt, E.F., *Ethical and Political Thinking* (Clarendon Press, Oxford, 1947), Ch. 9.
Cooper, D.E., 'Hegel's Theory of Punishment' in *Hegel's Political Philosophy*, ed. Z.A. Pelczynski (University Press, Cambridge, 1971).
Day, J.P., 'Threats, Offers, Law, Opinion and Liberty', *American Philosophical Quarterly*, Vol. 14 (1977), pp. 257-72.
Del Vecchio, Giorgio, 'The Struggle Against Crime', tr. A.H. Campbell, in *The Philosophy of Punishment*, ed. H.B. Acton (Macmillan, London, 1969).
Demos, Raphael, 'Some Reflections on Threats and Punishments', *The Review of Metaphysics*, Vol. 11 (1958), pp. 224-36.
Doyle, J.F., 'Justice and Legal Punishment', *Philosophy*, Vol. 42 (1967), pp. 53-67.
Eckhoff, Torstein, *Justice* University Press, Rotterdam, 1974), Chs. 1, 2, 5-7.
Eglash, Albert, 'Creative Restitution', *British Journal of Delinquency*, Vol. 10 (1960), pp. 114-19.
Ewing, A.C., 'Armstrong on the Retributive Theory', *Mind*, Vol. 72 (1963), pp. 121-4.
Ezorsky, Gertrude, 'The Ethics of Punishment' in *Philosophical Perspectives on Punishment*, ed. G. Ezorsky (State University of New York, Albany, 1972).
Feinberg, Joel, *Social Philosophy* (Prentice-Hall, Englewood Cliffs, 1973), Ch. 7.
Flew, A.G.N., 'The Justification of Punishment', *Philosophy*, Vol. 29 (1954), pp. 291-307.
Fry, Margery, *Arms of the Law* (Gollancz, London, 1951). Ch. 5.
Green, T.H., *Lectures on the Principles of Political Obligation* (Longmans, London, 1937), lecture L.
Guest, A.R. (ed.), *Anson's Law of Contract*, 24th edn (Clarendon Press, Oxford, 1975), pp. 25-7, 544-8.
Hart, H.L.A., 'Are There Any Natural Rights?' *Philosophical Review*, Vol. 64 (1955), pp. 175-91.
—— *The Concept of Law* (Clarendon Press, Oxford, 1961), Chs. 2-4, 8.
—— *Punishment and Responsibility* (Clarendon Press, Oxford, 1968).
Hart, H.L.A. and Honoré, A.M., *Causation in the Law* (Clarendon Press, Oxford, 1959), Ch. 1.
Hegel, G.W.F., *Philosophy of Right*, tr. T.M. Knox (Clarendon Press, Oxford, 1942),

paras. 82-104.

Hobbes, Thomas, *Leviathan*, ed. Michael Oakeshott (Blackwell, Oxford, 1947), Chs. 26-8.

Honderich, Ted, *Punishment* (Penguin, London, 1961), Chs. 1-3, 7.

Jacob, B.R., 'Reparation or Restitution by the Criminal Offender to his Victim', *The Journal of Criminal Law, Criminology and Police Science*, Vol. 61 (1970), pp. 152-67.

Kant, Immanuel, *The Metaphysical Elements of the Theory of Right*, in *Kant's Political Writings*, ed. Hans Reiss, tr. H.B. Nisbet (University Press, Cambridge, 1970), pp. 154-60.

Kassman, Alec, 'On Punishing', *Aristotelian Society Proceedings*, Vol. 77, (1977), pp. 221-46.

Lamont, W.D., 'Justice: Distributive and Corrective', *Philosophy*, Vol. 16 (1941), pp. 3-18.

Mabbott, J.D., 'Punishment', *Mind*, Vol. 48 (1939), pp. 152-67.

McLean, Ian and Morrish, Peter (eds.), *Harris's Criminal Law*, 22nd edn (Sweet and Maxwell, London, 1973), pp. 820-5.

McTaggart, J.E., 'Hegel's Theory of Punishment', *International Journal of Ethics*, Vol. 6 (1896), pp. 479-502.

Mill, J.S., *Utilitarianism* (Longmans, London, 1861), Ch. 5.

—— *An Examination of Sir William Hamilton's Philosophy*, 3rd edn (Longmans, London, 1867), Ch. 26.

—— Speech in Defence of Capital Punishment in Ezorsky, op. cit. 'The Ethics of Punishment'.

Moore, G.E., *Principia Ethica* (University Press, Cambridge, 1903), Ch. 6.

Rashdall, Hastings, *The Theory of Good and Evil*, 2nd edn, Vol. 1 (Clarendon Press, Oxford, 1924), Ch. 9.

Rogers, W.H.V. (ed.), *Winfield and Jolowicz on Tort*, 10th edn (Sweet and Maxwell, London, 1975), Ch. 27.

Ross, W.D., *The Right and The Good* (Clarendon Press, Oxford, 1930), Ch. 2, App. 2.

Schafer, Stephen, *The Victim and his Criminal* (Random House, New York, 1968), Chs. 1, 3.

Sharp, F.C. and Otto, M.C., 'A Study of the Popular Attitude towards Retributive Punishment', *International Journal of Ethics*, Vol. 20 (1910), pp. 341-57.

Stephen, J.F., *A History of the Criminal Law of England*, Vol. 2 (Macmillan, London, 1883), Chs. 17, 18.

Sutherland, E.H. and Cressey, D.R., *Principles of Criminology*, 6th edn (Lippincott, Chicago, 1960), Chs. 1, 14-17, 29.

Westermarck, Edvard, 'The Essence of Revenge', *Mind*, Vol. 7 (1898), pp. 289-310.

Wilson, John, 'The Need for a New Kind of Justice for Vandals', *The Times* (24 May 1977), p. 10.

5   COMPENSATORY DISCRIMINATION

1. Introduction

Like theories of punishment, theories of reverse (positive) discrimination can usefully be divided into forward-looking (teleological) ones and backward-looking (compensatory/retributive) ones.[1] (See Sec. 1 of Essay 4.) One example of the former type of theory is Dworkin's, who defends the policy on the ground that it will (perhaps) produce 'a more equal society'.[2] Another is Sher's, who defends it on the ground that it increases equality of opportunity.[3] This essay is an examination of the latter type of theory.[4] Compensatory discrimination is related, then, to discrimination thus: discrimination is the genus, of which reverse discrimination is a species, of which compensatory discrimination is a sub-species. It will be convenient to proceed by examining successively the ideas of discrimination, of compensation, and of compensatory discrimination.

2. Discrimination

The questions to be answered here are about the meaning of 'discrimination', the causes of discrimination, and the reasons for and against discrimination.

2.1 The Meaning of 'Discrimination' and the Causes of Discrimination

Our attitude to discrimination is ambivalent, and I think that the reason for this is to be found in an ambiguity in the word 'discrimination'. On the one hand, to call A a man of discrimination (or of nice discernment, or of good judgement) is to describe him as adept in discerning (or distinguishing) *between* X and Y (say, different teas). This is the sort of discrimination which interests students of perception. It is considered a good capacity. Similarly, to be indiscriminate in, say, love and friendship is considered bad. For indiscriminateness consists in disregarding relevant differences, and is therefore to be contrasted with impartiality (fairness, justice), which consists partly in disregarding irrelevant differences and partly in paying regard to relevant differences.[5]

On the other hand, however, 'discrimination' means 'the practice of discriminating *against* A or B' (see below). It is discrimination in this second sense which concerns us here. *Examples*: (1) 'Erewhon's appointer of bus conductors discriminated against applicant Baba Nanak because he is a Sikh'; (2) 'Erewhon's appointer discriminates against Sikh applicants because they are Sikhs'; (3) 'Erewhon's appointer discriminates against male Sikh applicants because they are long-haired'.

The vocabulary in this area has always been pleonastic, and is becoming more so. For since 'discrimination' (in this sense) means 'discrimination-against', and since to discriminate against Fs is to favour — Fs, we do not need both 'favouritism' ('preferential treatment') and 'discrimination'. And since the neologisms 'reverse discrimination' and 'positive discrimination' mean 'discrimination-for', i.e. 'favouritism', we do not need them either.

Discrimination-against, or favouritism, is considered bad. As Thomson points out, 'discrimination' in the relevant sense means not only 'discrimination-against' but also 'unfair discrimination-against'.[6] So our ambivalent attitude towards discrimination proceeds from our failure to discriminate between discriminating-between and discriminating-against.

The *formula* for discrimination in example (3) is (i) 'A discriminates against Fs because Fs are G'. (*Example* (2) is a special case of *example* (3) in which G = F.) First, then, what are the ranges of the variables A and F? This may be called (*pace* Lenin) 'the who/whom question'. Evidently, persons; discrimination is one kind of interpersonal transaction. Specifically however, persons-in-roles. For discrimination occurs in institutional and hence rule-governed settings, such as competitions (*examples* (1)-(3) above). Thus, typical values of A are appointers, selectors and governments. *Example* (4) 'The government of Ruritania discriminates against Protestant citizens by taxing them more heavily than non-Protestant citizens'. Correspondingly, typical values of Fs are applicants, candidates and citizens.

Next, when does A discriminate against Fs? As a first approximation, let us say when and only when A deprives Fs more than — Fs because Fs are G. This provisional analysis will be completed later (Subsec. 2.2, end). In *examples* (1)-(4), the deprivations consist in withholding appointments and taking away money.

There is a distinction of great importance between conscious discrimination and unconscious discrimination. Conscious discrimination is intended and practised as a policy. Here, the 'because' in *formula* (i) means 'for the reason that'. Unconscious discrimination is unintended and is caused mainly by prejudice. It is unconscious because the existence and operation of prejudice is itself unconscious. Here, the 'because' in *formula* (i) means 'as a result of the fact that'.

A is prejudiced against B, or Fs, when and only when: (1) A believes some generalisation which is not supported by evidence, e.g. 'priests are crafty'; (2) A is emotionally resistant to evidence against the generalisation; and (3) A is hostile to priests because of his belief. A's irrational belief and hostile attitude may be acted out in various ways, one important sort of which is discrimination.[7]

On the causes of prejudice Allport writes: 'We may lay it down as a general law applying to all social phenomena that *multiple causation* is invariably at work, and nowhere is the law more clearly applicable than to prejudice'.[8]

The following illustration of the existence and operation of prejudice will serve. Erewhon's appointer is a member of an in-group which he sees as threatened in the competition for jobs by an out-group, Sikhs. His fear causes an aversion from Sikhs and a desire to exclude them from jobs, which in turn causes him to discriminate against Sikhs when appointing conductors. In reality, the threat is much less than he believes; and he is unconscious of the facts that he sees Sikhs as a threat, that he fears them and hates them and desires to exclude them, and that he discriminates against them.

It is not easy to prove, e.g., that the appointer is prejudiced against Sikh applicants. Plainly, the fact that he is unconscious of his prejudice does not prove that he does not have it; to suppose that it does is simply to beg the question. On the other hand, the fact that he appoints no male Sikh applicants does not prove that he is prejudiced against male Sikh applicants. For the explanation of this fact may be that he is prejudiced against long-haired males, and that the class of male Sikhs is included in the class of long-haired males. In principle, perhaps, his unconscious wish to exclude Sikhs from jobs could be revealed by psychoanalysis; but the practical difficulties are obvious.

In the rest of this essay, we shall be concerned only with conscious discrimination. But it is essential to notice the existence of unconscious discrimination for two reasons. First, newspapers reveal that, in courts and before tribunals, charges of unconscious discrimination in the fields of employment, housing, education, etc., are being made increasingly frequently. And, of course, some of these charges may be the effect of prejudice against those who allocate jobs, houses, schooling, etc. Secondly, unconscious discrimination bears very importantly on compensatory discrimination. For it is more than a bare possibility that some of those who claim to discriminate consciously in favour of Negroes or

Catholics on the ground that these groups ought to be compensated for wrongful deprivations, are really discriminating unconsciously against WASPs, because they are prejudiced against that group. With these, their claim is simply rationalisation. However, to recognise that this is true of some advocates or practitioners of compensatory discrimination is not to say that it is true of all or most of them. Consequently, we shall have to consider the arguments for compensatory discrimination on their merits.

There is another cause of unconscious discrimination which is particularly relevant to this inquiry because it is a cause of unconscious compensatory discrimination. This is what McKenzie calls 'subjective guilt', which is the feeling of guilt which interests the psychologist, as contrasted with the fact of guilt ('objective guilt') which interests the jurisprudent and the moralist.[9] For A can, of course, feel guilty of doing X without being guilty of doing X; just as he can be guilty of doing X without feeling guilty of doing X. Moreover, as there is a difference between A's being guilty and feeling guilty of wronging B; so there is a difference between B's being wronged and feeling wronged by A. We shall see the significance of the latter distinction below (Subsec. 4.2). The following definitions of 'guilt' bring out clearly the difference between objective and subjective guilt. 'The having committed a specified or implied offence; criminality, culpability' (*The Concise Oxford Dictionary*). 'Sense of wrong-doing, as an emotional attitude, generally involving emotional conflict, arising out of real or imagined contravention of moral or social standards, in act or thought' (James Drever, *A Dictionary of Psychology*).

Subjective guilt is also called 'the consciousness of guilt'; but Freud points out that this name is paradoxical, since 'the patient does not feel it and is not aware of it'.[10] Thus, as unconscious prejudice can cause unconscious discrimination, so unconscious subjective guilt can cause unconscious compensatory discrimination. The following illustrates the process. Erewhon's non-Sikh appointer has an unconscious feeling of guilt about having discriminated against Sikh applicants, which arouses in him an unconscious need to 'punish' himself retributively for having wronged them. But he projects the feeling and the need on to non-Sikh applicants, and unconsciously discriminates against them in order to 'punish' them vicariously for having wronged the Sikh applicants. However, in unconsciously 'punishing' non-Sikh applicants retributively by withholding jobs from them, he *eo ipso* unconsciously compensates Sikh applicants by giving the jobs to them.[11] I enclose the word 'punish' in inverted commas because, speaking strictly, the appointer cannot punish himself or non-Sikh applicants because he is not in authority over either.

The cause of subjective guilt is fear.[12] In the example just given, that which the appointer fears is the resentment of the Sikh applicants against whom he feels guilty of having discriminated. I shall discuss the causes of resentment later (Subsec. 4.2, end).

2.2 *The Reasons For and Against Discrimination*

In Section 4, I shall examine the case for compensatory discrimination, which is the most often attempted and the most interesting justification of reverse discrimination. Here, we will consider two other arguments, one for and one against any form of discrimination.

A possible argument in favour of discrimination proceeds via a justification of prejudice. For if prejudice is good, then the discrimination in which, as we have seen, prejudice is often expressed, is also good (Subsec. 2.1). But is prejudice ever good? The most famous defence of prejudice in politics is widely held to be that advanced by Burke, who writes: 'Prejudice is of ready application in the emergency; it previously engages the mind in a steady course of wisdom and virtue, and does not leave the man hesitating in the moment of decision, sceptical, puzzled, and unresolved. Prejudice renders a man's virtue his habit; and not a series of unconnected acts. Through just prejudice, his duty becomes a part of his nature.'[13]

The odd feature about this passage is that in it Burke seems to be extolling the habit of acting in accordance with precedent; which, however, is incompatible with acting from prejudice, which means acting on an unreasoned belief, and which is therefore considered bad (Subsec. 2.1). I believe that the explanation of the apparent paradox is that Burke is using the word 'prejudice' in its original sense of 'precedent'. The Latin '*praejudiciuim*' means 'a previous decision affecting a case under consideration', i.e. 'a precedent'. The history of the meanings of words is often curious, and 'prejudice' provides a striking example of this truth, since the meaning of the modern 'prejudice' is virtually the opposite of that of the original '*praejudicium*'. In the original sense of the word, Burke's defence of prejudice fits in perfectly with prominent features of his social philosophy which he shares with other eminent conservative thinkers. His defence of habit or custom is common ground with Hume, and his advocacy of acting in accordance with precedent or tradition aligns him with those, such as Maine, who find their ideal of decision-making in the procedures of the common law of England. This argument therefore fails through equivocation on the word 'prejudice'.[14]

The answer to the question of the justification of discrimination seems to me to be as follows.[15] Discrimination against Fs is unfair to Fs under either of two conditions: (a) When the division is irrelevant to the purpose of the selection: e.g. the Sikh/non-Sikh division is irrelevant to the purpose of excluding bad conductors, because being a Sikh is irrelevant to being a bad conductor. (b) When the purpose of the selection is unfair to Fs: e.g. when the purpose of the selection is to exclude Sikhs. In practice, condition (a) holds more commonly and is more important than condition (b). Discrimination under both conditions is unfair because it breaks part of Aristotle's Rule of Justice, 'to treat alike (equally) those who are the same in relevant respects'.[16]

Suppose now, however, that Erewhon's appointer rejects applicant David Evans because he is a thief. His action is justified, indeed his duty, because being a thief is relevant to being a bad conductor. But in this case the appointer is not said to discriminate against David Evans. As was pointed out above, 'discrimination' means '*unfair* discrimination-against'. So we can now replace our first approximation to the answer to the question, when does A discriminate against Fs?, by the following complete answer. A discriminates against Fs when and only when (1) A deprives Fs more than — Fs because Fs are G; and (2) Gness is irrelevant to Hness, where Hness is some property that appointees ought to possess or not to possess: e.g. Erewhon's appointer discriminates against male Sikh applicants if he appoints none of them because they are long-haired, and being long-haired is irrelevant to being a bad conductor. In this way, it is necessarily true that all discrimination is unjustified, and the question of the meaning of 'discrimination' and the question of the justification of discrimination are inseparable. (The relation of discrimination to comparative injustice is discussed in Subsec. 2.2 of Essay 8.)

3. Compensation

Compensation is both a moral and a legal right, and the correlative obligation may be called, as it is in Scots law, 'the obligation of reparation'. As with other rights, such as justice and property, the questions which arise respecting it are those of meaning, justification and distribution.[17]

3.1. The Meaning of 'Compensation'

The *formula* for compensation is (ii) 'A gives back an equivalent of X to B in return for the X of which A deprived B'. *Example* (5). If A borrows

B's umbrella and loses it, then A has an obligation to return to B as soon as possible an equivalent in kind or in cash. Compensation must be distinguished from restitution, where the X which A returns to B is numerically the same as the X of which A deprived B. The variables A and B in *formula* (ii) range over persons-in-roles, not plain persons. For the compensator must be identical with the depriver, and the compensatee must be identical with the deprivee. Compensation is made *by* the depriver *to* the deprivee *for* a deprivation of some good. Such deprivations are called 'wrongs', 'harms' or 'injuries', which mean 'violations of some right', e.g. a property-right. For the argument of this essay, it will be convenient to take as paradigm of a wrong the following example of MacCormick's.[18] *Example* (6). In backing his car hastily out of his drive in good visibility, A unintentionally collides with and damages his neighbour B's car, which is parked on the opposite side of the road.

The preceding account needs to be amplified and qualified as follows. Legally considered, the wrong in *example* (6) is not a crime, but a tort, because it was not intended. If A had collided with B's car deliberately or recklessly (with *mens rea*), that would have been a criminal wrong.

In *example* (6), A's fault is negligence, specifically, neglect of his 'duty of care'. This is both a moral and a legal fault. It is also objective, in the sense that it is defined as a lapse from 'a certain "objective" standard of care not calculated in terms of what this or that individual was subjectively capable of achieving in given circumstances, but calculated in terms of what a "reasonable person" could and would achieve given the degree of risk of a certain kind of harm occurring in given circumstances'.[19]

A is responsible *for* the wrong to B, in that he *caused* it. That he caused it unintentionally does not alter this fact. However, responsibility-for is limited by the restriction that the causal connection must not be too indirect.[20] In neglecting his duty of care, A also fails in his duty of responsibility *to* B.[21] Responsibility-to is related to responsibility-for as follows. First, if A is responsible for X, then A must logically be responsible to someone (not necessarily the immediate victim) for X. But further, secondly, unless A knows that he will normally be held responsible for any wrong that he may do, A is unlikely to behave responsibly towards other persons.

The statement (above), that the compensator must be identical with the depriver and the compensatee with the deprivee, needs qualification. Thus, if one boy injures another boy, then the father of the first boy has a moral and legal obligation to compensate the second boy. And if the second boy dies of the injury, then the father of the first boy has an obligation to compensate the second boy's next of kin. In the case of corporations, such as joint-stock companies or nation-states, the company or state which compensates now can of course be the same company or state as did the wrong then, even though the members of the company or state are all different.[22]

Finally, compensation can be either voluntary or non-voluntary. If A does not compensate B voluntarily for his damage to B's car, then B may sue A, and the court may order A to compensate B. If, but only if the damage was malicious so that the wrong is criminal, the court's order is a retributive and deterrent political punishment of A.[23]

3.2 The Justification of Compensation

This question has to be considered in terms of the distinction just drawn between voluntary and non-voluntary compensation.

First, as to voluntary compensation. The question, 'Why has A a moral obligation to compensate B for violating some right of B?' sounds almost as oddly as does 'Why ought A to be moral?'[24] It seems obvious that A has such an obligation. But here, as often, the psychologically obvious has a logical basis. For the existence of the right to compensation can be inferred immediately from the existence of the violated right: i.e. to say 'B has a property-right in this car but no right to compensation by A for damage which A does to it' is illogical. It is a matter of 'obvious because true', not of 'obvious therefore true', as Descartes would have it. (To be exact, that which is true is not of course the immediate inference, but the implication which corresponds to it.)

The justification of non-voluntary compensation is similar. The state's obligation to make unwilling A compensate B for damaging B's car follows immediately from the state's obligation to protect A's property-right in his car. For the protection of the rights of its citizens is the fundamental duty of a state, to which its duty to pursue the public interest (common good, general happiness, etc.) is generally subordinate.[25]

Happily, the obligation of reparation is sanctioned by a strong natural tendency which Klein discerns even in young children. The process of 'identification' is central; the depriver 'puts himself in the place of' the deprivee.[26] The existence of A's natural tendency to give back a good to B in return for the evil which (A believes that) A gave to B, is interesting. We are much more familiar, of course, with A's strong natural tendency to give back an evil to B in return for the evil which (A believes that) B gave to A. We shall have occasion to discuss this latter tendency below (Subsec. 4.2).

3.3 The Distribution of Compensation

This is the question of what kind and amount of compensation should be made. The general rule is that the depriver ought to compensate the deprivee as nearly completely as the depriver can. This is both a legal and a moral rule. When the wrong is a tort, it is called the Rule of Complete Compensation and is not penal; but when the wrong is a crime, it is called the Rule of Retributive Justice and is penal.[27]

These rules sound simple, but actually involve many and great difficulties. To name but a few: to decide whether a monetary compensation ('damages') or some other form of compensation is appropriate; to put a monetary value on an injury to reputation (see below); to classify deprivations into different types (e.g. defamation, loss of prospective earnings through physical injury); to ensure that deprivations of the same type are compensated approximately equally; to ensure that the depriver's dependants are not seriously deprived by too liberal an estimate of what the depriver 'can' pay in compensation to the deprivee.

These rules also reveal one important connection between justice and equality, in that ideally the compensation is equal in value to the good of which the deprivee was deprived. This point is illuminated by a consideration of over-compensation, of which 'exemplary (punitive) damages' in the English law of defamation provide a classic illustration. This is the practice whereby, in cases of grave defamation, the court orders the defendant to pay to the plaintiff damages larger than the full monetary equivalent of the injury to reputation, for deterrent reasons. Now, where there has been serious defamation, there may well be a case for making the defendant pay more than full compensation, for deterrent or preventive reasons. But the surplus ought to be paid to the state in the form of a fine, and not to the plaintiff in the form of additional damages. In my terminology, the institution of exemplary damages errs in treating as wholly retributive punishment what ought to be treated as partly retributive punishment and partly protective punishment.[28] (On the principle of complete compensation see Subsec. 2.2 of Essay 8. On the relation of justice to equality see Subsec. 2.3 of Essay 8. On the relation of retributive punishment to protective punishment see Sec. 5 of Essay 4.)

4. Compensatory Discrimination

It is desirable to discuss the case for and against compensatory discrimination by considering first disadvantages which could not have been prevented, and then disadvantages which could have been prevented. We shall find, however, that this distinction is not watertight.

4.1 Non-preventable Disadvantages

Take the following case. *Case (1)*. There are two competitors for one place in a medical school, C1 who is female and C2 who is male. C2 obtains better grades in the entrance test, but the admitter awards the place to C1 on the ground that C1 was disadvantaged by being female, and has a right to be compensated for being thus disadvantaged. For in the society in question, females are regarded and treated as inferior to males; and this has bred in C1 a sense of inferiority, which has led in turn to a lack of self-confidence, and so to inferior performance in examinations. If C1 had been male, urges the admitter, C1 would have obtained better grades than C2, so that it is only fair that C1 should have the place.

Here, being female is regarded as a disadvantage of the same sort as being born incurably blind. But we need to notice that non-preventable disadvantages may cease to be such. Thus, it may become possible to control the sex with which an infant is born.

It is possible and profitable to take a short way with the admitter's argument. We have seen that, as a general rule, the compensator must be identical with the depriver (Subsec. 3.1). Consequently, where there is no deprivation, the question of compensation cannot arise. This is so in *case (1)*. C1's being female is not the consequence of any act of commission or omission by any person or persons. Hence, being female is C1's misfortune, not any person's (including her own) fault.

Of course, this is not to say that nothing should be done about C1's bad luck. But if she is given the place on this ground, it is a matter not of compensation, but of aid, assistance, benefit or relief. These are the names which are usually given to institutional relief on grounds of public policy. The name for private relief of misfortune on moral grounds is 'charity'; and charity (in the sense of the corresponding disposition), or beneficence, is rightly accounted a paramount virtue. The essential difference is that, whereas compensation is a right to which there exists a correlative obligation of reparation, relief and charity are not rights to which there exist correlative obligations. If charity were an obligation, it could be enforced, as can e.g. compensation (Subsec. 3.1). But 'enforced charity' is not charity.[29]

Nevertheless, misfortune is often mistaken for maltreatment, and there seem to be two principal causes of this confusion of ideas. First, the unlucky are often called 'victims of misfortune'. Here, their disadvantages are seen as deprivations inflicted on them by a supernatural agent, viz. the indiscriminate and fickle goddess, Fortune.[30] Secondly, there is a widespread misunderstanding of the concept, 'accident'. Many so-called accidents, e.g. motoring accidents, are occurrences in which some person is at fault; e.g. MacCormick's negligent motorist (Subsec. 3.1). Some accidents, on the other hand, are 'pure' accidents in which no one is at fault. But men seem reluctant to allow the existence of this second type of accident; we are only too ready to believe that somebody can and should be held responsible for every untoward event. The 'victims of misfortune' fallacy rests on a failure to grasp the concept of chance.[31] The 'no pure accidents' fallacy rests on a failure to appreciate the large part which chance plays in our lives, and on our deplorable proclivity to blame another whenever we are hurt.

4.2 Preventable Disadvantages

Take now the following case. *Case (2)*. There are two competitors for one place in a medical school, C3 who has attended a bad secondary school, and C4 who has attended a good secondary school. C4 obtains better grades in the entrance test, but the admitter awards the place to C3 on the ground that C3 was disadvantaged by his inferior secondary schooling, and has a right to be compensated for being thus disadvantaged. If C3 had attended C4's secondary school or an equivalent school, the admitter urges, C3 would have obtained better grades than C4; so that it is only fair that C3 should have the place.

In criticising compensatory discrimination (or any controversial policy, for that matter), it is prudent to proceed by first advancing as strong a case for it as is possible. I think that this is best effected by representing *case (2)* as being on all fours with the case of MacCormick's negligent motorist (Subsec. 3.1). The deprivee is C3, and the depriver is 'society' or 'the community'. Society's fault is its failure to take due care of C3 in the matter of his secondary education. The fault is unintended, and is an act of omission rather than of commission. Since there is no *mens rea* the fault is in no way criminal; rather, society is seen as being, like the motorist, an unintentionally negligent tortfeasor. But is this analogical argument convincing?

First, here too it is possible to take a short way with the admitter's argument (cf. Subsec. 4.1). This consists simply in pointing out that, since all discrimination is unjustified (Subsec. 2.2), and all compensatory discrimination is discrimination (Sec. 1), all compensatory discrimination is unjustified. It will be instructive, however, to set aside this objection and to draw attention to some others.

Secondly, it is questionable whether C3's disadvantage was indeed preventable. In the case of *some particular* C3, perhaps so; but it must be remembered that the argument is supposed to be of general application; and the proposition is surely false of *any* C3. Given the different abilities of teachers, etc., it is clearly impossible for all secondary school students to attend 'equivalent' secondary schools. Consequently, there cannot be an obligation on society to ensure that they do so. We have seen that what are now non-preventable disadvantages may cease to be so in the future (Subsec. 4.1). We now see further than what are believed to be preventable disadvantages may not be so in reality. This relates to a significant fact about compensatory discrimination. Those who advocate it tend to be collectivists (socialists), who entertain a greatly exaggerated idea of what 'society' *can* do. For the basic fallacies of collectivism are the following false beliefs. First, that the only possible kind of social order is artificial (man-made) and not natural. (Hayek distinguishes these two types of order as *taxis* and *kosmos* respectively.)[32] Secondly, that any kind and any amount of artificial order can be imposed on any society by political coercion. The belief in the possibility of equalizing opportunity in secondary education is a consequence of this second belief.

Thirdly, one must question the admitter's counterfactual judgement, that if C3 had attended either the same secondary school as C4 or an equivalent school, then C3 would have obtained better grades than C4 in the entrance test. Thus, compare the following case. *Case (3)*. In a running-race between two competitors, C5 and C6, the organiser makes a faulty arrangement whereby C5 has to run 20 yards farther than C6. C6 finishes 1 foot in front of C5; but C5 appeals successfully against the decision that C6 has won on the ground that C5 was unfairly handicapped; and that if C5 had had to run the same distance as C6, then C5 would have finished in front of C6. This counterfactual judgement is practically certain; but the corresponding counterfactual judgement in *Case (2)* is anything but certain. For C3's performance in the test will have been determined not only by the quality of his schooling, but also by his genetic endowment, his home background, etc.

Fourthly, the admitter breaks the Rule of Complete Compensation (Subsec. 3.3). For a good tertiary education is no equivalent of a good secondary education; especially since the natural result of 'depriving' C3 of the latter is to render him incapable of benefiting from the former. Other writers on compensatory discrimination find a difficulty in the idea that jobs, or places in law schools or medical schools, are compensations which are equivalent to the goods of which those such as C3 have allegedly been deprived.[33]

But the main weakness in the admitter's argument seems to me to reside in his contention that society has neglected its duty of care towards C3. The following remarks of Hayek's are very much to the point:

> Evidently, not only the actions of individuals but also the concerted actions of many individuals, or the actions of organisations, may be just, or unjust. Government is such an organisation, but society is not. And, though the order of society will be affected by actions of government, so long as it remains a spontaneous order, the particular results of the social process cannot be just or unjust . . . We shall see that what is called 'social' or 'distributive' justice is indeed meaningless within a spontaneous order and has meaning only within an organization.[34]

What Hayek says here respecting the right to distributive justice is equally true of the right to compensation. A member of 'society' holds these rights against 'society' only when the society is one which is organised, notably by a government (political authority) into a 'state'. If the analogy between 'society' and MacCormick's motorist is to hold good, then the society must be an organised one, among the duties of which is a responsibility to ensure equal secondary education to all its members; i.e. in effect, a social society. Only then does it make sense to speak of society having a duty of care towards C3 in this matter, and of it having an obligation of reparation to C3 if it neglects that duty. But if, as is usual, the society in question is one which is largely free, and which has no such responsibility, then the fact that C3's secondary education is inferior to C4's is C3's bad luck, like being female. And, as we have seen, there is no right to compensation for misfortune (Subsec. 41). The use of the vague word 'society' in this connection obscures the vital point, which is whether the society in question is organised in the relevant respect, or free.

A further objection to the admitter's argument is that the compensator (himself) is not identical with the alleged depriver (society). Others, e.g. Fiss, have found this difficulty with compensatory discrimination.[35] It has been replied to this objection that, provided the medical school is public, the admitter acts as an agent of society in admitting C3. But this reply calls for two connected comments. First, the relation of the admitter to society is not like that of the father to his young son, who injures another boy (Subsec. 3.1). For the father has a clearly defined and generally recognised moral and legal responsibility for the wrong; whereas the admitter has not. Secondly, Hayek's point about what *kind*

of society we are talking about is again relevant. It is, of course, possible for a society to be so organised that admitters at public medical
schools are explicitly charged with the responsibility for compensation
which is here at issue. But it is surely most unusual, even in highly collectivist societies. And in a largely free society where medical schools
are independent, this reply to the objection has no force at all.

Alternatively, the transaction may be regarded, not as a voluntary
compensation by the admitter, but as a non-voluntary compensation
imposed by the admitter (Subsec. 3.1). But this view of the matter is
exposed to the same objections, that the compensator is not identical with
the alleged depriver. For, on this view, what ought to happen is that
the admitter makes society give back the place to C3 in return for the
good secondary education of which society deprived C3. But what
in fact happens is that the admitter deprives C4, not society, of the
place.[36]

The upshot is, then, that the argument for compensatory discrimination in cases of preventable disadvantage, as well as of non-preventable
disadvantages, fails.

In conclusion, I shall propound a strong objection not only to the practice, but also to the profession of the theory, of compensatory discrimination. This objection rests on the tendency of both its practice and its profession to arouse resentment. Other students of reverse discrimination,
e.g. Nagel, have objected to it on this ground, but have not spelled out
the objection in detail.[37] A principal reason for this, no doubt, is that
resentment, like prejudice, is a complex social fact. It is desirable,
therefore, to begin by explaining it, and then to proceed to show its connection with the practice and profession of the theory of compensatory
discrimination.

An initial difficulty is posed by the fact that the phenomenon in question is not always discussed under the name of 'resentment'. It is so by
older authors (e.g. Butler, Westermarck), but nowadays it is treated of
under the name of 'reactive (defensive) aggression' (by, e.g., Allport,
Fromm).[38] Fromm gives the following account of reactive aggression,
which *Homo sapiens* shares with all animals. It is a phylogenetically pro-
grammed impulse to attack or to flee when vital interests are threatened.
It is 'benign', since it conduces to the survival of the individual and the
species; it is biologically adaptive; and it ceases when the threat has ceased
to exist. Further, it is an instinct (organic drive), which originates in
Man's psychophysical constitution. Naturally, this impulse is not always
acted out in behaviour. The emotions associated with it are anger, hatred
and fear. Unlike other animals, however, Man reacts to imagined

threats as well as to real ones. Indeed, with resentment as with prejudice and subjective guilt, the phenomenological aspect is all-important; what matters is whether A sees (imagines) himself as threatened by B. Again as with subjective guilt, displacement (projection) is important. For A's resentment is often displaced from B, the real threatener, on to C, a scapegoat. Finally, when the impulse is expressed in behaviour, counter-behaviour tends to follow. Thus, if A attacks B reactively, then B tends to attack A counter-reactively. Consequently, 'the more aggression is expressed, the more of it there will be'.[39] Fromm's mention of threats reminds us that, although the object of resentment is often some person who is seen as the doer of a past or present injury, it is also often some person who is seen as the doer of a future injury, i.e. as a threatener.

But here an obvious objection suggests itself. If resentment is 'benign', because it conduces to the survival of the individual and the species, how can the practice and profession of compensatory discrimination be faulted on the score that they tend to arouse resentment? The reply to this objection is that it fails to distinguish between resentment itself and its effect. Butler makes the point clearly: 'The good influence which [resentment] has in fact upon the affairs of the world, is obvious to everyone's notice. Men are plainly restrained from injuring their fellow-creatures by fear of their resentment; and it is very happy that they are so, when they would not be restrained by a principle of virtue . . . This however is to be considered as a good effect, notwithstanding it were much to be wished that men would act from a better principle, reason and cool reflection.' That is to say, (1) A's injuring B followed by B's reactive aggression (involving anger) at the injury is better (or less bad) than (2) A's injuring B followed by no such reaction by B. For (1) will cause A (and C, D . . .) to fear B's reactive aggression if they injure him again. But it neither follows nor is true that B's anger and A's (and C's, D's . . .) fear are good in themselves. On the contrary, they are bad; indeed, paradigms of those 'passive emotions' which, Spinoza teaches, keep men in 'human bondage'.[40]

It is now possible to sketch the sort of way in which the practice and profession of compensatory discrimination tends to generate resentment, and to indicate why this is a bad thing. (The picture is deliberately over-drawn in order to bring out clearly the dangers in compensatory discrimination.). Consider again *case 2*, in which the admitter awards the place in the medical school to C3, despite the fact that C3's inferior secondary education is a misfortune and not a wrong. C4 resents this, because he sees himself as wronged by the admitter, since no compensation is due to C3. Further, C4 displaces his resentment from the admitter on to C3, and expresses it, e.g., by ostracising C3. But if C3 has been told by an advocate of compensatory discrimination that he has been wronged by society's neglect of its duty of care of him, so that compensation is in fact due to him, he is only too ready to believe that it is he and not C4 who has a right to the place. For among what Butler calls 'abuses of deliberate resentment' he rightly gives a prominent place to 'partiality to ourselves'. Consequently, C3 regards C4's resentment, as expressed by his ostracism of C3, as unjustified; counter-resents it; and acts out his counter-resentment in, say, antilocution against C4. But since C4 believes that it is he who has a right to the place, he regards C3's counter-resentment and antilocution as unjustified; counter-counter-resents it; and acts out his counter-counter-resentment in, say, antilocution against C3 as well as in ostracism of him. And so on in corrosive escalation, with C3 and C4 hating and maltreating one another more and more. Evidently, the key factors in this process of escalation are the phenomenological aspect, displacement, and the tendency of expressed aggression to generate more aggression.

5. Conclusion

This essay is conceived in the spirit of Allport's study of prejudice, Eckhoff's of justice,[41] Fromm's of aggression and McKenzie's of guilt; viz. as interdisciplinary. For compensatory discrimination is illuminated not only by philosophers but also by jurisprudents and psychologists. The contribution of the philosophers (e.g. Nagel, Thomson) naturally consists in clarifying the concepts involved and in either advancing arguments of their own for or against compensatory discrimination, or criticising the arguments of others. The contributions of the jurisprudents are of two kinds. Some (e.g. Eckhoff, MacCormick, Vecchio) elucidate the connected ideas of retributive justice and the right to compensation. Others (e.g. Dworkin, Fiss) elicit and debate the principles implicit in some leading cases in the USA. What the psychologists have to offer is insight into the causes and effects of compensatory discrimination. But in the numerous recent discussions of compensatory discrimination their contribution has been ignored, so that these otherwise excellent papers are unbalanced and incomplete. Consequently, I have had in this essay a dual aim. Primarily, of course, to forward the philosophical work as just described, taking due account of the jurisprudents' contributions. But also, secondarily, to repair the omission of the psychological dimension of our problem. For it is my submission that compensatory discrimination is not only a highly controversial policy which needs to be justified or condemned, but also a complex and significant phenomenon which requires to be understood.[42]

APPENDIX

Valuable discussions of some of the issues treated in this essay will be found in W.T. Blackstone and R.D. Heslep (eds), *Social Justice and Preferential Treatment* (The University of Georgia Press, Athens, Georgia, 1977).

Notes

1. A.H. Goldman, 'Affirmative Action', *Equality and Preferential Treatment*, Marshall Cohen and Thomas Scanlon (eds) (University Press, Princeton, 1977), p. 192.

2. Ronald Dworkin, *Taking Rights Seriously* (Duckworth, London, 1977), pp. 223-39.

3. George Sher, 'Justifying Reverse Discrimination in Employment', Cohen and Scanlon, *Equality and Preferential Treatment*, pp. 49-60.

4. I advance a strong teleological objection to compensatory discrimination in the conclusion of Subsection 4.2. Nathan Glazer presents another powerful teleological objection to reverse discrimination in his 'Individual Rights Against Group Rights' in *Human Rights*, Eugene Kamenka and A.E. Tay (eds) (Edward Arnold, London, 1978), pp. 87-103.

5. See Essay 2, note 13; Joel Feinberg, *Social Philosophy* (Prentice-Hall, Englewood Cliffs, 1973), p. 100; Giorgio del Vecchio, *Justice* (University Press, Edinburgh, 1952), pp. 51, 169.

6. J.J. Thomson, 'Preferential Hiring', Cohen and Scanlon, *Equality and Preferential Treatment*, p. 39.

7. G.W. Allport, *The Nature of Prejudice* (Doubleday, New York, 1968), pp. 3-16. See also G.C. Field, *Prejudice and Impartiality* (Methuen, London, 1932).

8. Allport, *Prejudice*, p. 212. Here is one more confirmation of the truth of Mill's assertion that 'of all effects, none depend on so great a complication of causes as social phenomena'. He continues 'social phenomena are those in which plurality of causes prevails in the utmost extent'. Allport's study does indeed show that prejudice is caused, e.g., sometimes by the authoritarian personality of the subject, sometimes by a tradition of anti-clericalism in the subject's society, and sometimes by both. But it is the third possibility which he finds to be much the most important one (J.S. Mill, *Logic*, 8th edn, VI, vii, 1, 4; cf. III, x, 5-8).

9. J.G. McKenzie, *Guilt* (Allen and Unwin, London, 1962), pp. 20-4.

10. Sigmund Freud, *An Outline of Psycho-Analysis* (Hogarth Press, London, 1949), p. 45.

11. H.D. Lewis, 'The Problem of Guilt', *Aristotelian Society Supplement*, Vol. 21 (1947), pp. 175-96; McKenzie, *Guilt*, pp. 25-8. On the correlativity of non-voluntary compensation and retributive punishment see Essay 4; also Subsec. 3.1 below.

12. McKenzie, *Guilt*, pp. 29-57.

13. Edmund Burke, *Reflections on the Revolution in France*.

14. The anthropologist Arthur Keith presents a qualified, Darwinian defence of ethnic prejudice in the modern sense of 'prejudice' in *The Place of Prejudice in Modern Civilization* (Williams and Norgate, London, 1931). But his argument is unconvincing.

15. Cf. O.M. Fiss, 'Groups and the Equal Protection Clause', Cohen and Scanlon, *Equality and Preferential Treatment*, pp. 85-97; 'School Desegregation', Cohen and Scanlon, *Equality and Preferential Treatment*, pp. 161-2.

16. Feinberg, *Social Philosophy*, p. 100; cf. Subsec. 2.1, above, on impartiality and indiscriminateness. Aristotle, *Nicomachean Ethics*, V; *Politics*, III.

17. See Sec. 1 of Essay 4.

18. D.N. MacCormick, 'The Obligation of Reparation', *Aristotelian Society Proceedings*, Vol. 78 (1978), pp. 175-93. See also Martin Wasik, 'The Place of Compensation in the Penal System', *The Criminal Law Review* (1978), pp. 599-611.

19. MacCormick, *The Obligation of Reparation*, p. 181.

20. Thomas Nagel, 'Equal Treatment and Compensatory Discrimination', Cohen and Scanlon, *Equality and Preferential Treatment*, p. xi.

21. McKenzie, *Guilt*, pp. 97ff.

22. John Locke, *An Essay Concerning Human Understanding*, II, xxvii, pp. 4-8.

23. See Sec. 2 of Essay 4.

24. F.H. Bradley, *Ethical Studies* (Clarendon Press, Oxford, 1927).

25. This argument is additional to and more basic than the two advanced in Sec. 3 of Essay 4. On the primacy of the state's duty to maintain civil rights, see also Dworkin, *Taking Rights Seriously*, especially Ch. 7.

26. Melanie Klein, 'Love, Guilt and Reparation' in Melanie Klein and Joan Riviere, *Love, Hate and Reparation* (Hogarth Press, London, 1937), pp. 65ff.

27. See Sec. 4 of Essay 4.

28. Another unsatisfactory feature of the English law of defamation is that here it is left to the jury and not to the judge to decide the amount of the damages. Three recent cases, those of Savalas, *alias* Kojak, Ryder and the Redgraves, illustrate how this practice can lead to plaintiffs being paid far too much or far too little. See the leading article, 'Damages are not for Juries to Assess', *The Times* (11 November 1978).

29. For some interesting reflections on the relationship between justice and rights on the one hand and assistance and charity on the other, see Ch. Perelman, *The Idea of Justice and the Problem of Argument* (Routledge and Kegan Paul, London, 1963), pp. 23, 40f.; Vecchio, *Justice*, pp. 148ff.; S.I. Benn, 'Human Rights — for Whom and for What?', *Human Rights*, Kamenka and Tay, pp. 68-71; Philippa Foot, 'Euthanasia', *Philosophy and Public Affairs*, Vol. 6, No. 2 (1977), pp. 85-112. It should be added that there is a moral as well as a prudential obligation to insure oneself and one's dependants against misfortune, so as not 'to come upon the parish'.

30. See Essay 2, note 13.

31. It is, after all, quite a new idea. 'The decade around 1660 is the birthtime of probability' (Ian Hacking, *The Emergence of Probability* (University Press, Cambridge, 1975), p. 11).

32. F.A. Hayek, *The Mirage of Social Justice* (Routledge and Kegan Paul, London, 1976).

33. Sher, 'Justifying Reverse Discrimination', p. 51f.; Robert Simon, 'Preferential Hiring: A Reply to Judith Jarvis Thomson', Cohen and Scanlon, *Equality and Preferential Treatment*, p. 40.

34. Hayek, *Social Justice*, pp. 32f.; cf. pp. 67ff.

35. Fiss, 'School Desegregation', p. 159.

36. 'The Criminal Injuries Compensation Board' is in fact a misnomer. For its members are obviously not identical with the deprivers, who are the murderers, muggers and rapists with whose misdeeds they deal. Consequently, the payments out of public funds which the Board makes to the victims are properly called, not 'compensation', but rather 'relief' or 'aid'. Notice, in this connection, that although all relief of misfortune is charity or assistance (Subsec. 4.1), the converse is not true. The Board's payments are relief and not compensation; but the deprivations sustained by the victims are of course wrongs and not misfortunes. Indeed, any righting of a wrong except that effected by the wrongdoer is charity

or assistance. It is possible to be misled on this point by the fact that it is correct to say of, e.g., the traveller who was aided by the Good Samaritan 'he had the misfortune to fall among muggers' (*Luke*, x, 30-7).

37. Nagel, 'Equal Treatment', p. 17.

38. The qualifying adjectives are needed in order to distinguish this type of aggression from what Fromm calls 'malignant aggression', which is not reactive or defensive. Thus, according to Freud's later writings, 'the love instinct' and 'the death instinct' are Man's two basic organic drives (Freud, *An Outline*, Ch. 2). But other psychologists question whether there really is any such 'death instinct'. Allport, e.g., maintains that 'love is a precondition of hate', so that all aggression is reactive (op. cit., p. 342). However, this interesting controversy does not concern us, since our business is exclusively with reactive aggression, the reality of which has never been in doubt. See Allport, *Prejudice*, pp. 335-44; Joseph Butler, 'Upon Resentment' in *Fifteen Sermons*; Erich Fromm, *The Anatomy of Human Destructiveness* (Cape, London, 1974); Edvard Westermarck, 'The Essence of Revenge', *Mind*, Vol. 7 (1898), pp. 289-310; P.F. Strawson, 'Freedom and Resentment', *British Academy Proceedings*, Vol. 48 (1962), pp. 187-211.

39. Allport, *Prejudice*, p. 338.

40. Benedict de Spinoza, *Ethics*, IV. Plainly, Bishop Butler is sharply at variance with Christian orthodoxy respecting the duty to 'love your enemies' (*Matthew*, v, 43-5). This is because he considers, rightly, that 'in dealing with this problem we must take Man as he is, not inquire why he is not different'.

41. Torstein Eckhoff, *Justice* (University Press, Rotterdam, 1974).

42. If my introduction of such considerations is objected to as irrelevant psychologism, I reply that there are many precedents. To cite a single, but classic one: consider how Mill finds the sanction of the Principle of Utility in the social feelings, and that of retributive justice in both them and the resentment which is discussed in Subsec. 4.2 of this essay (J.S. Mill, *Utilitarianism*, Chs 3, 5). I am grateful to Professor Herbert Hart for suggesting amendments on some points of law and jurisprudence.

6 INDIVIDUAL LIBERTY

The philosophical problems of liberty may be classified as those of definition, of justification and of distribution. They are so complex that there is a danger of being unable to see the wood for the trees. It may be helpful, therefore, to provide an aerial photograph of a large part of the wood, namely, the liberty of *individual persons*, But it is, of course, a photograph taken from an individual point of view, as Leibniz would have put it.

1. The Problem of Definition

The chief questions here are those of *the subjects* of liberty and of *the truth-conditions* of liberty.

The subjects of the predicate 'free' are *events* involving *things, actions* of persons, and *persons*. Thus, we speak of the degrees of freedom of movement of bodies, of free contracts, of free men, and of free churches. The last two illustrate the distinction between *individual liberty* and *collective liberty*. In this lecture I shall discuss only the former. The significance of attributing freedom to events involving things will appear shortly. But the important subjects of liberty are individual persons and organisations of persons

Different answers are given to the question, When is an individual person, A, truly said to be unfree to do X? According to *the positive or intrapersonal concept of liberty*, A is unfree to do X if A is 'a slave to his passions', i.e. is prevented from doing X by some emotion or desire; e.g. A is unfree to work effectively because A is made unable to do so by his addiction to alcohol.

The creator of the positive concept of individual liberty was Plato, who modelled it on his positive concept of collective liberty. That is, he maintained that the good or free person is isomorphic with the good or free state, in that in both the best part keeps the worst part in subjection. It is, therefore, an essentially political concept. Other protagonists of positive liberty are Spinoza, Rousseau, Kant and Hegel.[1] Of these Spinoza is especially interesting since he offers a programme of emancipation from slavery to the passions, which he calls 'human bondage', that anticipates interestingly modern psycho-therapeutic techniques.[2]

Some contemporary philosophers also favour this concept of liberty.[3] (In fact, it is necessary to distinguish Plato's and Spinoza's definition from Rousseau's and Kant's definition. According to the former, the free man is the self-controlled man. But according to the latter, the free man is the autonomous man. However, self-control and autonomy are closely related, which is doubtless why the two definitions tend not to be distinguished. For, first, the autonomous man or organisation is self-controlled in that he or it is subject to rules (laws) imposed on him or it by himself or itself and not by rules imposed on him or it by some other person or organisation, which is heteronomy. Secondly, on both definitions liberty is intrapersonal and not interpersonal. See Secs. 2 and 5 and Appendices 1 and 2 of Essay 10, Essay 13.)

Nevertheless, this answer to the question of the truth-conditions of liberty is false. For liberty is *a moral right*, and A can possess a right only against some other person, B, and not against A or part of A. (See Sec. 2.) Liberty is therefore an interpersonal concept and not an intrapersonal one.

According to *the negative or interpersonal concept of liberty*, A is unfree to do X if A is restrained from doing X by B. The name 'negative liberty' was coined by Bentham to indicate that liberty means *the absence of coercion*.[4] B coerces A if B *restrains* A from doing X or if B *compels* A not to do X. (Since these are equivalent, we do not need both 'restrains' and 'compels'.)

B restrains A from doing X if and only if B *makes A unable* to do X. There is a difficulty here, since persons differ in their abilities. It is met by employing the concept of *objective (intersubjective) human possibility* rather than that of subjective human possibility. For example, B is deemed to make A unfree to move if B binds A in a way that would make *the average man* unable to move.

B makes A unfree to do X if and only if B makes A unable to do X with *the intention* of making A unable to do X. For example, if B locks A in a room unintentionally, B makes A unable to leave the room, but not unfree to do so. The reasons for this are that all coercive acts are violations of the moral right to liberty; that all violations of a moral right are morally right or wrong acts; and that all morally right or wrong acts are intentional acts. A violation of a moral right is morally right if and only if the moral obligation to respect the right is overborne by some stronger moral obligation.

Some think that 'free' is *univocal*, so that in the above positive and negative accounts of the truth-conditions of unfreedom 'if' should be replaced by 'if and only if'. But others think that 'free' is *equivocal*, so that the above accounts can stand. Among these are those who think that there are more than two concepts of liberty. Oppenheim has recently distinguished five.[5] But one main thesis of this lecture is that 'free' is univocal and that the negative concept is the only concept of liberty.

The creator of the negative concept of individual liberty was Hobbes, who formed it by analogy with the concept of freely moving bodies. His is an essentially physical concept, and its introduction was causally connected with the then rapidly rising science of dynamics. Hobbes' other great achievement in this field was to dissolve *the* (so-called) *problem of free will* by showing that an action can be both negatively free and also determined by law: that negatively free human actions can be explained and predicted by the laws of the social sciences in substantially the same way as the falls of the stones which Galileo dropped can be explained and predicted by his law of falling bodies. With important qualifications, Locke, Hume, Bentham and Mill accept both Hobbes' concept of liberty and his view of the free will question. Respecting the latter, they share Hume's opinion that 'the whole controversy has . . . turned merely upon words'.[6]

Consider now the values that can be taken by the variables A and B in the above negative account of the truth-conditions of unfreedom. The most important value of B is a sovereign, *Rex* (R), a political authority; when the corresponding value of A is a citizen (C). The species of liberty involved here is *political liberty*. There is also non-political liberty, because coercion is also exercised by, e.g., parents and teachers on children. Again, C1 may make C2 unfree by kidnapping him, and it is one of R's duties to deter or prevent such violations of liberty by his subjects. Mill considered 'the coercion of public opinion', i.e. *social liberty*, to be as serious a matter as political coercion; but he lacked our sad experience of how coercive governments can be.[7] If the state should wither away, political liberty would cease to be the most important species of liberty. At present, however, it is so; just as political justice is the most important sort of justice, and political punishment is the most important sort of punishment.[8]

R coerces any C in three main ways. First, by *simple coercion*, e.g. incarceration. Here, R restrains some C from doing *a simple action*, namely, moving out of prison.

Secondly, by *legislation*, above all by *criminal law*. For example, R addresses to all C a command not to kill any fellow-C, and backs his command with *a threat* that he will *punish* any C who disobeys it by killing him. It is the effective threat and not the command which coerces all C, and it does this by restraining any C from doing *a complex (conjunctive) action*, namely, both taking a fellow-C's life and also keeping his own life. The effect of this restraint is *to deter* any C from doing the simple action, killing a fellow-C.[9] Coercion by legislation is therefore *complex coercion*.

Thirdly, by *manipulation*. Here, R proceeds typically as follows. He covertly compels all C to hear the proposition, P, that any C who kills a fellow-C will die immediately. He also covertly prevents all C from hearing not-P. Consequently, all C believe P, and so desire not to kill any fellow-C, and so refrain from doing so. Note that P is *a prediction*, and not a threat. Moreover, since R is engaged in political propaganda, it is a prediction which he knows to be probably false. If R were to compel all C to hear the proposition, Q, that any C who kills a fellow-C will die immediately *by R's hand*, that would be in effect coercion by legislation, not coercion by manipulation, and identical with the example of it given above. Like incarceration, eviction, etc., coercion by manipulation is simple coercion.

The differences between coercion by legislation and coercion by manipulation are therefore as follows. First, in coercion by legislation, R prevents all C from doing a complex action, whereas in coercion by manipulation R restrains all C from doing a simple action; for example hearing not-P. Secondly, in coercion by legislation, any C who wants to kill a fellow-C is made *to feel unfree* by R's threat of punishment, because he is restrained from doing what he wants to do, namely, both to take a fellow-C's life and also keep his own life. But in coercion by manipulation, no C is made to feel unfree, because all C do what they want to do, namely, refrain from killing any fellow-C. Thirdly, coercion by legislation must be overt, since R's threat will not deter unless it is published to all C. But coercion by manipulation must be covert, since R's propaganda will not work if all C realise that they are being manipulated by him.

Which of the three modes of political coercion now curtails liberty most? Not simple coercion, such as incarceration, since the proportion of all C whose liberty is curtailed in this way is relatively small even in extreme tyrannies. Coercion by manipulation is superior to the other two modes. For whereas incarceration and legislation normally make some C feel unfree to do X and so disposed *to resist* R, manipulation makes no C feel unfree to do X and so disposed to resist R. It is not surprising, therefore, that it is coercion by manipulation which has fired the public imagination.[10] But, while the present power of propaganda, brainwashing, etc., should not be underestimated, the full exploitation of these techniques lies in the future. Today, coercion by legislation is still the main cause of unfreedom. Indeed, the situation in this respect has long been deteriorating. The monstrous multiplication of possible offences in this and other countries in modern times is due chiefly to R's obsessions with internal and external security (the public safety) and with collectivism. These obsessions in turn have been created mainly by the two world wars. This, therefore, is the problem which I address in the present lecture.

2. The Problem of Justification

It is necessary to distinguish, first, arguments for *liberty* (singular) from arguments for *liberties* (plural); and secondly, arguments for liberty as *a moral right* from arguments for liberty from *consequences*. It will be convenient to discuss the second distinction first.

Political liberty is *a negative, general, individual, moral right*. It is individual, because it is held by individual persons.[11] Since political liberty is the subject under discussion, the right is held by an individual in his role as a C, and is held by him against R. The right is general, because it is held by any C in his role as a citizen, and not because of some special relationship between him and R. Such a special relationship would exist if, for example, R had promised all C that he would assure their political liberty.[12] General rights are therefore also called 'human rights', 'natural rights' or 'the rights of man and the citizen'. Finally, it is negative, because it is *a right not to be injured. A positive right* is *an (alleged) right to be benefited*. I shall touch on the subject of positive rights later. (See Sec. 3.)

Arguments for liberty as a moral right preceded arguments for it from consequences. The notion that political liberty is a negative, general, individual, moral right is causally linked with the connected phenomena of Protestanism and capitalism.[13] Locke, who first claimed political liberty as a natural right, was sympathetic to both these movements. From him, the idea passed into the English, American, French and other classic declarations of the rights of man and of the citizen.[14]

Consequential arguments for liberty were introduced by Bentham and Mill.[15] They are intended to show that negative individual political liberty benefits all C (is in the public interest, that is, promotes the general happiness or common good). So the essential difference between arguments for such liberty as a right and arguments for it from consequences is as follows. The former are designed to show that such liberty *averts injury from each C individually*, whereas the latter are designed to show that it *confers benefit on all C collectively*.

Let us consider first an argument for liberty in general (singular) which is an argument for it as a moral right. When R coerces all C by legislation, they often feel unfree. But the feeling of unfreedom, or frustration, is painful and injurious.[16] This argument is sound, but subject to the important qualification that a C does not always feel unfree when R makes him unfree. First, a C does not feel unfree to do X when R restrains him from doing X if that C believes falsely that he is free to do X. Secondly, a C does not feel unfree to do X when R restrains him from doing X if that C does not desire to do X.

Confusion between feeling unfree and being unfree vitiates the Stoic theory of individual liberty. The slave Epictetus taught that the remedy for a slave is to suppress his desire to be free.[17] But although a slave who did that would cease to feel unfree, he would not cease to be unfree. (See the Appendix to Essay 1.)

The facts that coercion tends to make coercees feel frustrated and that liberty is a moral right justify Mill's judgement that 'all restraint, *qua* restraint, is an evil'. They also justify *the presumption* in favour of liberty which imposes *the burden of justification* on the coercer.[18]

I turn now to arguments for liberties (plural). Liberties are differentiated as liberties *to do X, to do Y, to do Z*, etc.; where doing X, doing Y, doing Z . . . etc., are *sorts of actions*, not *particular actions*. We shall need to consider the liberty of expression, 'the liberty of tastes and pursuits';[19] the liberty of association, religious liberty and economic liberty.

The expression *religious liberty* is ambiguous. Usually it means *ecclesiastical liberty*, which is the liberty of a Church *vis-à-vis* R.[20] This is a collective liberty, consideration of which lies outside the scope of this lecture. Sometimes, however, 'religious liberty' means the liberty of an individual to join any Church or none, or to leave any Church. This falls under the liberty of association, which I shall discuss shortly. (Religious liberty is treated of in Essay 11.)

Economic liberty, too, is a collective liberty, since economic operations are carried on mostly by organisations, such as family businesses, partnerships and joint-stock companies, rather than by individuals. Discussion of this liberty therefore also falls outside the scope of this lecture. (Economic liberty is treated of in Essay 12.)

The argument for *the liberty of expression* as a right consists in pointing out that not only the professional author (*the individual producer*) but also the common speaker need to express their thoughts. If R deters or restrains them from doing so, he injures them by denying their need and by frustrating their potentiality for self-development. But Mill, in in his classic defence of this liberty, uses consequential arguments which point out the benefit of this liberty to all readers (*the consumers collectively*). If R deters or prevents geneticists from publishing their results, the progress of the science of genetics towards *truth* will be slowed or arrested. If he disallows criticism of religious doctrines, they will lose their *meaning* and become 'dead dogmas'.[21]

Similarly, the argument for the *liberty of tastes and pursuits* as a right consists in pointing out that R injures each individual C if R deters or prevents him from his *pursuit of happiness*. But Mill emphasises the public benefit of R's respecting this right, since the happy few who realise their potentialities will set the rest 'the example of more enlightened conduct, and better taste and sense in human life.'[22]

The liberty of association (singular) is the *individual* liberty of each C to associate or not to associate with, or to dissociate from some other C. It must be distinguished from *the collective liberty of associations* (plural) to do X, to do Y, to do Z . . . etc., e.g. the liberty of Churches to profess their faiths and to practise their rites, and the liberty of joint-stock companies to engage in free enterprise and free trade. The argument for the liberty of association as a right consists in pointing out that each C is a social animal who needs the company of his fellows in clubs, etc. More importantly, that each C can only achieve many of his main goals in co-operation with others. He cannot play cricket without being a member of a team, and he cannot engage in economic operations on any scale without joining a partnership or a joint-stock company. Hence, R will injure each C gravely if he does not respect this right. Consequential arguments for this liberty point out the benefit to all C of free associations, such as joint-stock companies and trade unions. Showing that joint-stock companies and trade unions benefit the public is a matter of justifying collective economic liberty. Here, the point is simply that, without the individual liberty of association, such organisations could not exist.[23]

3. The Problem of Distribution

This problem is that of deciding what *kinds* and what *amount* of each kind of liberty are morally justified. Important principles have been proposed to answer it.

The most famous of these is Mill's 'principle of individual liberty', which he applied to social liberty as well as to political liberty.[24] (See Sec. 1.) Being interested only in political liberty, I shall consider (1) *the* (corresponding) *principle of negative individual political liberty*. This states that, if any C does not injure some other C by doing X, then R is not morally justified in legislating against any C doing X.

The following remarks will clarify the meaning of principle (1). First, 'some other C' means not only some other individual C, but also alternatively some proper subset of the set of all C, or the set all C. Secondly, 'some other C' excludes any C himself. So, since the principle says nothing about cases where some C does not injure himself or others, or about cases where some C does injure himself but not others, it is against legal paternalism. (See principle (4), below.) Thirdly, the principle states that harm to another is a necessary condition, not a sufficient condition of morally justified political coercion. The following examples illustrate this point. (i) A penal law against homosexual conduct between consenting adults. Since such conduct harms no other, the principle applies and condemns such a law as morally unjustified.[25] (ii) A penal law against murder. Since murder harms another, the principle does not apply. (But the law is morally justified because it is R's duty to maintain the right to life of all C.) (iii) A penal law against economic competition. Since such competition harms others, namely, the losers, the principle does not apply. (But Mill, as a classical economist, maintains that this law is not morally justified because free competition is in the general interest.[26])

The truth of principle (1) is contested. I shall consider the commonest objection to it with a view both to defending it and to bringing out an important point which tends to be overlooked in these debates.

Consider a penal law which requires motor-cyclists to wear protective helmets. Some say that this law is not morally justified because a motor-cyclist who has no dependants and who does not comply with it is likely to harm himself but not others. The commonest objection to this claim is that, on the contrary, his conduct is likely to harm others. For if he is injured as a result of not wearing a helmet, other C will have to pay for his medicare in taxation; which involves violating their property-right and their liberty to dispose of their property as they wish. But the reply to this objection is that it is true only in a collectivist state with socialised medicine. It is true because it is made to be true by political coercion. The important general point is that principle (1) applies only to states which are free, in the sense that all C already have a large amount of negative individual political liberty.

I turn now to (2) *the principle of Good Samaritan legislation*. This states that R is morally justified in legislating so as to benefit some proper subset of the set all C at the expense of the complementary set of that subset: for example, in providing education for the children of those

C who cannot afford to pay for it by taxing the other C.

Like principle (1), principle (2) is highly controversial. It is implicit in the laws of some collectivist states, such as the people's democracies of Eastern Europe, but not in those of mainly non-collectivist states such as Great Britain and the USA.[27]

A common defence of it is the contention that there is a positive right to be benefited. (On the difference between positive and negative rights see Sec. 2.) A typical negative right is the right to life, and a typical alleged positive right is the right to the means of livelihood. There are two essential differences between them. First, in the case of the right to life, there is a perfect reciprocity between right-bearers and right-respecters. Every C can and ought to respect every other C's right to life. Similarly with liberty and other negative rights. But in the case of the right to the means of livelihood, there is no such reciprocity. Some C cannot, and so have no obligation to, contribute to the means of livelihood of other C.[28] Similarly with the right to holidays with pay and other alleged positive rights. Secondly, if R coerces C1 in order to deter C1 from violating C2's right to life, R violates no right of C1, since C1 has no right to violate C2's right to life. Similarly with liberty and other negative rights. But if R coerces C1 in order to deter C1 from not contributing to C2's means of livelihood, R does violate some right of C1, namely, his property-right. Similarly with the right to holidays with pay and other alleged positive rights.[29]

Principle (2) must therefore be justified, if at all, by consequential argument and not by argument from rights. I submit that the true principle is *the principle of the coincidence of particular and general interests*. This states that principle (2) is true only if such legislation also benefits the set all C.[30] This principle of coincidence is satisfied in the education example (above), since it is to the interest of all C that all C should be educated. But this principle is not satisfied if R imposes a protective tariff on footwear of foreign manufacture. The essential difference between the two cases is as follows. In the education case, the complementary set are not injured, since it is to the interest of all C that all C should be educated, and they are a proper subset of the set all C. But in the tariff case, the complementary set are injured, since they have to pay more for their footwear than they need to do, and receive no benefit in return for this injury. A subsidy to General Motors by the US government would be justified if what is good for General Motors in this respect is indeed good for the USA. Bentham called particular interests which do not coincide with the public interest 'sinister interests'. The purpose of most lobbies and pressure groups is to promote sinister interests.

(The education example is called by political economists a 'neighbourhood effect'. Such effects can be bad as well as good. See e.g. M. Friedman, *Capitalism and Freedom*, Reissue (University of Chicago Press, Chicago, 1982).)

According to (3) *the principle of utilitarian legislation*, R is morally justified in legislating so as to benefit all C at the expense of some pro- per subset of the set all C, e.g. in conscripting young C for the defence of the realm, or in taxing C who are not poor in order to provide and maintain roads. As these examples suggest, this principle applies par- ticularly to the provision of goods and services which benefit all C collectively.

We have just seen that principle (3) is justified by the fact that the proper subset are not injured precisely because, being a proper subset of the set all C, they too receive benefit in return for their injury. We have also just seen that principle (3) justifies a qualified version of prin- ciple (2) by the mediation of the principle of the coincidence of particular and public interests.

The difficulty with it lies in achieving an equitable trade-off between the public interest and individual rights, e.g. *how far* may R justifiably violate the property-rights of some proper subset of all C by taxation in order to provide and maintain roads? It is not possible to answer such a question by appeal to any one principle. One has to appeal to a number of fairly obvious considerations, such as that the level of taxation imposed by R on some proper subset of all C for all goods and services which benefit all C collectively must not be so high as to deter that subset from producing the wealth out of which the taxes must be paid.

I pass now to (4) *the principle of paternalistic legislation*. This states that, if any C injures himself by doing X, then R is morally justified in legislating against any C doing X. Thus R would be morally justified in legislating against C taking heroin. This principle seeks to mandate *prudence*. The commonest liberal objection to it is based on *the principle of rational self-interest*. This asserts that A is the best judge of A's interests; so that R does not know what is good for any C better than he himself does. But the reply to this objection is that, as a matter of fact, the gentleman at Westminster does know best.

I have three observations to offer on this dispute. First, the principle of rational self-interest is often rendered 'A knows best what A wants'. But 'A wants X' means either 'A desires X' or 'It is in A's interest that A should have X'. It is approximately true that A knows best what A desires, so that the principle may look obvious. However, the principle is in fact about A's interests and not his desires. And it is questionable whether it is approximately true that A knows best what A's interests are. Secondly, Mill uses this principle to justify economic liberty or *laisser-faire*. He therefore means by it that A is the best judge of A's *economic interests*. This may be true, and yet it may be false that A is the best judge of A's non-economic interests. On the other hand, thirdly, there is no reason to believe that R, the political authority, possesses *as such* expert knowledge of, e.g., the educational needs of any child of any C. If he has it, it is because he has consulted an expert on this subject. But any C can do this himself, and satisfy his children's needs accordingly. Such a system is superior in point of cost, flexibility and preservation of liberty to one in which R monopolises the supply of education.[31]

In any case, there is a deeper objection to legal paternalism which bypasses this controversy. Even if R were to know what is good for any C better than he himself does, it would not follow that R ought to legislate against actions whereby any C injures himself. For it is assumed that all C are adults; and if adults are treated as children, children they will remain. It is an essential part of growing-up and of education that A should learn from his own mistakes. Indeed, he is unlikely to learn in any other way. For, although A can learn from A's mistakes, he is unlikely to learn from B's mistakes.[32]

The last principle of distribution for consideration is (5) *the principle of moralistic legislation*. According to it, if any C acts immorally in doing X, then R is morally justified in legislating against any C doing X. As principle (4) seeks to mandate prudence, so principle (5) seeks to mandate *morality*.[33] Moreover, these two principles are compatible. The puritans who foisted prohibition on the USA seem to have been at least as much interested in saving their fellow-Cs' souls as their bodies.

Like principles (2), (3) and (4), principle (5) is exposed to the objection that it curtails liberty. But there are two further strong objections to it. First, it is impracticable. Certainly, some immoral acts, such as murder, can be and are also treated as crimes. But it is equally certain that other immoral acts cannot be so treated. Ingratitude is a black vice; but the notion that acts of ingratitude could be treated as legal offences is too obviously absurd to require discussion.[34] Secondly, principle (5), which is intended to strengthen morality, actually weakens it. For suppose it were practicable to mandate gratitude: for R to threaten C1 with punishment if C1 fails to return good to C2 in return for the good which C2 gave to C1. Then C1's returning good to C2 would be less meritorious than it would be if there were no such penal law; since at least part of C1's motive would be a desire to avoid punishment as opposed to a desire to discharge a moral obligation to C2. A similar objection applies to principle (4). Moderation in drinking, as in other things, is commendable; but it is less commendable when the motive for practising it is, at least in part, a desire to escape punishment.

Although legal moralism is usually discussed with reference to criminal law, it is important to note that civil law too mandates morality. Consider the moral obligation to fidelity. Suppose C1 knows that, if C1 breaks his contract with C2, then C2 can sue C1 for damages; and that, if C1 fails to pay the damages which R awards to C2, then R will punish C1 for contempt. Clearly, C1 has a strong motive for honouring his contract with C2. (See note 9.)

In conclusion, I shall touch on a principle of individual liberty which is not a principle of distribution but a principle of historical interpretation. Mill believed in a 'general tendency . . . towards a better and happier state'.[35] Now, as he understood 'happiness', more happiness involves more negative individual liberty as a necessary condition thereof. Many other liberals of Mill's time accepted this *negative individual liberal interpretation of history* and conception of *progress*. We have noticed, however, that in fact the general tendency has long been towards more political coercion. (See Sec. 1, end.) Yet Mill's belief was natural, since his life coincided with a period of individualism. Only after his death was this succeeded by a period of collectivism which has endured until very recently.[36] For there is now mounting evidence that men, disillusioned by the failure of more than a century of collectivism to yield its promised benefits, wish to revert to a freer political order. Yet the obstacle in the way of doing so should not be underrated. For, 'as our history only too clearly shows, it is comparatively easy to make criminal law and exceedingly difficult to unmake it'.[37]

APPENDIX I: INDIVIDUAL LIBERTY AND LEGAL PATERNALISM

At the beginning of Sec. 3 I say that Mill's 'principle of individual liberty' commits him to opposition to legal paternalism. This statement is true, but only with substantial qualification. For consider the following *locum classicum*:

> . . . it is a proper office of public authority to guard against accidents. If either a public officer or any one else saw a person attempting to cross a bridge which had been ascertained to be unsafe, and there

were no time to warn him of his danger, they might seize him and turn him back, without any real infringement of his liberty; for liberty consists in doing what one desires, and he does not desire to fall into the river. Nevertheless, when there is not a certainty, but only a danger of mischief, no one but the person himself can judge of the sufficiency of the motive which may prompt him to incur the risk: in this case, therefore (unless he is a child, or delirious, or in some state of excitement or absorption incompatible with the full use of the reflecting faculty) he ought, I conceive, to be only warned of the danger; not forcibly prevented from exposing himself to it.[38]

It calls for two comments. First, a human action may be unsatisfactory in respect either of its consequences or of its antecedents. The traveller's attempt to cross the bridge in Mill's example is unsatisfactory in both respects. It has the bad consequence that he falls into the river, and it has the (clearly implied) bad antecedent that he acts in ignorance of a vital fact, namely, that the bridge is unsafe. In the parenthesis in his third sentence Mill indicates other bad antecedents which render an action unsatisfactory. It is desirable to distinguish accordingly *strong paternalism* from *weak paternalism*. Weak paternalists hold that B is morally justified in restraining or deterring A from doing X if (1) A's doing X has the bad consequence of harming A, and (2) A's doing X has some bad antecedent, e.g. A does X in ignorance of some vital fact. Strong paternalists hold that B is morally justified in restraining or deterring A from doing X if only condition (1) is satisfied. What is true is that Mill is opposed to strong legal paternalism. But the parenthesis indicates that he is not opposed to weak legal paternalism. In his example, therefore, one would expect him to conclude that any other person is morally justified in restraining the traveller from attempting to cross the bridge because weak paternalism is a true doctrine.[39]

But, secondly, the conclusion which Mill actually draws is that any other person is morally justified in restraining the traveller from attempting to cross the bridge because he is not 'really' restraining the traveller at all by doing so. This, however, is simply false. The cause of Mill's mistake is his false definition of 'liberty' in his second sentence as 'doing what one desires'. It is easy to see that this definition is false. Suppose, e.g., that A is B's slave and that B brainwashes A into desiring to remain so enslaved. Then, by Mill's definition, A is free. But the expression 'free slave' is self-contradictory. In fact, A can be free to do X and A can be unfree to do X when A desires to do X, when A does not desire to do X and when A is indifferent to doing X. The cause of Mill's false

definition of 'liberty' is in turn his confusing A's being unfree to do X
with A's feeling unfree to do X. For it is indeed true that if A is unfree
to do X but A does not desire to do X, then A will not feel unfree to
do X.[40]

APPENDIX II: QUALIFIED FREEDOM

Oppenheim writes 'We do say currently that a speeder does something
he is officially (i.e. legally) unfree to do' (parenthesis added).[41] So *A*
is *legally* unfree to do *X* means 'There is a *legal* rule prohibiting *A* from
doing *X*', and '*A* is *legally* free to do *X*' means 'There is no *legal* rule
prohibiting *A* from doing *X*'.

Conceding for argument's sake (what may well be doubted) that we
do say this, the objections to taking it literally are as follows.

First, there will be as many sorts of unfreedom and of freedom (or
meanings of 'unfree' and of 'free') as there are sorts of rules prohibiting
A from doing X. Thus, *A* is: *morally* unfree to treat animals cruelly,
aesthetically unfree to write consecutive fifths, *prudentially* unfree to
live beyond his means, *etiquettely* unfree to wear cricket-boots with a
dinner-jacket . . . and so on. But in fact there is only one meaning of
'unfree', namely 'restrained (coerced)'. There are not even, as is often
alleged, two different meanings of 'unfree', viz. 'restrained' (negative
unfreedom) and 'heteronomous' (positive unfreedom). (See Essay 10,
Sec. 5.)

Secondly, if *A* is legally unfree to speed, then *A* is unfree to speed.
Then *A* is restrained from speeding. Then *A* is unable to speed. But *A*
can and often does speed, i.e. does break the legal rule prohibiting him
from speeding. Similarly, *mutatis mutandis*, with moral, aesthetic,
prudential, etc. prohibitions.

Thirdly, it is false that *A* is legally free to speed if and only if there
is no legal rule prohibiting *A* from speeding. For if *A* is legally free to
speed, then *A* is free to speed. Then *A* is not restrained from speeding.
Yet *A* may be restrained from speeding by *B* who has fixed *A*'s car so
that it will not go fast.

A fourth objection to the Qualified Freedom Thesis is as follows.
There is a moral rule prohibiting *A* from treating *B* ungratefully but no
legal rule (law) prohibiting *A* from doing this. So, according to this thesis,
A is legally free to treat *B* ungratefully but morally unfree to do this.
So what is the answer to the simple question, Is *A* free to treat *B*
ungratefully? According to this thesis, no answer to this simple

question can be given. One has to say that, although *A* is legally (and prudentially etc.) free to do this, he is morally unfree to do it. And yet, of course, an answer to this simple question can be given. Namely, *A* is free to treat *B* ungratefully if and only if *A* is not restrained from doing so by *B*.

Notes

1. See Plato, *Republic* (*c.* 360 BC); B. de Spinoza, *Ethics* and *Political Treatise* (1677); J.J. Rousseau, *Social Contract* (1762); I. Kant, *Foundations of the Metaphysics of Morals* (1785); G.W.F. Hegel, *Philosophy of Right* (1821) and *Lectures on Philosophy of History* (2nd edn, 1840); I. Berlin, 'Two Concepts of Liberty' in *Four Essays on Liberty* (Oxford University Press, London, 1969). Kant uses the expression 'a positive concept of freedom'.
2. See S. Hampshire, *Spinoza* (Penguin Books, Harmondsworth, 1951), esp. Ch. 4.
3. See, e.g., L.H. Crocker, *Positive Liberty* (Nijhoff, The Hague, 1980); C. Taylor, 'What's Wrong with Negative Liberty' in *The Idea of Freedom*, A. Ryan (ed.) (University Press, Oxford, 1979).
4. See D.G. Long, *Bentham on Liberty* (University Press, Toronto, 1977), p. 54.
5. F.E. Oppenheim, *Political Concepts: A Reconstruction* (Blackwell, Oxford, 1981).
6. See T. Hobbes, *Leviathan* (1651); J. Locke, *Second Treatise of Civil Government* (1690) and *A Letter concerning Toleration* (1689); D. Hume, *An Enquiry concerning the Principles of Morals* (1777); J. Bentham, *An Introduction to the Principles of Morals and Legislation* (2nd edn, 1823) and *Of Laws in General* (1782); J.S. Mill, *On Liberty* (1859) and *A System of Logic* (8th edn, 1872); D.J. O'Connor, *Free Will* (Macmillan, London, 1972), esp. Ch. 9.
7. *On Liberty*, Ch. 1.
8. Bentham uses the expressions 'political liberty' and 'political punishment', Plato and Godwin use the expression 'political justice'; see note 29 and Appendix 3 to Essay 11.
9. This account of a penal statute is due to Bentham, who created *the imperative theory of law*. See Bentham, *An Introduction*; H.L.A. Hart, 'Bentham's *Of Laws in General*', *Rechtstheorie* 2 (1971). On how threats coerce, see Essay 3. Although criminal law is the chief instrument of political coercion, it must be remembered that *civil law* is also coercive, since the orders of civil courts are backed by a threat of punishment for contempt in the event of recalcitrance.
10. See, e.g., A. Huxley, *Brave New World* (Chatto & Windus, London, 1932) and *Brave New World Revisited* (London, 1959); G. Orwell, *Nineteen Eighty-four* (Secker & Warburg, London, 1949); V. Packard, *The Hidden Persuaders* (Longman, London, 1957). Rousseau was the first to grasp the concept of political coercion by manipulation; see his *Discourse on Political Economy* (1758). Bentham calls it 'indirect legislation'; see Long, *Bentham on Liberty*, Ch. 8. B.F. Skinner's reflections on social control provide the most thorough contemporary treatment of the topic; see his *Beyond Freedom and Dignity* (Cape, London, 1971).
11. There are also alleged to be *collective rights* held by groups, e.g. women and Negroes. See N. Glazer, 'Individual Rights Against Group Rights' in *Human Rights*, E. Kamenka and A.E. Tay (eds) (Arnold, London, 1978). (But the rights of such unorganised sets are reducible to the rights of their individual members. See Subsec. 2.2 and Appendix 2 of Essay 11.)
12. See Hart, 'Are There Any Natural Rights?', *Philosophical Review*, Vol. 64 (1955). One consequence of the theory of *a contract of government* is that it transforms liberty and other natural rights from general political rights into special political rights.

13. See M. Weber, *The Protestant Ethic and the Spirit of Capitalism*, trans. T. Parsons (Unwin, London, 1930); R.H. Tawney, *Religion and the Rise of Capitalism* (Murray, London, 1926).

14. See Locke, *Second Treatise*; E. Kamenka, 'The Anatomy of an Idea', in Kamenka and Tay, *Human Rights*.

15. But there is a strong utilitarian (consequential) strand in Locke's political thought too, e.g. 'The public good is the rule and measure of all law-making' (*A Letter concerning Toleration*).

16. See J.P. Plamenatz, *Consent, Freedom and Political Obligation* (University Press, Oxford, 1938), Ch. 6.

17. *Discourses* (*c.* 100).

18. *On Liberty*, Ch. 5. See also S.I. Benn and R.S. Peters, *Social Principles and the Democratic State* (Allen and Unwin, London, 1959), Ch. 10; Day, 'Presumptions', *Proceedings of the Fourteenth International Conference of Philosophy*, Vol. 5 (Herder, Vienna, 1968).

19. Mill, *On Liberty*, Ch. 1.

20. Locke uses the expression 'ecclesiastical liberty' in his *Letter concerning Toleration*.

21. *On Liberty*, Ch. 2; see also T. Scanlon, 'A Theory of Freedom of Expression', *Philosophy and Public Affairs*, Vol. 1 (1972).

22. *On Liberty*, Ch. 3.

23. On the liberties of association and of associations, see A.V. Dicey, *Law and Opinion in England*, 2nd edn (Macmillan, London, 1914), introduction to 2nd edn, lectures 5, 6, 8, appendix, note 1; Benn and Peters, *Social Principles*, Ch. 13; *Nomos XI: Voluntary Associations*, J.R. Pennock and J.W. Chapman (eds) (Atherton Press, New York, 1969).

24. *On Liberty*, Ch. 1.

25. See Hart, *Law, Liberty and Morality* (Oxford University Press, London, 1963).

26. *On Liberty*, Ch. 5.

27. See S.I. Benn, 'Human Rights — for Whom and for What?', in Kamenka and Tay, *Human Rights*; E. Mack, 'Bad Samaritanism and the Causation of Harm', *'Philosophy and Public Affairs*, Vol. 9. (1980).

28. See Antony Flew, 'What is a Right?', the *Georgia Law Review*, Vol. 13 (1979).

29. The spread of the belief in positive rights is obviously connectged with the growth of the welfare movement; see Benn (note 27, above). But in England, the belief is already to be found in the writings of, e.g., Paine and Godwin, and in legislation of the sixteenth century. See Thomas Paine, *The Rights of Man* (1792), Pt 2, Ch. 5; William Godwin, *Enquiry Concerning Political Justice* (3rd edn, 1798), Bk 2, Ch. 5 and Bk. 8; Elie Halévy, *The Growth of Philosophic Radicalism*, trans. M. Morris (Faber and Faber, London, 1928), Pt 2, Ch. 2, Sec. 1.

30. This principle should not be confused with *the principle of the natural identity of particular and general interests*. This states that individuals and organisations promote the general interest by pursuing their particular interests. Its most famous formulation is A. Smith's doctrine of 'an invisible hand' in his *Wealth of Nations* (1776). An essential difference between the two principles is that Smith's is descriptive whereas mine is normative. Different again is *the principle of the artificial identification of particular and general interests*. This states that the legislator ought to enact penal laws which will make it to the interest of individuals and organisations to promote the general interest; and that the instructor ought to inculcate in his pupils beliefs which will make them desire to promote the general interest, and consequently do so. Plainly, this Benthamite view of *education*, which derives from C.A. Helvétius, represents it as propaganda, i.e. as a sort of coercion by manipulation. (See Sec. 1.) This principle too is normative and not descriptive. See Halévy, *The Growth of Philosophic Radicalism*, Pt. 1, Ch. 1.

31. See Mill, *Principles of Political Economy* (7th edn, 1871), Bk 5, Ch. 11; Dicey, *Law and Opinion in England*, lecture 6; Essay 1, above.

32. I am grateful to Professor E. Mack for pointing out to me this deeper objection

to legal paternalism. See also J. Feinberg, *Social Philosophy* (Prentice Hall, Englewood Cliffs, 1973), Ch. 3.

33. See J.F. Stephen, *Liberty, Equality, Fraternity*, 2nd edn (Smith Elder, London, 1874); P. Devlin, *The Enforcement of Morals*; Hart, *Law, Liberty and Morality*; Feinberg, *Social Philosophy* (University Press, Edinburgh, 1952).

34. In fact, that is. In fiction, things are different — 'Among the Lilliputians ingratitude was a capital offence' (A.D.M. Walker, 'Gratefulness and Gratitude', *Aristotelian Society Proceedings*, Vol. 80 (1980).

35. *A System of Logic*, Bk 6, Ch. 10.

36. See Dicey, *Law and Opinion in England*.

37. Hart, *Law, Liberty and Morality*, Preface. I am grateful to Professors A.G.N. Flew, H.L.A. Hart and J.O. Urmson for their commments on an earlier version of this lecture.

38. *On Liberty*, Ch. 5.

39. See J. Feinberg, 'Legal Paternalism', *Canadian Journal of Philosophy*, Vol. I (1971); C.L. Ten, *Mill on Liberty* (Clarendon Press, Oxford, 1980), Ch. 7; J. Lively, 'Paternalism', *Of Liberty*, A. Phillips Griffiths (ed.) (University Press, Cambridge, 1983).

40. See Sec. 2, above: also Essay 1 and Essay 3, Sec. 2.

41. F. Oppenheim, *Political Concepts* (Blackwell, Oxford, 1981), p. 57.

7 CIVIL LIBERTY AND THE RULE OF LAW

1. The Meaning of 'The Rule of Law'

Aristotle poses the question 'Is it more expedient to be ruled by the one best man, or by the best laws?' He answers it thus: 'The rule of law is preferable to that of a single citizen: even if it be the better course to have individuals ruling, they should be made law-guardians or ministers of the laws'. He does so in a discussion of kingship, where he opposes the view advanced by Plato in the *Republic*. There, Plato maintains that ideally government should be left to the free initiative and the discretion of the philosopher-king (or kings), who should be untrammelled by laws. Aristotle, on the other hand, considers that legislators themselves ought to be subject to the laws.[1] The contrast may be expressed by saying that Plato favours the personal rule of men whereas Aristotle favours the impersonal rule of law. By 'a law' (*nomos*) Aristotle understands 'a general rule'. Laws are impersonal because they proceed from reason (*logos*) and not from some person, since it is the office of the legislator to discover and declare them rather than to make them.

However, Aristotle makes two concessions to Plato's view. First, absolute monarchy would be justified in a society where some person 'is of merit so outstanding as to surpass that of all the rest'. Secondly, since law is necessarily general, it is correct only as a general rule, that is for usual cases. But it may be incorrect for exceptional cases, so that law ought sometimes to be overridden by equity (*epieikeia*) in order to achieve 'a correction of law where law is defective owing to its generality': that is, in exceptional cases it may be the legislator's duty to override a general rule of law by a particular decree.[2]

Aristotle, then, is clear about the meaning of 'the rule of law'. His ideal was very influential down the ages, but with the passage of time its meaning became obfuscated, so that an authority on constitutional law finds that 'this principle has been used from time to time to convey quite different ideas'.[3] The present situation in this respect is so bad that it has moved Raz to a justified protest against 'the promiscuous use made in recent years of the expression "the rule of law" '.[4]

Raz finds an acceptable formulation of the ideal of the rule of law in the following words of Hayek's: 'Stripped of all technicalities, this means that government in all its actions is bound by rules fixed and

118

announced beforehand — rules which make it possible to foresee with fair certainty how the authority will use its coercive powers in given circumstances, and to plan one's individual affairs on the basis of this knowledge'.[5] He develops this formulation as follows.

The meaning of 'law' is understood in the lawyer's and jurisprudent's sense as anything which satisfies the conditions laid down in a legal system's rules of recognition or other rules.[6] This is wider than the layman's sense of a set of open, general and relatively stable rules. For law in the lawyer's sense includes particular legal orders as well, for example conditions imposed in trading licences.

The purpose of law is to enable those who are subject to it to know where they stand and to plan their affairs accordingly. Raz's conception of law is therefore instrumental. It is also formal, since it says nothing about how laws ought to be made or what their content ought to be.

The moral virtues of law are various. For example, it is one moral virtue in a legal system that it protects human rights. Another is the rule of law, the basic idea of which is that the law must be such that it can enable those who are subject to it to plan their affairs. From this basic idea certain principles follow. For example, the meaning of all laws must be clear, that is they must not be ambiguous, vague, obscure or imprecise. Again, laws should be relatively stable, that is they should not be changed too often. Yet again, the making of particular orders should be guided by open, clear and stable general rules. Naturally, the satisfaction of these conditions is largely a matter of wise governmental policy. Both legal systems and single laws can conform more or less to the rule of law. But 'complete conformity is impossible (some vagueness is inescapable) and maximal possible conformity is on the whole undesirable (some controlled administrative discretion is better than none)'.[7]

Like law's moral virtues, its specific virtues are various. But the most important of them is the rule of law. This follows from Raz's instrumental conception of law (see above). For the greater the degree in which laws are clear, stable etc., the better citizens will be able to take note of them and guide themselves accordingly.

This is the interpretation of 'the rule of law' which I shall follow in this essay, with one important exception. We have seen that Raz interprets 'law' widely, so as to include not only general rules but also particular orders, such as injunctions. For Aristotle and Hayek, on the other hand, laws are necessarily general (see above, and Sec. 2 below). This narrower interpretation of 'law' is the one which is taken in the traditional theory of liberal constitutionalism,[8] and it seems best to adhere to it — the purpose of laws is to provide for *classes* of persons, things and events. It has been suggested that the wider interpretation rests on a confusion between *being law* and *having the force of law*. Thus, a family law relating to divorce may be a general rule that a successful petitioner is entitled to receive as maintenance one-third of the joint income of the petitioner and the respondent. In application of this law, a court may make an order directing a particular respondent to pay to a particular petitioner a particular sum at a particular time. This order has the force of a law, but it is not itself a law. It has been suggested further that this confusion has been created by Bentham's and Austin's imperative theory of law, which represents both laws and orders made under laws as 'commands'; and by Kelsen's theory, which represents both of them as 'norms'.[9]

2. Hayek on Civil Liberty and the Rule of Law

Hayek writes:

> The conception of freedom under the law that is the chief concern of this book rests on the contention that when we obey laws, in the sense of general abstract rules laid down irrespective of their application to us, we are not subject to another man's will and are therefore free . . . As a true law should not name any particulars, so it should especially not single out any specific persons or groups of persons . . . The requirement that the rules of true law be general does not mean that sometimes special rules may not apply to different classes of people if they refer to properties that only some people possess . . . Such distinctions will not be arbitrary, will not subject one group to the will of others, if they are equally recognized as justified by those inside and those outside the group.[10]

Consider, then, the following case. A law of a certain state provides that all fit male citizens shall do military service; that any such citizen who does not report for military service when called up shall be imprisoned; but that female citizens are exempt from military service. Both the male citizens and the female citizens recognise that this arrangement is justified. Then, according to Hayek, this law does not make the male citizens unfree.

But this is false. It is necesssary to be clear, however, about how this law does make the male citizens unfree. Many, perhaps most, believe that the threat of imprisonment which backs this rule, if it is effective, curtails the male citizens' liberty by making them unable not to report for military service when called up. But this, too, is false. What the threat really makes the male citizens unable to do, if it is effective, is both to fail to report for military serivce when called up and to remain unimprisoned. But by *restraining* (that is intentionally preventing) the male citizens from performing this *complex* (conjunctive) action, the effective threat *deters* them from performing the *simple* action, not reporting for military service when called up. It is the restraint, not the deterrence, which curtails their liberty. (Compare Sec. 4, below.)[11]

The cause of Hayek's mistake is a familiar one, namely, confusing not *being* unfree with not *feeling* unfree. Since the male citizens are content with the arrangement, they do not desire both not to report for military service when called up and to remain unimprisoned. Consequently, the threat which backs the law does not cause them to feel unfree. For, generally, A does not feel unfree to do X when B restrains A from doing X if A does not desire to do X. But that does not alter the fact that the threat causes the male citizens to be unfree.[12]

This criticism of Hayek presupposes that 'liberty' means 'absence of coercion (or restraint)', and that 'civil liberty' means 'absence of coercion of the citizen by the state'. But it has been objected that this criticism is an *ignoratio elenchi*, because what Hayek calls 'the conception of freedom under the law' (above) is different from this conception of civil liberty.

In order to understand and to meet this objection, it is necessary to examine the source of what Hayek calls 'the traditional doctrine of liberal constitutionalism', which is known in Germany as the theory of the *Rechtsstaat*. This source is Montesquieu's *Spirit of the Laws*. There, Montesquieu distinguishes (1) 'political liberty in relation to the subject' from (2) 'political liberty with regard to the constitution'. As to (1), 'it is . . . on the goodness of criminal laws that the liberty of the subject principally depends'. But (2) 'arises from a certain distribution of the three powers (namely, legislative, executive and judiciary)', and 'it is the disposition only . . . of the fundamental (i.e. constitutional) laws that constitute liberty in relation to the constitution'. Specifically, in order to assure the latter sort of liberty, it is necessary that the three powers should be separated. The objection under consideration maintains that my criticism of Hayek takes his conception of liberty to be (1), whereas it is in fact (2).

The reply to this objection is that it confuses the question of different *meanings of 'liberty'* with the question of different *means to liberty*.

To Montesquieu, 'political liberty' means only one thing: 'the political liberty of the subject is a tranquillity of mind arising from the opinion each person has of his safety'.[13] But 'political (or civil) liberty' cannot be defined as 'the citizen's sense of security from tyrannical or arbitrary coercion by the state', since the citizen is unfree when the state's coercion of him is not tyrannical as well as when it is tyrannical, and when he does not feel coerced as well as when he does feel coerced (see above). The correct definition of 'civil liberty' is therefore that given above. But what Montesquieu's theory is about is how this liberty is to be assured. It will be assured if for example there is no criminal law which makes it an offence for a citizen to criticise the law-maker. This is indeed true, because the most important sort of political coercion is that exerted by the threats which back criminal laws (see above). How, then, can it be ensured that there will not be such a law? One way would be to have for law-maker a philosopher-king who recognised the citizen's moral right to free expression, and who therefore would not make such a law. (See Sec. 1, above.) But when, as usually happens, the law-maker is less sublime, another way of securing the desired result would be as follows. First, to have a constitutional law providing that such a criminal law is unconstitutional. Second, to have a separation of legislative and judicial powers so that, if the legislature does make such a criminal law, the judiciary will strike it down as unconstitutional. This is in fact the situation in the United States, where the First Amendment provides that 'Congress shall make no law . . . abridging the freedom of speech, or of the press . . .', and where the Supreme Court is separate from the Congress.

The objection to my criticism of Hayek on the ground that the theory of liberal constitutionalism employs a different conception of liberty from mine accordingly fails.

3. Raz on Civil Liberty and the Rule of Law

Raz claims that the rule of law has three values. It curbs arbitrary power, it protects individual liberty, and it protects human dignity. The second of these is the greatest. The rule of law protects individual liberty by making 'the law . . . a stable and safe basis for individual planning'.[14]

Consider, then, the following two cases. *Case (1)*. At t_1, there is no rule of law in a certain state because the laws are unstable, since the law-maker is constantly and unpredictably changing them. But at t_2, there is rule of law in that state, because it now has a reforming law-maker who has made the laws stable with the intention of enabling the citizens to plan their lives effectively. The law-maker's action has increased the citizens' *power*, because before the reform they were *unable* to plan effectively. *Case (2)*. At t_1, there is no rule of law in a certain state because the laws are unstable, since the law-maker is constantly and unpredictably changing them with the intention of preventing the citizens from planning their lives effectively. But at t_2, there is rule of law in that state, because the law-maker has undergone a change of heart and keeps the laws stable with the intention of enabling the citizens to plan their lives effectively. The law-maker's action has increased the citizens' *liberty*, because before the reform they were *unfree* to plan effectively.

Case (2) shows that Raz is right to the extent that the rule of law *can* promote liberty. On the other hand, Case (2) is exceptional, since it is most unusual for the reason for the absence of the rule of law to be the law-maker's intention to baffle the citizens. Case (1) is the usual case. The conclusion is, therefore, that what the rule of law usually protects or promotes is not liberty but power. Liberty is not the same as power because liberty *presupposes* power. That is, if X is the sort of thing that the average person cannot do, then the question of A being free to do X or unfree to do X does not arise.[15]

The chief value of the rule of law, then, is not that it protects citizens' liberty but that it augments citizens' power. For the fact that Man often abuses his power does not mean, of course, that the increase of it is not a good thing.

When we think of the augmentation of human power, we are naturally reminded of Bacon's aphorism, 'human knowledge and human power meet in one'.[16] The sort of knowledge which he has in mind is, of course, the know-how imparted by applied natural science, that is by arts or techniques. But the fact that human power is substantially increased by the rule of law reminds us that it can also be augmented massively by social institutions and practices. Indeed, the technical know-how to which Bacon refers itself presupposes certain vital social institutions. For applied natural science presupposes pure natural science, and advanced pure natural science is not possible without some natural language, such as English, without the artificial language of mathematics, and without organisations for the advancement and dissemination of knowledge, such as research institutes and universities.

From this point of view, it is instructive to compare the value of the rule of law with that of the law itself, that is with the value of legal systems. In discussing the variety of laws, Hart draws a fundamental distinction between laws which impose obligations and laws which 'provide individuals with facilities for realising their wishes, by conferring legal powers upon them to create by certain specified procedures and subject to certain conditions, structures of rights and duties within the coercive framework of the law'.[17] The paradigm of the first sort of law is a penal statute, which fits best Bentham's and Austin's imperative theory of law as a general order addressed by a sovereign to his subjects which is backed by a threat of punishment in the event of recalcitrance. Tort laws also fit, though less well, into this division. Paradigms of the second sort of laws are contract laws. These sorts of laws are 'one of the great contributions of law to social life',[18] and such basic economic operations as giving, buying and selling would not exist without such power-conferring rules. In truth, it is easy to see that the business world could scarcely operate, or indeed exist, without the law of contract.

It seems to me, however, that the social function of both sorts of laws is to protect or increase citizens' power. Contract laws do this by conferring on citizens legal powers to make promises which are enforceable by the courts. Criminal laws protect citizen A's power by deterring citizen B from harming A and thereby reducing A's power. Tort laws protect citizen A's power by making citizen B, who has harmed A, compensate A fully; so that — ideally, at least — it is as if B had never reduced A's power by harming A at all.

However, it would not be true to say that the social function of all laws is to protect or increase citizens' power. Thus, in elaborating Hart's ideas on the classification of laws, Raz distinguishes the following additional social functions of law: providing services and redistributing goods; settling unregulated disputes; laying down procedures for changing the law; and laying down procedures for enforcing the law.[19] The discharge of none of these functions has the effect of maintaining or augmenting citizens' power. But it suffices to have shown that the chief value of a great deal of law is the same as that of the rule of law.

Hart in fact divides laws according to their form as well as according to their function. Thus, the function of criminal laws and tort laws is to protect citizens from harm, and they have the form of the general categorical imperative. Let A do X! For example, 'Let any citizen not murder any other citizen!'; 'Let any citizen not defame any other citizen!'. But the function of contract laws and other empowering laws is to furnish citizens with facilities, and they have the form of the general

general hypothetical imperative, If *A* desires to do *X*, then let *A* do *Y*! For example, 'If citizen *B* desires to make a legally binding contract with citizen *A*, then let *B* promise *A* a consideration if *A* does *X*, and let *B* have *A* promise *B* a *quid pro quo* if *B* does *Y*!'; 'If any citizen desires to make a legally valid will, then let him have his signature to it witnessed by two persons!'.

4. Coercion and Intention

In the Case (1) discussed in Sec. 3 (above), the reason why the citizens are *unable* at t_1 to plan effectively is that it just so happens that the laws are unstable. By contrast, in Case (2), the reason why the citizens are *unfree* to plan effectively is that the law-maker keeps the laws unstable with the intention of making the citizens unable to do so. For '*A* is unfree to do *X*' is true if and only if '*B* intentionally makes *A* retrievably unable to do *X* by doing *Y* to *A*' is true. For example, *B* intentionally makes *A* retrievably unable to escape by binding *A*. I shall now discuss the relation of intention to coercion in order to complete the analysis of the concept of civil liberty which the argument of this essay requires.[20]

In a letter which he sent to John Lind in 1776, Bentham writes of 'a kind of discovery (he) thought (he) had made'. This is that the idea of liberty is a negative one, namely, the absence of coercion. He continues that he takes 'coercion' to mean 'restraint or constraint', and adds that this definition of 'liberty' is 'one of the cornerstones of (his) system: and one that (he knows) not how to do without'.[21] *The Concise Oxford Dictionary* gives 'to force' as a synonym of 'to coerce'. *B* restrains *A* *from* doing *X* if and only if *B* constrains *A* not *to* do *X*. The following expressions therefore all mean the same: 'to coerce', 'to force', 'to restrain', 'to constrain', 'to compel', 'intentionally to make retrievably unable' and 'to make unfree'.

Bentham's account of the meaning of 'to coerce' is correct, and it will be convenient to concentrate on 'to restrain'. This is one of the many verbs which, like 'to lie', have intention included in their meaning. As one must distinguish from the genus 'saying what one knows to be untrue' the species 'saying what one knows to untrue with intent to deceive' (which equals 'lying'); so one must distinguish from the genus 'preventing' the species 'intentional interpersonal prevention' (which equals 'restraining'). When *B* sits on a certain chair, he thereby prevents or stops *A* from sitting on it. This may be intentional, but usually it is not

But if *B* restrains *A* from sitting on a certain chair, that is necessarily intentional. The notion of unintentional preventing or stopping is purely physical. *B* prevents *A* from sitting on the chair by getting there first and sitting on it, thereby making *A* unable to do so. But the notion of restraining is mental as well as physical, because intending is a mental act.

The subjects of restraint are necessarily persons. This is because restraint is necessarily intentional and only persons have intentions. Moreover, the objects of restraint are normally persons. This is because 'to restrain' means 'to make unfree' and freedom (which equals negative freedom) is interpersonal. (Positive freedom, on the other hand, is intrapersonal.) (On positive freedom see Sec. 1 of Essay 6, Essays 10, 13.) Consider the following examples. *Example (1)*. *B* restrains *A* from escaping (that is *B* makes *A* unfree to escape) by binding *A*. But *Example (2)*, *B* does not restrain a door from closing by wedging it in the open position; he thereby stops it from doing so. Nor, *Example (3)*, does a flood restrain *A* from travelling along a certain path; it prevents him from doing so. *A fortiori*, *Example (4)*, the chain which attaches a chandelier to the ceiling does not restrain it from falling; it thereby stops it from doing so.[22]

There is another important difference between restraint and prevention which is conceptually connected with the fact that both the subjects and the objects of restraint are normally persons, whereas this is not true of prevention. This difference turns on the crucial distinction between action and behaviour. In Example (1), *B* acts intentionally (binds *A*) so as to restrain *A* from acting intentionally (escaping). But in Example (2), *B* acts intentionally (wedges *X*) so as to prevent *X* from behaving (closing). In Example (3), *X* behaves (bars the path) so as to prevent *A* from acting intentionally (travelling along the path). In Example (4), *X* behaves (retains *Y*) so as to prevent *Y* from behaving (falling). So restraint necessarily involves two intentional actions, whereas prevention does not.[23]

The most important sort of unfreedom is civil (or political) unfreedom, in which the state makes the citizen unfree. And the most important sort of political coercion is coercion by legislation.[24] As we have seen (Sec. 2, above), this sort of coercion makes the citizen unfree because an effective threat which backs a law restrains him from doing a complex (conjunctive) action. The facts that all threats attempt to restrain, and that all restraint is intentional, explain why all threats are intentional. But when the law-maker threatens the citizens, his intention to restrain them from some complex action is not his primary intention. His primary intention is to deter them from some simple action. He attempts to restrain them from the complex action only as a means to deterring them from the simple action, so that his intention to restrain them is secondary.

Deterrence by threat is necessarily intentional because threatening, as we have just seen, is necessarily intentional. Deterrence by threat is not the only sort of deterrence. There are also deterrence by reward, by warning, by dissuasion and by advice. But deterrence by threat is the only one of these five modes of deterrence which curtails liberty, because effective threats curtail liberty. The subjects and objects of deterrence by threat are necessarily persons, because threat necessarily involves attempted restraint, and restraint is necessarily interpersonal.

Both 'to restrain' and 'to deter by threat' are what Ryle calls 'achievement words', and so, consequently, are all the equivalents of 'to restrain' listed above, e.g., 'to make unfree'.[25] But 'to threaten' is not an achievement word because, when *B* threatens *A*, *B* *attempts* to restrain *A* from performing some simple action. However, *B* may resist *A* successfully, so that *B*'s threat *actually* restrains and deters *A* if and only if it is effective.

But why is intention included in the meaning of 'to restrain'? The analogue given above, 'to lie', provides a clue. The fact that lying is necessarily intentional is essentially connected with its moral aspect, namely, that it is judged to be presumptively immoral — similarly with 'to restrain'. For the reasons why 'to restrain' is necessarily intentional are given in the following sorites:

(1) All acts of restraint are violations of a moral right
(2) All violations of a moral right are presumptively immoral acts
(3) All presumptively immoral acts are intentional acts
Therefore
(4) All acts of restraint are intentional acts.

The validity of this argument is unlikely to be impugned, but its premisses call for comment.

As to premiss (1), all acts of restraint violate the general moral right to liberty. This is why 'all restraint, *qua* restraint, is an evil',[26] and why there is a presumption *pro* liberty.

It may be objected that to imprison a murderer is not to violate his moral right to liberty, because his imprisonment is morally justified. But the true account of this matter is not that all *morally unjustified* acts of restraint are violations of a moral right. It is that the moral obligation to respect the murderer's right to liberty is outweighed by the moral obligation to maintain the other citizens' right to life. Thus, in premiss (2), the expression 'presumptively (or prima facie) immoral' allows for the possibility that the moral obligation to respect a right may be overborne by some stronger moral obligation.

As to premiss (3), it is necessary to meet three objections to its truth. The first is that we do sometimes speak of *B* doing the morally right (or wrong) thing unintentionally. The reply is that '*B* did the morally right thing unintentionally' must be interpreted counterfactually as meaning '*B* acted as *B* would have acted if *B* had done the morally right thing', where it is understood that 'had done the morally right thing' has its normal meaning of 'had done the morally right thing intentionally'. *Example.* On Monday, *B* promises *A* to give *A* £10 on Saturday. But *B* does not keep his promise to *A* on Saturday because *B* has forgotten it. Nevertheless, *B* gives *A* £10 on Saturday as a present, because *B* is fond of *A*. Similarly, *mutatis mutandis*, with doing the morally wrong thing unintentionally.

The second objection is that a law-maker may repeal a law because he finds that a (by him) unforeseen and unintended consequence of it is that it curtails liberty; which (by premisses (1) and (2)) is a presumptively immoral act.[27] *Example.* He finds that a law which he intended to deter one category of persons from entering his realm has the unintended consequence of deterring another category of persons from doing so. In reply to this objection, consider the following cases. *Case (1).* A sovereign imprisons a citizen for two years for robbery with the intention of preventing that citizen from moving out of the prison for two years. *Case (2).* A sovereign imprisons a citizen for two years for robbery with the intention of preventing that citizen from robbing outsiders for two years. *Case (3).* A sovereign imprisons a citizen for two years for robbery with the intention of preventing that citizen from committing any offence against outsiders for two years. *Case (4).* A sovereign imprisons a citizen for two years for robbery with the (by him) unforeseen and unintended consequence of preventing that citizen from attending a football match for which he had bought a ticket. Case (1) is a paradigm; here, the sovereign makes the citizen unfree to move out of the prison. Case (4) is also a paradigm; here, the sovereign is not correctly said to make the citizen unfree to attend the football match, though he certainly makes him incapable of doing so. This disposes of the objection. But Cases (2) and (3) illustrate a significant point about liberty. In both cases, it is correct to speak of the sovereign abridging the citizen's liberty. Nevertheless, we feel less confident about these cases than we do about Case (1), and it is important to understand why this is so.

In Case (1), the sovereign is naturally said to deprive the citizen of his freedom of movement. But in Cases (2) and (3) the sovereign is not naturally said to deprive the citizen of his freedom to rob or of his freedom to commit crimes. For we do not normally speak of *A* being unfree to do *X* unless *X* is the sort of thing that the normal, reasonable man both desires to do and judges it desirable to do. Freedom of movement is both generally desired and generally judged desirable, but freedom to commit a crime or crimes is neither generally desired nor generally judged to be desirable.[28]

The third objection to the truth of premiss (3) turns on negligence.[29] *Example.* In backing his car fast out of his drive in good visibility, *B* unintentionally collides with and damages his neighbour *A*'s car, which is parked on the opposite side of the road. In thus damaging *A*'s car, *B* does *A* an unintentional wrong. The reply to this objection is that this wrong is a legal one (a tort) but not a moral one. It is not a moral wrong precisely because it was not intended. The objection rests on a failure to appreciate the facts that *B* not only does *A* an unintentional legal wrong, but also does something which is morally as well as legally wrong, namely, neglects his duty of care. His negligence is morally wrong precisely because it is intentional. For *B* — we will suppose — is in a hurry to get to the hospital to visit his wife, and to this end he intentionally takes any necessary risk, such as driving faster than is safe in the prevailing conditions, cutting corners, and so on.[30] Different notions of responsibility are associated with the negligence and with the tort. *B* is morally responsible for his neglect of his duty of care, and so may be blamed for it. But his responsibility for damaging *A*'s car is not moral responsibility but liability-responsibility. Consequently, *B* may be required to compensate *A* for the tort, but he may not be blamed or punished for it.[31]

Finally on premiss (3), the converse of its obverse, 'No unintentional acts are presumptively immoral acts', requires a comment. Although it makes no sense to require or to give *excuses* for unintended harms, it does make sense to require or to give *explanations* of them. E.g., *B* explains, but does not excuse, his unintentionally locking *A* in a room by pointing out that he did not know that *A* was there.

There is a temptation to believe that the problem of the meaning of 'liberty' can be solved without consideration of the problem of the value of liberty. But this belief is false.[32] For the fact that liberty is a general moral right entails two vital points about the meaning of 'free'. First, that liberty is necessarily interpersonal, since a right is always held by some person *A* against some other person *B*. This decides the issue in

Civil Liberty and the Rule of Law

favour of Bentham's negative concept of liberty and against Plato's and Rousseau's positive concepts.[33] Secondly, as the foregoing argument has shown, that coercion (which is making unfree) is necessarily intentional.

5. Conclusion

It is important to understand why the rule of law is valuable, and how it is related to civil liberty. Naturally, this cannot be done unless we are clear about the meaning of 'the rule of law', and we have to thank Hayek and Raz for the fact that we now are so. But although this is necessary it is not sufficient. It is equally necessary to be clear about the meaning of 'civil liberty', so that my chief task in this essay has been to provide the needed elucidation of this cardinal concept.[34]

APPENDIX: THE TRADITIONAL DOCTRINE OF LIBERAL CONSTITUTIONALISM

In Sec. 2 I say that the source of this theory is Montesquieu's *Spirit of the Laws*. In fact it originates in Livy and Cicero. A notable exponent of it is Machiavelli in his *Discourses on Livy*. Contemporary adherents of it are, besides Hayek, Taylor and Skinner. See C. Taylor, 'The Nature and Scope of Distributive Justice' and 'Kant's Theory of Freedom' in his *Philosophical Papers*, Vol. 2 (Cambridge University Press, Cambridge, 1985); Q. Skinner, 'The Idea of Negative Liberty' in R. Rorty, J.B. Schneewind and Q. Skinner (eds), *Philosophy in History* (Cambridge University Press, Cambridge, 1984).

Notes

1. In the *Laws*, Plato naturally finds an extensive place for law. But for this very reason he considers the state projected in that dialogue to be a 'second best' to the Utopia delineated in the *Republic*.
2. See *The Politics of Aristotle*, translated with an Introduction, Notes and Appendices by Ernest Barker (Clarendon Press, Oxford, 1946), pp. liv and lv, 137-53, 362-72; *Aristotle's Politics Books III and IV*, translated with an Introduction and Comments by Richard Robinson (Clarendon Press, Oxford, 1962), pp. 49-66. Compare Locke's remarks on royal prerogative in secs. 159 and 160 of his *Second Treatise of Civil Government*.
3. C.E.P. Davies, 'The Relation of Law and the Constitution' in *Law*, edited by R.H. Graveson (Routledge & Kegan Paul, London, 1967), p. 48. Compare J.R. Lucas, *The*

Principles of Politics (Clarendon Press, Oxford, 1966), p. 107.

4. Joseph Raz, 'The Rule of Law and its Virtue' in his *The Authority of Law* (Clarendon Press, Oxford, 1979), p. 211.

5. F.A. Hayek, *The Road to Serfdom* (Routledge & Kegan Paul, London, 1944), p. 54.

6. See Hart, *The Concept of Law*, pp. 97-120.

7. J. Raz, *The Authority of Law*, p. 222.

8. See Franz Neumann's Introduction to Montesquieu, *The Spirit of the Laws*, translated by Thomas Nugent (Hafner, New York, 1949), pp. lxii and lxiii.

9. See A.D. Woozley, *Law and Obedience: The Arguments of Plato's Crito* (University of North Carolina Press, Chapel Hill, 1979), pp. 38, 41 and 42.

10. F.A. Hayek, *The Constitution of Liberty* (Routledge & Kegan Paul, London, 1960), pp. 153, 154. In *Law, Legislation and Liberty*, Vol 1 (Routledge & Kegan Paul, London, 1973), pp. 1-7, Hayek expresses dissatisfaction with 'the traditional doctrine of liberal constitutionalism' expounded in his earlier book, but maintains nevertheless that the revised conception of law which is expounded in the later book leads to the conclusion expresses in the passage just cited from the earlier book (p. 107). See J.N. Gray, 'F.A. Hayek on Liberty and Tradition', *The Journal of Libertarian Studies*, 4 (1980), pp. 119-37, especially p. 126; Lucas, 'Liberty, Morality and Justice', in *Liberty and the Rule of Law*, edited by R.L. Cunningham (Texas A and M University Press, College Station, Texas, 1979), especially pp. 160-6.

11. See Sec. 3 of Essay 3.

12. See Essay 1.

13. See Montesquieu, *The Spirit*, bk. xi, secs. 1-6; bk. xii, secs. 1-4, 12 and 13: Neumann, Introduction, pp. xlix-lxiv. For Bentham's criticism of Montesquieu's theory, see Elie Halévy, *The Growth of Philosophic Radicalism*, translated by Mary Morris (Faber & Faber, London, 1934), pp. 408, 409.

14. Raz, *The Authority of Law*, p. 220.

15. See Sec. 4 of Essay 3.

16. Francis Bacon, *Novum Organum*, aphorism III. Those who have discussed human power in recent times have tended to confine their attention to questions of interpersonal power, i.e., the power which B wields over A. See, e.g., Bertrand Russell, *Power* (Allen & Unwin, London, 1938); Bertrand de Jouvenel, *Power*, translated by J.F. Huntingdon (Hutchinson, London, 1945); Steven Lukes, *Power* (Macmillan, London, 1974); D.H. Wrong, *Power* (Blackwell, Oxford, 1979).

17. Hart, *The Concept of Law*, p. 27. Compare Joseph Raz, *The Concept of a Legal System* (Clarendon Press, Oxford, 1970), pp. 147-67.

18. Hart, *The Concept of Law*, p. 28.

19. See Raz, 'The Function of Law', in *The Authority of Law*, pp. 163-79.

20. See J.N. Gray, 'On Negative and Positive Liberty', *Political Studies*, 28 (1980), pp. 521-3; D.M. White, 'Negative Liberty', *Ethics*, 80 (1970), pp. 191-6.

21. See D.G. Long, *Bentham on Liberty* , (University of Toronto Press, Toronto, 1977), pp. 54, 55.

22. As often happens, (some) animals present an interesting intermediate case between persons on the one hand and things and events on the other hand. Thus — as Dr B.J. Smart has pointed out to me — it is correct to speak of a rider restraining his horse. This is because horses are deemed to be sufficiently like humans to qualify as proper objects of restraint. But they are not deemed to be sufficiently like humans to qualify as proper subjects of restraint. For it is not correct to speak of a spurred horse that will not budge as *restraining* its rider from advancing. It only *prevents* him from doing so. This is precisely because horses, unlike their riders, have no intentions.

23. See Gray, 'On Negative and Positive Liberty', p. 515.

24. Political coercion by legislation needs to be distinguished from, e.g., political coercion by manipulation. This distinction is explained in Sec. 1 of Essay 6. Civil liberty must be distinguished from social (or natural) liberty, in which society makes some member

of it unfree. Civil liberty (singular) also needs to be distinguished from civil liberties (plural), a name which is used in these days for diverse alleged rights, such as those to privacy and non-discrimination. Priestley distinguishes civil liberty from political liberty, meaning by the former the concept defined in the text, and by the latter the autonomy or self-government of a political society or state (i.e. democracy). The former is therefore identical with what Berlin, like Bentham, calls 'negative liberty' (see above). But the latter is identical with what Berlin calls 'positive liberty'. Hume, however, uses 'civil liberty' in the same sense as Priestley's 'political liberty'. Since this essay is concerned only with civil liberty, it is not necessary to consider how, if at all, liberty or liberties (without qualification) differ from so-called 'free will' or from what lawyers call 'liberties'. See Hume, 'Civil Liberty', in his *Political Discourses*; Joseph Priestley, 'A Sermon preached before the Congregation of the Old and New Meetings at Birmingham, November 5, 1789'; Mill, *On Liberty*, Ch. 1; Isaiah Berlin, 'Two Concepts of Liberty' in *Four Essays on Liberty* (Oxford University Press, London, 1968); Neil MacCormick, *Civil Liberties and the Law* (Heriot-Watt University, Edinburgh, 1977), pp. 5-13: James Dybikowski, 'Civil Liberty', *American Philosophical Quarterly*, Vol. 18 (1981), pp. 339-46.

25. See G. Ryle, *The Concept of Mind* (Hutchinson, London, 1949), pp. 149-53.

26. Mill, *On Liberty*, Ch. 5. On general and special moral rights, see Hart, 'Are There Any Natural Rights?', *Philosophical Review*, Vol. 64 (1955), pp. 175-91.

27. I am obliged to Dr John N. Gray for proposing this objection.

28. See S.I. Benn and W.L. Weinstein, 'Being Free to Act and Being a Free Man', *Mind*, Vol. 80 (1971), pp. 194-211; Sec. 2 of Essay 3. White, 'Negative Liberty'.

29. I am obliged to Mr Jeremy Shearmur for proposing this objection.

30. See A.C. Guest, 'Common Law and Equity' in Graveson, *Law*, pp. 63-8; Hart, *The Concept of Law*, pp. 168, 169; Neil MacCormick, 'The Obligation of Reparation', *Aristotelian Society Proceedings*, Vol. 78 (1978), pp. 175-93.

31. On these and other distinct concepts of responsibility, see L.A. Hart, *Punishment and Responsibility* (Clarendon Press, Oxford, 1968), pp. 210-30.

32. As Gray makes very clear; see 'On Negative and Positive Liberty', pp. 513-17.

33. See the *Republic*, pp. 430 and 431. Compare Subsec. 6.4 of Essay 3.

34. I am particularly indebted in this essay to the writings and comments of Prof. Herbert L.A. Hart and Dr. Joseph Raz.

8 THE INDEFEASIBILITY OF JUSTICE

1. Introduction

My texts and questions in this essay are as follows:

(a) Socrates has a Principle of the Indefeasibility of Justice, 'In no way ought one to . . . act unjustly' (*Oudamos . . . dei adikein*) (Plato, *Crito*, p. 149). Woozley comments that it is 'the fundamental principle of the *Crito*, on which stands each of the three arguments against disobedience to law', and also 'one of the main themes of Socrates' defence in the *Apology*' (Woozley 1979, pp. 49 and 135).

(b) Kant also has a Principle of the Indefeasibility of Justice, 'Let justice be done though the world perish!' (*Fiat justitia, pereat mundus*) (Kant, p. 179).[1]

(c) Mill too has a Principle of the Indefeasibility of Justice which he expounds as follows:

> It appears from what has been said, that justice is a name for certain moral requirements, which, regarded collectively, stand higher in the scale of social utility, and are therefore of more paramount obligation, than any others; though particular cases may occur in which some other social duty is so important, as to overrule any one of the general maxims of justice. Thus, to save a life, it may not only be allowable, but a duty, to steal, or take by force, the necessary food or medicine, or to kidnap, and compel to officiate, the only qualified medical practitioner. In such cases, as we do not call anything justice which is not a virtue, we usually say, not that justice must give way to some other moral principle, but that what is just in ordinary cases is, by reason of that other principle, not just in the particular case. By this useful accommodation of language, the character of indefeasibility attributed to justice is kept up, and we are saved from the necessity of maintaining that there can be laudable injustice. (Mill, *Utilitarianism*, p. 59)

(d) Woozley comments on Socrates' Principle as follows:

> What Socrates never questioned was the alleged absoluteness of the obligation to refrain from acting unjustly. . . Here many would want to disagree with him, for it does seem that no such obligation could be absolute or, without exception, morally binding. It is, unfortun-

ately, true that human life is a messy business, with valid claims being
sometimes in competition with one another, so that sometimes it is
impossible to avoid doing injustice to somebody; or it may happen
that the demands of social benefit may have to be preferred to those
of justice. No doubt the reasons in favour of a course of action which
involves treating some people unjustly have to be very strong before
that course can be justified, and attempts to represent them as being
very strong must be very carefully, even sceptically, scrutinised before
they are to be accepted. But they can be strong enough for that; and,
if they are, then what the agent is morally bound to perform is the
action which involves some injustice, not the alternative action which
avoids it. (Ibid, pp. 26 and 27)

The questions which I shall address are two. First and primarily, are
Socrates' and Kant's Principles true or, as Woozley claims, false?
Secondly and secondarily, what exactly does Mill's Principle establish?
But it is necessary to consider first two preliminary questions, viz., the
meaning of 'Justice' and the value of Justice.

2. The Meaning of 'Justice'

According to a competent authority, 'not a few people now regard the
incredibly complex concept of justice as hopelessly beyond rational
analysis' (Kelbley, p. 1). But in this they are quite wrong.

2.1 Just Action

Our starting-point must be the formula 'B ϕd A unjustly (or unfairly),'
where A and B are person-variables and ϕ is an action-variable. It may
be read 'B treated (or dealt with) A unjustly (or unfairly).' For, as it
is truly said, Justice must be *done*; so that we are concerned with a kind
of activity, indeed an art, viz., fair dealing (Kamenka, pp. 14 and 15;
Tay, p. 96).

The first question, then, is what substitutions may be made on the
variable ϕ. The answer appears to be very many, but not all transitive
verbs. One can make sense of, e.g., 'B married A unfairly,' but not
of 'B admired A unfairly.' However, the *important* substitutions are fairly
few. For the sorts of unfair treatment that persons are in fact concerned
about are unfair: distribution, legislation, competition, exchange, compensation, punishment, blame and criticism. The sort of Injustice which
attaches to, e.g., punishment and compensation is Reciprocative

Injustice. For punishment and compensation are sorts of reciprocative action, which is something which B does to A because of, or in *consideration* of, something which A has done or suffered. Thus, B punishes A for an offence which A has committed; and B compensates A for a harm which A has suffered from B. But the sort of Injustice which attaches to distribution may be either Reciprocative or Non-reciprocative Injustice. If B distributes X to A and C according to their contributions to the making of X, and gives more of X to C than to A although A's contribution is greater than C's, that is Reciprocative Injustice. But if B distributes X to A and C according to their needs of X, and gives more of X to C than to A although A's need is greater than C's, that is Non-reciprocative Injustice. For B is not acting in consideration of anything that A and C *have done* (or had done to them), but in consideration of what they *are*, viz. needy (See Subsec. 2.2, below; cf. Eckhoff, pp. 3-10).

In elucidating the idea of Justice, it is profitable to concentrate on unjust treatment rather than on just treatment (Mill, *Utilitarianism*, p. 39; Woozley 1973, p. 109). Similarly, in elucidating the idea of liberty, it is profitable to concentrate on coercion (= making unfree).

Just treatment and unjust treatment are contraries, not contradictories. For if B treated A generously, then he treated him neither justly nor unjustly (Woozley 1973, pp. 109 and 110; Frankena, p. 2).

There are degrees of Injustice but not of Justice. Consequently, there are no comparative judgements of the form 'B treated A more justly than he treated C;' but there are comparative judgements of the form 'B treated A more unjustly than he treated C.' Judgements of the latter type are often encountered, e.g. in discussions of sentencing-policy. This discrepancy reflects the important fact that, where just/unjust action is concerned, there is only one way of getting things right, but indefinitely many ways of getting things wrong, of which some are worse than others. The existence of the expressions 'perfect justice' and 'rough justice' does not indicate that there are degrees of Justice. It indicates the further important fact that very often, indeed usually, the best that we can achieve is not Justice (= 'perfect justice') but an approximation to it (= 'rough justice').

We speak of A being unfairly treated only if he is disadvantaged, e.g. when his punishment is too severe or his compensation too small. If he is advantaged by too light a punishment or too great a compensation, we call the punishment 'inadequate' and the compensation 'excessive,' but we do not call them unfair. Or, if we do call an excessive compensation 'unfair,' we mean that it is unfair to the compensator, not to the compensatee.

Injustice is a narrower notion than Unfairness, in fact a species of it. The specific difference is that — as might be expected — we only speak of Injustice in legal or quasi-legal contexts. If B fouled A in a competitive game of skill, or cheated him in a game of chance, we say that B treated A unfairly, not unjustly. But the referee's failure to penalise B for his foul is called indifferently unfair or unjust. So paradigms of what are called unjust are laws, rules and regulations, judicial punishments or damages, headmasters' punishments, and umpires' penalties. This is a genuine distinction, but not an essential one, so that in this essay I shall treat Injustice as identical with Unfairness. (Cf. Lucas, p. 2.)

The next question, then, is what substitutions may be made on the variables A and B. These are individual persons or sets of persons (e.g. children, Asians).[2] B is the subject or agent of unfair treatment, and A its object or patient. The latter, not the former, is the central figure, and I mark this fact by designating him 'A.' (See Subsecs. 3.1 and 3.2.) Similarly with Liberty; the coercee, not the coercer, holds the centre of the stage. The possible ranges of A and B are very wide; in the example 'B married A unfairly' the only restrictions are, e.g., the legal ones that B and A should be of different sexes and of marriageable age. But in the *important* cases of unfair treatment these values are narrowly restricted, since A and B have to stand in natural or artificial special relationships. If a tax-law is unfair, then B must be a law-maker and A must be B's subject; if a punishment is unfair, then A must be an offender and B must be an authority who is competent to punish A; and so on. It is not that these special relationships produce just or unjust treatment of A by B; it is that the question of just or unjust treatment *does not arise* outside these contexts (Woozley 1973, p. 118).

Here lies the answer to interesting questions about Justice between generations and between states (Barry). Is this generation treating the next one unfairly by consuming more than its share of irreplaceable fossil fuels, granting for argument's sake that the generations are equal in the relevant respect, say, need of fossil fuels? A mother treats her child unfairly if she fails to give him an equal share of her food, if they are equal in the relevant respect, say, need of the food. But parent/child is a natural special relationship, whereas this generation/next generation is not, so that in the case of the latter the question of just or unjust treatment does not arise.[3] Similarly, B does not treat A, the only other occupant of a train-compartment, unfairly if he does not offer him a share of his sandwiches. If A is obviously hungry or undernourished, then B's treatment of him is uncharitable, or even cruel; but it is not unfair.

Again, are some rich northern countries treating some poor southern ones unfairly by paying them too little for their tea? If B underpays his employee A, or dismisses him for not working when he has in fact worked, then B treats A unfairly. But the relationship between an employer and his employee is an artificial special relationship, whereas the relationship between a rich northern country and a poor southern one is no sort of special relationship, so that in the latter case the question of just or unjust treatment does not arise. This is not to say that there is nothing wrong in rich countries so treating poor ones. It is to say that the wrong is not an injustice.

We speak of many other things besides B's treatment of A as just or unjust. Yet these all reduce to the justice or injustice of some individual person's, B's, treatment of some other individual person, A. When we call B himself unjust, we mean that he is disposed to treat A, C, D *et al.* unjustly. (See Subsec. 3.2.) Injustice to a set, e.g., Jews, is simply injustice to the individual members of that set. When we call unfair a law which, say, taxes Catholic citizens more heavily than non-Catholic ones, we mean that the law-maker treats unfairly the members of the set, Catholic citizens. An authority who makes an unfair arrangement for a competitive game treats unfairly those individual competitors who are disadvantaged by his arrangement. As to unjust procedures, if, say, a sovereign decrees that those of his subjects who are accused of blackmail shall be tried by ordeal, then he treats unjustly any individual subject who may be so accused.

Today, many claim that society (or social institutions) is (or are) preeminently that which is just or unjust, and the justice (= justness) of a just society is designated 'Social Justice.' Thus, according to Rawls, 'justice is the first virtue of social institutions' (Rawls, p. 3; Frankena, pp. 1 and 2). Miller expands this notion as follows. 'Social justice . . . concerns the distribution of benefits and burdens throughout a society, as it results from major social institutions — property systems, public organisations, etc.' (Miller, p. 22; cf. Vecchio, pp. 37-9). But a society, or a social institution, can only be just or unjust if it is organised or 'planned,' because just or unjust institutions are the products of just or unjust action and, as we shall see, just or unjust action is necessarily intentional (Subsec. 2.4). This is highly significant, because even in the most *dirigiste* states most institutions are largely 'unplanned' or natural growths (Hayek, pp. 67-70; but cf. Lucas, p. 5, n. 8).

Social Justice must be distinguished from Political Justice, which is the supremely important sort of Justice in which the agent of just treatment is the government and the patient is the citizen. Political punishment, e.g., can be politically just or unjust. Like Rawls, Plato believes that society is the most important subject of Justice.[4] On his idea of the just society he models his idea of the just (or virtuous, or free) man, one who is not a slave to his passions. His conceptions of both Justice and Liberty are therefore intrapersonal (*Republic*, pp. 119-43). But this is wrong on both counts, since treating unjustly and making unfree (= coercion) are both interpersonal, i.e involve at least two persons. However, although the man who is a slave to his passions is not identical with the unjust man, he is prone to be unjust. For insofar as he is moved by love, hate, prejudice etc. he will not be impartial, and so will tend to treat persons unfairly. (See Subsecs. 2.3 and 3.2. Appendix I to Essay 10.)

2.2 Principles and Species of Justice

When is B truly said to treat A unjustly? When B, in his treatment of A, flouts some Principle of Justice. This introduces the connected topics of the Principles of Justice and the species of Justice. There is an important distinction between Formal and Substantive (or Concrete, or Material) Principles of Justice (Perelman; Feinberg 1973, pp. 99-102).

The true Formal Principle of Reciprocative Justice is Simonides' Definition 'Justice is returning to every man his due' (*To ta opheilomena ekasto apodidonai dikaion esti.*) (Plato, *Republic*, p. 9).[5] Substantive Principles of Reciprocative Justice give content to Simonides' Definition by specifying what is due to A, from whom, and why. E.g., it is a generally accepted principle that there is due to A from the competent authority, B, a punishment with degree of severity n, because A has committed an offence with degree of gravity n. This is the principle of making the punishment fit the crime. But it is not a generally accepted principle that there is due to A from the competent authority, B, a punishment with degree of severity $n + m$, because A has committed an offence with degree of gravity n which is widely prevalent — say, mugging. This is the principle of exemplary punishment. Again, it is a generally accepted principle that there is due to A from B a compensation of value n because B has done A a harm the cost of repairing which is n. This is the principle of complete compensation. But it is not a generally accepted principle that there is due to A from B a compensation of value $n + m$ because B has done A a harm the cost of repairing which is n and which is widely prevalent — say, serious defamation. This is the principle of exemplary (or punitive) damages.

'A is entitled to X' (= 'X is due to A') does not mean the same as 'A deserves X', and the resemblances and differences between the two formulas illuminate the notion of the due. First, desert resembles dueness in that it is backward-looking. For A deserves X because A has done Y. With desert, Y must be either a morally good thing (good desert) or a morally bad thing (bad desert). This is sometimes the case with dueness too, as when we speak of 'due reward' and 'due punishment'. But not always. In exchange, for instance, A's transfer of X to B is usually morally indifferent, since economic goods are usually not moral goods. Again, when B compensates A, A is not an agent at all but a patient. Secondly, 'X is A's due' entails 'A has a right to X'. A must hold this right against some other, B, from whom X is due to A. But 'A deserves X' does not entail 'A has a right to X'. E.g., if A has been grievously injured in heroically saving B's life, it may be said of A that he deserves the best medical treatment that money can buy. Yet A has no right to receive this benefit from B or from anyone else. Since 'X is A's due' entails 'A has a right to X' whereas 'X is a A's desert' does not entail this, it follows that when X is A's due, it is *too weak* to say that X is A's desert.

Since we speak of A being duly punished or reprimanded, there are bad dues as well as good dues, just as there are bad deserts as well as good deserts. Hence A can have a right to an evil as well as to a good. This seems paradoxical, since we ordinarily speak of A having a right to a good but not to an evil. However, this is simply an interesting instance of the quite common situation in which ordinary language needs to be methodised and corrected in the interests of general coherence. Hegel's opinion that an offender has a right to his punishment is generally considered to illustrate his love of paradox (Hegel, pp 64-74). But the preceding observations show that this criticism is unjust.

Another significant point respecting the relation of the due to the unfair is this. When we speak of an exchange or a compensation as unfair, we always mean that, say, employer B underpaid his employee A; or that B undercompensated A whom he had harmed. We do not mean that there was overpayment or overcompensation in these cases. Similarly, unfair punishment and unfair criticism always mean excessive punishment and excessive criticism. Nevertheless, speaking strictly, A does not receive his due when he is overpaid, or overcompensated, or underpunished, or undercriticised; just as when he is underpaid, or undercompensated, or overpunished, or overcriticised.

So if A voluntarily overcompensates C does A treat himself unfairly? Aristotle maintains that unjust treatment is an irreflexive relation. But he confuses two different points. He says truly that (1) 'the just and the unjust always involve more than one person' (1138a 19-20), and infers from this that 'there must be someone (B) to treat him (A) unjustly' (1136 b 11-14). But (2) does not follow from (1), nor is it true (Gewirth, p. 125). Respecting (1), Justice is naturally and best thought of as triadic, i.e as involving three persons, with B treating A and C justly. This is the view of Justice presented in the traditional image, where the sublime goddess *Justitia* (B), with her scales, blindfold and sword, deals even-handedly with A and C. The case of reflexive injustice given above is the special case of the general case in which B=A. (On the iconography of Justice, see Vecchio pp. 169-73.) It may be objected that, although Civil Justice involves three persons, namely, judge, plaintiff and defendant, Criminal Justice is dyadic, i.e. involves only two, namely, B (the punitive authority) and C (the putative offender). But the reply is that, in the opinion of many, the principal weakness of Criminal Justice is precisely that A, C's victim, has been squeezed out by B. As Hegel saw, Criminal Justice ought to resemble Civil Justice, in that its chief aim should be to right the wrong, or to restore the *status quo*, by making the criminal compensate fully the person whom he has harmed. (See Vecchio, Appendices I and II; Essay 4.)

The true Formal Principle of Non-reciprocative Justice is Aristotle's Principle of Justice: Treat equally (alike) those who are equal in the relevant respects, and unequally (differently) those who are unequal in the relevant respects in direct proportion to the inequalities (differences) between them (Aristotle, 1131 a 19-24). Substantive Principles of Non-Reciprocative Justice give content to Aristotle's Principle by specifying the relevant respects in which A and C are alike or different. E.g., it is a generally accepted principle that, in distributing a divisible X between A and C, B should allocate equal shares of X to A and C if A and C are equal in respect of their degree of need of X; but that B should allocate a greater (or smaller) share of X to A than to C if A's degree of need of X is greater (or smaller) than C's. This is the principle of 'To each according to his need'. But it is not a generally accepted principle that, in the same situation, B should allocate equal shares of X to A and C if A and C are equal in respect of their degree of desire of X; but that B should allocate a greater (or smaller) share of X to A than to C if A's degree of desire of X is greater (or smaller) than C's. This is the principle of 'To each according to his desire'.

In the area of Reciprocative Justice, Aristotle's Principle is a consequence of Simonides' Definition (Miller, pp. 20 and 21). E.g., the reciprocative principle of making the punishment fit the crime (above) requires that, if A and C are equal in respect of degree of gravity of offence, then B should treat them equally in respect of degree of severity of the punishment which he inflcts on them; but that if they are unequal in the former respect, then B should treat them unequally in the latter respect in direct proportion to their inequality in the former respect.

However, Aristotle's Principle is derivative from Simonides' Definition only in the area of Reciprocative Justice. In the area of Non-reciprocative Justice, Simonides' Definition does not apply, so that Aristotle's Principle is there primitive. (Cf. Barry, pp. 73 and 74; Chapman.) To fix the ideas, it is best to bear in mind paradigms of Reciprocative Justice and Non-reciprocative Justice taken from the supremely important area of Political Justice. For Reciprocative Justice, these are, first, State-imposed compensation or damages, which is the field of Civil Law; and secondly, *political punishment*, which is the field of Criminal Law. For Non-reciprocative Justice, one should think, e.g., of a ministry devising and operating a national food-rationing scheme in time of war; or, for burdens as opposed to benefits, of a finance minister devising and operating a system of national taxation. (See Appendix I.)

The essential differences between Reciprocative Justice and Non-reciprocative Justice are as follows. We have seen that, with Reciprocative Justice, the problem is to determine what is due to A, from whom, and why. A typical answer is that the State ought to make C pay to A £1,000, because C has harmed A, and because £1,000 is the sum which is required to put A back where he was before C harmed him. But with Non-reciprocative Justice the problem is to determine what A ought to receive (not what is due to A) from the distributing authority, the ministry (not from some other individual citizen), and why. A typical answer is that the ministry ought to allocate to A 1 pint of milk *per* day because A is under 16 and needs the milk because she is still growing (not because A has done or had done to her something which makes the milk her due or right).

First, then, non-reciprocative transfer is simpler than reciprocative transfer, because the former involves only one action, whereas the latter involves either two actions or one action and one passion. For reciprocative transfer is always retrospective, looking back to what A *has done or has suffered*. But non-reciprocative transfer is inspective, since it takes no account of what A has done or has suffered, but simply considers what A *is*, viz. needy because poor, young, pregnant, etc. Secondly, this is why, although A ought to be allocated the milk, the milk is not A's due or right, because X is only due to A on account of something which A has done or suffered.

A distributing authority can use either Reciprocative or Non-reciprocative Substantive Principles in making its allocations. We have seen that 'To each according to his need' is non-reciprocative, as is also e.g., 'Women and children first' (Eckhoff, p. 234). But 'To each according to his work (= contribution)' is reciprocative. 'First come, first served' is interestingly ambiguous. If it means, as I think that it usually does, 'He who happens to come first will be served first', it is non-reciprocative (Eckhoff, p. 218). But if it means, as it might and perhaps sometimes does, 'He who succeeds in getting here first will be served first', it is reciprocative. The distinction between Reciprocative Justice and Non-reciprocative Justice is traditionally referred to as that between Reciprocative (or Commutative) Justice and Distributive Justice.[6] But since Reciprocative Substantive Principles as well as Non-reciprocative ones are used in distribution, it is undesirable to express the distinction in this way.

If employer B pays his employee A less than A's work (= contribution) is worth, that is Non-comparative Reciprocative Injustice (Feinberg, 1974). If B pays his employee A less than his employee C although A's contribution is greater than C's , that is Comparative Reciprocative Injustice. If B does both these things to A then B inflicts on A a Double Reciprocative Injustice. In the first case, B *exploits* A. In the second case, B *discriminates against* A. In the third case, B both exploits and discriminates against A.

We have seen that, if B does not allocate X to A in order to satisfy A's need of X, then B does not treat A unfairly, because X is not A's due. However, *if* B *does* allocate X to A and C according to their needs of X, but gives A the smaller part of (divisible) X although A's need of X is greater than C's, then B *does* treat A unfairly (Woozley 1973, pp. 111 and 112). This sort of Non-reciprocative Injustice is therefore always Comparative. (See Subsec. 2.3.)

Finally, the Comparative/Non-comparative division can be combined with the Reciprocative/Non-reciprocative division to yield four species of Injustice which can be ranked in descending order of moral iniquity as follows: (1) Comparative and Non-comparative Reciprocative Injustice (= Double Reciprocative Injustice); (2) Non-comparative Reciprocative Injustice; (3) Comparative Reciprocative Injustice; (4) Non-reciprocative Injustice.

Species (2) occurs if, e.g., A is B's sole employee, whom B underpays, but there is no other employee, C, whom B does not underpay. The logically possible combination in which there is no Non-comparative Reciprocative Injustice but there is Comparative Reciprocative Injustice does not in fact occur. For if, e.g., a grateful father, B, bequeathes his money to each of his children, A and C, in direct proportion to the good which they have done to him, but leaves the surplus to C and not to A, then B does not treat A unjustly (Woozley 1973, pp. 112 and 113).

As to the ranking, first, Reciprocative Injustice is morally worse than Non-reciprocative Injustice. E.g., it is worse that B should not assign (indivisible) X to A when A has contributed most to making X than it is that B should not assign X to A when A needs X more than any other claimant of X. Secondly, Non-comparative Reciprocative Injustice is morally worse than Comparative Reciprocative Injustice. E.g., it is worse that B should punish A with a degree of severity which is greater than the degree of gravity of A's offence than that B should punish A more severely than C although A and C have committed the same equally grave offence. Thirdly, Double Reciprocative Injustice is obviously morally worse than Single Reciprocative Injustice (Species (2) and (3)).

This ranking provides some, but very limited, assistance in dealing with the hard problems of conflicting claims which arise when, as very often happens, there are more than one relevant resemblances or differences between A and C. Thus, suppose that A's contribution to the making of divisible X is greater than C's, but that C's need of X is greater than A's. If these inequalities are equal, then B ought to allocate more of X to A than to C, because Comparative Reciprocative Injustice is morally worse than Non-reciprocative Injustice. But this may not be so when, as very often happens, these inequalities are not equal. For if A's contribution is only *a little greater* than C's, whereas C's need is *much greater* than A's, then Justice may require B to allocate more of X to C than to A (Chapman, pp. 160 and 161; Woozley 1973, p. 174).

2.3 Justice and Equality

We must now consider the relation of Justice to Equality. The essence of the situation is that, although the connexions between Justice and Equality are many, close and important, Justice is by no means the same thing as Equality (Flew, Stone). Thus, it is quite correct to say 'B divided X equally but unfairly between A and C', and 'B divided X fairly but unequally between A and C'. The most important difference between the two concepts is that Equality is descriptive whereas Justice is evaluative (Gewirth, p. 123). To call B's treatment of A unfair is to pass an unfavourable moral value-judgement on it. Consequently, 'B divided X equally (or unequally) between A and C' can be established easily by observation or measurement. But 'B divided X fairly (or unfairly) between A and C' cannot be so established. This is not to say, however, that observation plays no part in establishing it. For to establish it, one needs to know, e.g., (1) that the only relevant difference between A and C is that in respect of their needs of X; (2) that A's need of X is greater than C's; but (3) that B assigned a smaller share of X to A than to C. (3) can be established easily by observation or measurement. (2) can be established by observation, at least if need of X is a basic or genuine need, though even here not easily, since need is an empirical concept if a complex one (Miller, Ch. IV). But (1) cannot be decided by observation, and requires judgement. If one holds, as I do, that the only possible relevant differences between A and C in the allocation of benefits are those in respect of (*a*) contribution (cf. Taylor) and (*b*) compensatibility in the reciprocative area, and that in respect of (*c*) need in the non-reciprocative area, then he can establish (1) by establishing by observation that A and C are no different in respect of (*a*) and (*b*). But if another were to hold that another possible relevant difference between A and C is that in respect of their degree of desire for X, this difference between us could not be resolved by observation.

Next, the connexions between Justice and Equality. In Non-reciprocative Justice, Aristotle's Principle requires equal treatment of persons who are equal in the relevant respects. So if need of X is the only relevant resemblance or difference between A and C, and A's need of X is equal to C's, then Non-reciprocative Justice requires B to divide (divisible) X equally between A and C. Here, therefore, Justice requires both equality of things (shares of X) and also equality of treatment of persons. Similarly, Comparative Reciprocative Justice requires equality both of things and of treatmeant of persons. E.g., just punishment requires both that the degree of severity of the punishment should equal the degree of gravity of the crime (equality of things), and also that B should punish A and C equally severely if their offences are equally grave (equality of treatment, or uniformity in sentencing policy). Again, just non-voluntary compensation requires both that B should make C pay to A compensation equal in value to the cost of repairing the harm which C did to A (equality of things), and also that B should make A and C pay equal compensations to persons to whom they have done equal harms (equality of treatment, or uniformity in damages policy). Non-comparative Reciprocative Justice, on the other hand, requires only equality of things, not also of treatment of persons; e.g., as above, equality of punishment to crime, or equality of damages to harm. So Non-comparative Justice requires only equality of things, whereas Comparative Justice requires both equality of things and also of treatment of persons.

A sort of Equality that is intimately connected with Justice is Equality of Consideration (Benn; Benn and Peters, pp. 44-51, 110-11). In law, it is expressed in e.g. the Principle of Natural Justice, 'Hear the other party' (*Audi alteram partem*) (Hart, pp. 156, 202; Lucas, Ch. 4). Equality of Consideration applies only to Comparative Justice. It requires B to give equal consideration to the claims of A and C to X. Thus, in applying the relevant Substantive Principle of Non-reciprocative Justice 'To each according to his need,' B establishes carefully whether A and C both need X, and estimates carefully the degrees of their needs. The proper objects of equal consideration, then, are the claims which A and C have to X according to the relevant resemblances or differences between them. B first judges, say, that the only relevant resemblance or difference between A and C is need, and then properly gives equal consideration to the claims which A and C have to X according to this criterion. A has a claim to X if and only if A is in a position to lay a claim to X. And A is in a position to lay a claim to X if and only if he has some relevant property, such as need, on which to base his claim (Feinberg 1973, pp. 64-7).

Equality of Consideration has one peculiar and very interesting feature. B's giving equal consideration to A's and C's claims to X is a necessary, though not a sufficient, condition of B's treating A and C justly. Yet in giving equal consideration to A's and C's claims B is already treating A and C justly; he certainly treats them unjustly if he fails to do so. Equality of Consideration, then, is a sort of Non-reciprocative Justice which is an indispensable preliminary to doing further justice. It is a sort of Non-reciprocative Justice because B bestows the benefit of his equal consideration on A and C simply because of what they are, viz., persons who have claims to X according to the relevant resemblances or differences between them. It is not their due on account of something which they have done or suffered. For *having* a claim to X is not *laying* a claim to X; it is *being in a position to* lay a claim to X. A and C are simply *eligible recipients* of X according to the relevant criteria. Equality of Consideration therefore needs to be marked off as another sort of Justice additional to those already distinguished. An appropriate name for it is Preliminary Non-reciprocative Justice.

Of course, B's equal consideration of A's and C's claims to X on the basis of the relevant Substantive Principles of Justice is not a sufficient condition of B's allocating X justly. For B may give equal consideration to, say, A's and C's needs for X, but fail to appreciate that A's need is greater than C's. Or B may give equal consideration to A's and C's needs for X, correctly appreciate that A's need is greater than

C's, and yet perversely or maliciously assign (indivisible) X to C. But it may be objected to what I have said above that Equality of Consideration of claims is not a necessary condition of doing further justice either. For B may be Rabelais' Judge Bridlegoose, who decides cases by dicing. He assigns (indivisible) X to A if the die falls odd and to B if it falls even. And in so doing he may chance to treat A and C justly; since, as it happens, the relevant resemblance or difference between A and C is in respect of their contributions, and A's contribution to the making of X is equal to C's. The reply to this objection is that, although there is a weak sense in which B treats A and C justly in this example, in its strong and proper sense just or unjust action is necessarily intentional, and that equal consideration of claims is indeed a necessary condition of intentional just or unjust action. I shall return to this important point shortly (Subsec. 2.4).

We have seen that, generally speaking, Justice is not identical with Equality. But Comparative Preliminary Justice is one vital area in which Justice is identical with Equality. For just consideration of rival claims always means equal consideration of them. Another area in which Fairness is identical with Equality is games of pure chance. At roulette, e.g., croupier B cheats (treats unfairly) player A if he makes A's chance of winning less than player C's. For in such games of pure chance, the players ought to have an equal chance, or *equal opportunity*, of winning. Sometimes it is also fair to employ a random procedure for allocating X when X is an indivisible good, such as a theatre-ticket, rather than a divisible one, such as a loaf.[7] For if the relevant resemblance or difference between A and C is need of the ticket, and A's need of it is equal to C's, then B treats A and C fairly by giving them equal opportunities of obtaining it by deciding which of them receives it by throwing fairly a fair die. So there is a restricted area in which Judge Bridlegoose's procedure is fair.[8]

Equality and Inequality of Consideration are not the same things as Impartiality and Partiality. For the latter can occur in situations involving Non-comparative Justice. E.g., B underpays his sole employee, A, because B does not give impartial consideration to A's claim on the relevant ground, which is, say, A's contribution. This is, say, because A is an Arab, and B is prejudiced against Arabs. But Partiality can be favourable as well as unfavourable; indeed, 'partial to' normally means 'favourably partial to'. Equality of Consideration, then, is the species of Impartiality which occurs in situations involving Comparative Justice. As Equality of Consideration is necessary, but not sufficient, for B to treat A justly in situations involving Comparative Justice, so Impartiality is necessary, but not sufficient, for B to treat A justly in situations involving Non-comparative Justice. Preliminary Justice is therefore identical with Impartiality. As Mill truly says, Impartiality is 'a necessary condition of the fulfilment of the other obligations of justice' (Mill, *Utilitarianism*, p. 57).

As we have just seen, Preliminary Non-reciprocative Injustice can be either Comparative or Non-comparative. But Non-preliminary Non-reciprocative Injustice is always Comparative. The final tally of the species of Injustice is therefore as follows: (1) Comparative and Non-comparative Reciprocative Injustice (= Double Reciprocative Injustice); (2) Non-comparative Reciprocative Injustice; (3) Comparative Reciprocative Injustice; (4) Preliminary Non-reciprocative Injustice (= Partiality, Comparative or Non-comparative); (5) Non-preliminary Non-reciprocative Injustice (Comparative). (Cf. Subsec. 2.2.)

Two general findings emerge. First, in view of the many, close and significant connexions between Justice and Equality, it is not surprising that some have fallen into the error of believing them to be identical. Secondly, to anticipate the discussion in Sec. 4, our fourth species of Justice (above) is indeed indefeasible, in that all men have an absolute or unconditional right to have their claims considered impartially. (Cf. Feinberg 1973, p. 96.)

2.4 Justice and Intention

I turn now to the relationship between Justice (= just action) and Intention. In considering Judge Bridlegoose's procedure, we have seen that there is a weak sense of 'just treatment' in which B can treat A justly unintentionally. But in their full and proper sense, just and unjust action are necessarily intentional (Aristotle, 1138 a 20-1). The just man, who possesses the virtue of Justice (= justness), is he who is disposed to treat persons justly. One necessary condition of acting justly is intending to do so. But it is not a sufficient condition. For B may intend to treat A fairly, but believe falsely that the relevant resemblance or difference between A and C is need. Or he may believe truly that this is so, but judge wrongly that C's need of X is greater than A's. In either case, B will not treat A fairly. This shows that Intention is not the only necessary condition of just action, since Knowledge and Judgement are also required. (Cf. Lucas, pp. 35-46.) The object of knowledge must, of course, be true, so that there is an important connexion between Justice and Truth.[9] The fourth necessary condition of just action, as we have already seen, is Impartiality. These four conditions of just action are not only severally necessary but also collectively sufficient. These examples also show that there is a weak sense in which B can treat A unjustly without intending to do so. But in its full and proper sense, unjust treatment too is necessarily intentional. E.g., B knows that the relevant resemblance or difference between A and C is contribution to the making of (indivisible) X, and that A's contribution is greater than C's, and yet he allocates X to C in order to humiliate A of whom he is jealous.

The necessary intentionality of Justice (= justness) is clearly brought out in the definition into which Ulpian expanded Simonides' Definition: 'Justice is the settled and enduring intention of returning to every man his due (*Justitia est constans et perpetua voluntas jus suum cuique tribuendi*)' (Justinian, p. 2; Vecchio, p. 5; Vlastos, p. 53). It is conceptually connected with the fact that Justice (= just treatment) is a negative, general, moral right. (See Subsec. 3.1.) For one can neither respect nor violate a moral right unintentionally. There is a significant analogy here between Justice and Liberty. For Liberty too is a negative, general, moral right; in consequence of which Coercion (= making unfree), like Injustice (= treating unjustly), is necessarily intentional (Essay 7, Sec. 4; Essay 10, Sec. 4).

We have seen that 'X is due to A from B' entails 'A has a moral right to be given X by B' (Subsec. 2.2). This, however, applies only to Reciprocative Justice, e.g., in compensation. But the judgement 'A has a moral right to be treated justly by B' applies to Non-reciprocative Justice as well as to Reciprocative Justice, and it is this that is meant in saying that Justice (= just treatment) is a negative, general, moral right. Why, then, does Justice not figure in the famous declarations of natural or human rights, as Liberty does? Because its place in them has been usurped by Equality. But it is Justice which is the natural right, not Equality. These considerations lead naturally to the next division of our subject.

3. The Value of Justice

The goodness of Justice and the badness of Injustice have to be estimated from the standpoints of the patient A, the agent B, the other party C, and the general public.

3.1 The Right to Justice

In the expression 'the right to Justice' the word 'Justice' means 'just treatment'. It is the 'Justice' which Simonides' Definition defines (Subsec. 2.2). As Mill says, 'Justice (is) something which . . . some individual person can claim from us as his moral right' (Mill, *Utilitarianism*,

p. 46). Specifically, the patient A has a negative, general, individual, moral right to be treated justly by the agent B. The primary question considered in this essay is whether this right is also absolute or unconditional (Sec. 1).

The right is *individual* because it is held by individual persons. As said above, the rights of sets, such as Jews, reduce to the rights of individual Jews (Subsec. 2.1). This feature is characteristic of rights arguments generally, and contrasts them with consequential or utilitarian arguments which consider questions from the standpoint of how just and unjust action, for instance, affect the public good. This question is taken up in Subsec. 3.3. (Raphael, pp. v and vi.)

The right with which we are concerned is the *moral* right to Justice. Sometimes this moral right is also a legal right guaranteed by a constitutional law. An example is the equal protection clause of the Fourteenth Amendment, which provides that 'no State shall . . . deny to any person the equal protection of the laws'. It has been much used recently in arguments about discrimination (Fiss, Richards).

The right is *general* because it is held by A against B simply *qua* persons, not because of some special relationship between them. It may be objected that this conflicts with my having said earlier that the questions of B treating A justly or unjustly do not arise unless B and A stand in some special relationship, such as that of compensator to compensatee (Subsec. 2.1). The reply to this objection is that the general right to Justice is the right to Formal Justice. It is the rights to Substantive Justice which require B and A to stand in special relationships, such as that of compensator to compensatee in the case of the right to fair compensation, or that of authority to offender in the case of the right to just punishment.

In significant respects, 'A has a right not to be treated unfairly by B' is like 'A has a right not to be made unfree (= coerced) by B.' With both rights, two main questions are the problem of meaning and the problem of justification or value. But there are also two important differences. First, a third main question about the right to Liberty, as about the right to Property, is the problem of distribution, of how much liberty A ought to have. (See Sec. 3 of Essay 6.) But there is no corresponding problem about Justice because, as we have seen, Justice has no degrees (Subsec. 2.1). There are indeed questions about, e.g., how much punishment A ought to receive. But this, of course, is not a question about how much justice A ought to receive, but a question about how much punishment it is just for A to receive. Secondly, although Socrates and Kant have claimed that Justice is an absolute or unconditional right, nobody has claimed that Liberty — or any other negative, general, right, such as that to Life — is more than a presumptive or defeasible right.

The right to Justice is *negative* because it is a right not to be harmed. This distinguishes it from (alleged) positive (or welfare) rights, which are rights to be benefited, e.g. the right to holidays with pay. A's right to be treated justly by B arises exclusively from the fact that, since Justice and Injustice are contraries, B does not treat A unjustly if he treats him justly (Subsec. 2.1). For the vital consideration is not the good which B does to A if he treats him justly, but the harm which he does to him if he treats him unjustly.

When B treats A unjustly, he treats him with indignity and disrespect. But, as Kant taught, respect is due to all from all simply as persons. Kant also taught that persons ought not to treat one another as means. But when B treats A unjustly, he often does this. If B pays his employee A less than his contribution is worth, B treats A as a means to B's enrichment. If B imposes on A an exemplary punishment or exemplary damages, then B treats A as a means to deter C and others from a widely prevalent crime or tort (Lucas, pp. 143 and 144).

Unfair treatment arouses in A two successive feelings, both of which are very harmful and painful to him. First, a sense of humiliation at the disgrace. Second, a feeling of resentment or anger at the insult. The latter often harms C as well as A, when A transfers his resentment to C. This happens, e.g., when A and C are competitors for X, and B unfairly awards X to C. In such a case, A is apt to visit his anger on C as well as on B.

The sense of humiliation harms A by unjustifiably lowering his self-respect and self-confidence. For the successful conduct of life requires a measure of what Sterling calls 'pagan self-assertion' (Mill, *On Liberty*, p. 120). But sets, such as American negroes or Ulster Catholics, who have long been discriminated against, are prone to defeatism and self-pity. Alternatively, by over-reaction, they become aggressive.

When unjust treatment attains the pitch of *persecution*, its victims are liable to become paranoid. As 'discrimination-against' means *unfair* selection', so 'persecution' means '*unfair* pursuit' or 'hounding'. The patients of persecution are usually sets, such as Christians or Jews. Persecution involves Double Reciprocative Injustice. It involves Non-comparative Reciprocative Injustice, because the patient set are harmed although they have done no wrong. It also involves Comparative Reciprocative Injustice, because the patient set are treated worse than the complementary set although there is no relevant difference between them. As we have seen, Double Reciprocative Injustice is the morally worst sort of injustice, so that persecution is rightly judged to be the extreme form of unjust treatment.

The feelings of shock, humiliation and resentment which are caused by unfair treatment must be distinguished, or course, from feeling unfairly treated, which means believing that one is being unfairly treated. But this belief will cause the feelings of humiliation and resentment and their attendant bad consequences when it is false as well as when it is true. Those will be especially prone to hold this false belief who really have been unfairly treated in the past. Here, then, is another reason why Injustice is morally bad.

The proper response to moral Injustice, to treating a person with indignity, is moral Indignation. The essential differences between this and resentment are, first, that the latter is personal whereas moral Indignation is impersonal and disinterested. Whereas A resents B's injustice to A, C feels moral Indignation at B's unfair treatment of A, or of D, or of any other person similarly treated. Secondly, whereas resentment, being a purely natural reaction, is morally indifferent, moral Indignation is morally good.[10] So may not Injustice be defended on the score that it elicits this moral good?[11] The objection to this defence is that, although C, D *et al.* may feel moral Indignation and not resentment at B's injustice to A, A himself is most unlikely to do so. To suppose otherwise is to impute to him a superhuman capacity for detachment. Injustice will almost always arouse in its victims the very harmful and painful feelings of shock, humiliation and anger (Mill, *Utilitarianism*, pp. 47-9; Strawson 1962; Woozley 1973, pp. 121 and 122; Feinberg 1974, pp. 288-90).

The right to Justice is in the same class as the other classic negative, general, rights, e.g., those to Life and to Liberty. These rights are alike in the following respects. First, they are all negative, general, individual and moral rights. Secondly, being general, they are not specific. We have seen that the right to Justice is the right to Formal Justice, not the rights to Substantive Justice, such as the rights to fair compensation or to just punishment. Similarly, the right to Life is the right not to be killed, not the right not to be punished capitally or the right not to be conscripted; and the right to Liberty is the right not to be coerced, not the right to free expression or the right to freedom in respect of one's tastes and pursuits. Thirdly, they are all '*ideal directives* addressed to those in appropriate positions to do their best for a particular kind of human value, such as life, liberty,' or justice (Feinberg 1973, pp. 70 and 71).

But although the right to Justice shares these features with other rights, it is not identical with them. This needs to be said because it has been claimed that 'justice is coextensive with rights' (Raphael, p. 185). In fact, however, the right to Justice is simply one negative, general right among others. Some rights, e.g., those to Life and to Liberty, are not rights to Justice; and some wrongs (i.e. violations of some right) are not injustices. If B respects A's rights to Life and to Liberty, then B treats A rightly, but he does not treat him justly. And if B murders or kidnaps A, then B wrongs or maltreats A, but he does not treat him unfairly. The cause of this mistake is probably a confusion of *the unjustifiable* (= that which cannot be shown to be *just*).[12] B's murder or kidnapping of A are unjustifiable, but they are not unjusticizable.

3.2 The Virtue of Justice

In the expression 'the virtue of Justice' the word 'Justice' means 'justness', i.e. the quality which disposes a person to treat persons justly. It is the 'Justice' which Ulpian's Definition purports to define. It is the virtue which the agent B ought to display in his treatment of the patient A.

When, then, does a person possess this quality? When and only when he possesses three other qualities, two of which have been discussed already. First, the Just Will, i.e., the settled intention to act justly. For we have seen that, in the full and proper sense, just and unjust action are necessarily intentional (Subsec. 2.4). Secondly, Impartiality. For we have also seen that B will not treat A justly unless he considers A's claim solely in the light of the relevant resemblances or differences between A and C, and is not swayed by prejudice, sympathy or antipathy (Subsec. 2.3). Thirdly — and the name is surely significant — Judgement. It requires nice Judgement to determine with even rough Justice whether, when both contribution and need are relevant resemblances or differences, C's much greater need of X outweighs A's slightly greater contribution to the making of X; how much compensation is due for a serious defamation; how severely A should be punished in comparison with C, who has committed an offence which is somewhat, but not altogether, like A's; and so on.

These considerations show that Ulpian's Definition of 'Justice' (= 'justness') is too narrow. For the settled and enduring resolve of which he writes is not identical with Justness. It is simply one of the three necessary conditions of Reciprocative Justice. (Ulpian's Definition does not apply to Non-reciprocative Justness, because the concept of the due has no place in the area of Non-reciprocative Justice (Subsec. 2.2)). The three necessary conditions of the virtue of Justice are themselves virtues. In Aristotle's terminology, the Just Will, like Justice itself, is a moral virtue. But Impartiality and Judgement are intellectual virtues.[13]

These three collectively sufficient conditions of Justice (= justness) are not also the collectively sufficient conditions of Justice (= just action). For, as we have seen, Knowledge is a fourth necessary condition of just action (Subsec. 2.4). But a person can *be* just although the information on which he *acts* is incorrect. When this is so, he does not act justly and may *appear* to act unjustly. ('Just', 'Unjust', 'Not just' and 'Not unjust' are elucidated in Note 23 and Appendix II of Essay 9.) Their different relationship to Truth is an important difference between Justice (= justness) and Justice (= just action). It follows that 'Justice (= just action)' cannot be defined in terms of 'Justice (= justness)' as 'the treatment which the just person is disposed to accord to persons.' For the treatment which a just person who acts on incorrect information is disposed to accord to persons may well not be, indeed very probably will not be, just. On the contrary, as was said above, 'Justice (= justness)' has to be defined in terms of 'Justice (= just action)' as 'the quality which disposes a person to treat persons justly'. It is the notion of just action, not the notion of the virtue of Justice, which is fundamental for understanding the concept of Justice. (Cf. Subsec. 2.1.)

What is the value of Justness to its possessor? Justness and Unjustness are contraries, not contradictories, since the generous man, he who tends to treat others generously, is neither the just man, who tends to treat others justly, nor the unjust man, who tends to treat others unjustly. But the fact that B cannot be unjust if he is just is of great value to B. For even if Hume is right in accounting Justice a 'cautious, jealous virtue', it is certain that Injustice is a great vice (Hume, *Enquiry*, p. 184). The effect on B's character of his being consistently unjust will be to make him callous and insensitive to human dignity. For Socrates' paradox that 'to do . . . injustice to another is a far greater evil for the doer of the injustice than it is for the victim' is an exaggeration of an important truth (Plato, *Gorgias*, p. 87; Kelbley).

Justness is valuable to its possessor not only because it prevents him from being unjust, but on its own account. For Justness is indeed a virtue, and so are its conditions, Impartiality, Judgement and Just Will. They are all positively good qualities in a person. Here is another significant difference between Justice (= Justness) and Justice (= just action).

The low esteem in which Hume holds Justness contrasts sharply with the very high value placed upon it by Plato, Aristotle, Thomas and Mill. Part of the explanation of this disparity may be that the value of Justness to the patient is very different from its value to the agent. Hume is right in accounting it no great merit in B that he treats A fairly, whereas it is a considerable merit in B that he treats A generously. The former is the least that B can do, and he is morally and legally obliged to do it. Generosity, on the other hand, is supererogatory and not obligatory. But although it is of no great value to B that he treats A justly, it is of great value to A that B treats him thus, and so does not treat him unjustly. The situation here is the same with Justice as it is with, e.g., Life and Liberty. It is no great merit in B that he forbears to murder or to kidnap A, and he is morally and legally obliged so to forbear. Yet this forbearance is of very great value to A.

Another part of the explanation of this disparity of esteem of Justness is that Plato and Aristotle exaggerate its value by their doctrine of Justice as the universal virtue. As Aristotle puts it, quoting Theognis, 'In justice is all virtue found in sum' (Aristotle, 1129 b 30; Vecchio, pp. 18-41). But Justness is not identical with Righteousness (Vlastos, pp. 31 and 32). As it is incorrect to inflate Justice (= just treatment) into the sole right and Injustice (= unjust treatment) into the sole wrong, so it is incorrect to inflate Justice (= Justness) into the sole virtue and Injustice (= Unjustness) into the sole vice. Thus, Generosity is a virtue which is not the same as Justice, and meanness is a vice which is not the same as Injustice. For we have seen that if B treats A generously, then he treats him neither justly nor unjustly (Subsec. 2.1). Consequently, the disposition to treat others generously is different from the disposition to treat others justly.[14]

Finally, Justness is also a specific virtue. Specific virtues are those qualities which make a person or thing good of its kind. For instance, the specific virtues of a watch are accuracy and durability (Hare, p. 133). Those to whom the virtue of Justness is specific are chiefly legislators and, above all, judges. This is because of the prime importance of Political Justice (Subsec. 2.1). As the paradigm of the unfree man is the prisoner, so the paradigm of the victim of Injustice is the plaintiff or accused who is judged unjustly by an unjust judge. To be sure, judges ought also to possess other specific virtues, such as learning in the law. But above all they need the virtue of Justness and the three virtues on which that virtue depends, viz., Impartiality, Judgement and Just Will. (Cf. Lucas, p. 106.)

3.3 Justice and the Public Good

According to Locke and Hume, Justice is the bond without which no society or association can exist.[15] Once again, the point is seen more clearly from the standpoint of Injustice. It is not so much that Justice makes for social solidarity as that Injustice, especially to substantial and self-conscious minorities, is disastrously divisive. Just treatment of them is good because it excludes unjust treatment of them.

The most important form of such Injustice is Political Injustice, where the agent is government and the patient is, e.g., an ethnic or religious set. Even when the patient is an individual person, the injustice may really be of this kind, because the individual is seen by some set as typifying them. Thus, *l'affaire Dreyfus* was seen as an injustice to French Jews, and the Bakke case was regarded as an injustice to American whites. Such Injustice usually takes the form of discriminatory legislation, e.g., that enforcing segregation in schools or on trains.

But another significant species of such Injustice is Social Injustice, where the patient is again, e.g., an ethnic or religious minority, but the agent is the complementary majority, not government. Such Injustice usually takes the form of discriminatory practice, e.g., in employment policy.[16]

The divisive 'we/they' effect of this type of Political Injustice is very dangerous to a political society or State for two main reasons. First, it may make powerful minorities disloyal in times of emergency, such as war. Secondly, it may make for anarchy. For since these minorities are acutely conscious of the injustice of the laws which discriminate against them, they are liable to hold in disrespect 'the law' in all its aspects, not only the laws, but the courts, magistrates and police.

Discriminatory legislation which mandates segregation in schools and on trains violates a set's right to Liberty as well as to Justice. Similarly, unjust imprisonment violates an individual's right to Liberty as well as his right to Justice; and an unjust (excessive) fine violates an individual's right to Property as well as his right to Justice.

We have seen that Social Justice in my sense is different from Social Justice in Miller's sense (Subsec. 2.1). Miller's Social Justice is about Justice *in* a society as revealed by the distribution of benefits and burdens throughout it.[17] My Social Justice is about the Justice *of* a society as revealed by the treatment of minorities by the majority. This raises the question of the relation of Social Injustice in my sense to Social Injustice in Miller's sense. First, Social Injustice in my sense makes for Social Injustice in Miller's sense. If a majority discriminates against a minority over jobs, an unfair distribution of benefits will result. Secondly, and less obviously, the quest for Social Justice in Miller's sense makes for Political Injustice rather than Social Injustice in my sense. For, typically, this quest takes the form of government's practising reverse discrimination and collectivism. But reverse discrimination is unfair (Essay 5). Collectivism is usually criticised on the grounds that it tends to violate the rights to Liberty and Property. But it also tends to violate the right to Justice. For if a government taxes a minority unfairly (excessively) in order to benefit the majority or some other minority, an unfair distribution of burdens will result. These harms tend to be overlooked because, when they are appraising collectivist States, people tend to look to *the proclaimed intentions* of their governments rather than to *the actual consequences* of their governments' policies (Flew, Ch. VII).

4. The Indefeasibility of Justice

So much for the indispensable preliminaries. We are now in a position to answer the two questions to which this essay is addressed (Sec. 1).

We have seen already that Socrates' and Kant's Principles are true to the limited extent that there is one species of Justice the moral right to which is indeed indefeasible, viz. Preliminary Justice. B's moral obligation to give impartial consideration to A's claim to X according to the relevant criteria cannot be overborne by any other moral obligation (Subsec. 2.3). Our next question therefore is whether A's moral right to Non-preliminary Justice is similarly indefeasible.

In order to answer it, we must discover whether B's moral obligation to respect this right can be overborne by his moral obligation to respect (*a*) some other moral right of A; or (*b*) some other moral right of C; or (*c*) C's right to Non-preliminary Justice; or (*d*) the public good (Feinberg 1973, p. 95). Let us consider these possibilities in that order.

4.1 Indefeasibility by Rights

Possibility (*a*). Take the following *Case* (*1*). A is playing roulette and B is the croupier. A has been playing all evening with consistent success and is about to play again. But B knows, though A does not know, that C, who is insanely jealous of A's success, will kill A if he wins the play which he is about to make. B therefore fixes the wheel so that A has no chance of winning this play. Then does B treat A unfairly? The obvious and true answer is that he does, since he cheats A at a game of chance. But this is where Mill's Principle applies (Sec. 1, (*c*)). For we would never in fact allow (i.e. *say*) that B treated A unfairly in acting in such a way as to save his life.[18]

But how does this bear on Socrates' and Kant's Principles (Sec. 1, (*a*) and (*b*))? It shows that they are false. For it is incontrovertible that *in reality* B's moral obligation to play fair with A was overborne by his moral obligation to save A's life. Justice's 'character of indefeasibility' is specious, the mere effect of a linguistic convention. But many, perhaps most or even nearly all, less acute than Mill, have not seen this, and have concluded that the moral right to just treatment *really* is absolute. In this, they have been deceived by our manner of speaking; in which they have not been the first, nor will they be the last. One wonders, indeed, whether Socrates and Kant themselves may not have been deceived by it. However that may be, one must surely dissent from Mill's judgement that 'this accommodation of language', which is actually so misleading, is 'useful'.

Another likely cause of the false belief that Injustice cannot be justified is a confusion of justification with justicization. Injustice cannot, of course, be justicized, since 'justicized Injustice' is a contradiction in terms. But from this it may have been invalidly concluded that Injustice cannot be justified, which is false. (See Subsec. 3.1.)

Two notions which can be clarified in terms of the distinction between 'just' and 'justicized' on the one hand and 'right' and 'justified' on the other hand are 'a just war' and 'a just cause.' For 'a just war' means 'a justified war,' not 'a justicized war,' e.g., a war undertaken in self-defence; and similarly 'a just cause' means 'a rightful cause,' not 'an equitable (or fair) cause.'[19]

But the most likely cause of the false belief that unjust action cannot be morally justified is the confusion of unjust action with morally wrong action. The Greek word *adikein* in Socrates' Principle has both the wide meaning 'to act wrongly' and the narrow meaning 'to act unjustly' (Woozley 1979, pp. 18-21). Kant explains that his principle means that 'Political maxims must . . . proceed from the pure concept of the duty of right or (*sic*) justice (*Rechtspflicht*). . . the principle of which is given *a priori* by pure reason' (p. 180). But the German word *recht* has both the wide meaning 'right' and the narrow meaning 'just'.[20] In all probability, therefore, it is through an unconscious slide from the wide meanings of these words to their narrow meanings that the unassailable truism 'One ought never to act wrongly' has been transformed into the plausible but indefensible Principle 'One ought never to act unjustly.'

Possibility (b). Consider now the following *Case* (2). A is playing roulette, B is the croupier, and A is about to play again. But B knows that if A wins the play which he is about to make, A will use the money to buy a gun with which to kill C, of whose success at Roulette A is insanely jealous. B therefore fixes the wheel so that A has no chance of winning this play. Then does B treat A unfairly? This case is similar to Case (1), and Mill's Principle applies again.

Here another important principle is relevant. Case (2) is a case of conflicting moral rights, viz. A's right to Justice and C's right to Life. In such cases, it is generally believed that the stronger right ought to prevail, and there's an end on't. But MacCormick has recently pointed out that in fact this is not the end of the matter, since in such cases the bearer of the defeated right ought to be appropriately compensated. Let us call this MacCormick's Principle of the Compensatibility of Defeated Rights (MacCormick, pp. 175-7). So, in Case (2), ought A to be compensated for B's violation of A's right to fair play? Surely not, because he has forfeited that right by forming the intention to put the money to a wicked use if he won it. He *had* the right, but he has forfeited it.

MacCormick's Principle is an application to the case of defeated rights of an important Substantive Principle of Reciprocative Justice, namely, the Principle of Complete Compensation (Subsec. 2.2). Naturally, MacCormick's Principle does not apply to the right to compensation itself. Case (2) illustrates this point. If A's moral right to compensation is defeated, or forfeit, A has no moral right to be compensated for that.

Possibility (c). This is the alleged possibility that B's moral obligation to respect A's moral right to Non-preliminary Justice can be overborne by B's moral obligation to respect C's moral right to Non-preliminary Justice. Actually, this alleged possibility does not exist. Take the following two cases, which involve Reciprocative Justice and Non-reciprocative Justice respectively. *Case (3).* The relevant resemblance or difference between A and C is in respect of their contributions to the making of X, and C's contribution is greater than A's. Then B cannot, logically, treat A unfairly by giving indivisible X, or more of divisible X, to C than to A. *Case (4).* The relevant resemblance or difference between A and C is in respect of their needs of X, and C's need is greater than A's. Then B cannot, logically, treat A unfairly by giving indivisible X, or more of divisible X, to C than to A.

There is an important difference here between the right to Justice and other negative, general, moral rights. For although B cannot, logically, violate A's right to Justice by respecting C's right to Justice, he can violate A's right to Liberty by respecting C's right to Liberty. E.g., B respects C's right to free speech, knowing that C will abuse it by shouting A down, and intending that C shall so abuse it. (Feinberg 1973, p. 95.) Similarly with the right to Life. E.g., B respects C's right to Life, knowing that C will abuse it by taking A's life, and intending that C shall so abuse it.

This may seem to support Socrates' and Kant's Principles by showing that A's right to Justice cannot be defeated by C's right to Justice. But in fact it is fatal to them. For in the expression 'indefeasible right' the word 'indefeasible' may mean either 'logically indefeasible' or 'morally indefeasible'. What we have just seen is that A's right to Justice cannot *logically* be defeated by C's right to Justice. But Socrates' and Kant's Principles assert that A's right to Justice cannot *morally* be defeated by C's right to Justice. But since 'ought' implies 'can,' if it is true that B can not ever violate A's right to Justice by respecting C's right to Justice, then it is false that B ought not ever to violate A's right to Justice by respecting C's right to Justice. Here, however, is one more possible cause of the false belief in the indefeasibility of the moral right to Justice. Men may have been misled by mistaking logical indefeasibility for moral indefeasibility. Since A's right to just treatment by B logically cannot conflict with C's right to just treatment by B, A's right is neither morally defeasible nor morally indefeasible by C's, so that MacCormick's Principle does not apply.

4.2 Indefeasibility by Public Good

Take now *Case (5)*. A and the billionaire C are playing roulette, and B is the croupier. B knows that if and only if C wins the next play he will give his superb collection of paintings to the National Gallery. B therefore fixes the wheel so that C is certain to win the next play and A has no chance of winning it. Then does Mill's Principle apply here? I think not. What we would say in this case is not that B did not cheat A, but that he did cheat him, and that the unfairness was morally justified because the social benefit outweighed the individual harm. The discrepancy in this respect between Cases (1) and (2) on the one hand and Case (5) on the other is not a trivial linguistic nicety. On the contrary, and as is so often the case, it reflects a philosophically significant difference. Namely, that we judge B's moral obligation to respect A's and C's rights to Life (and their other negative, general, moral rights) as much stronger than his moral obligation to promote the public good. For, first, the moral obligation not to harm is stronger than that to benefit. Secondly, it is easier to be sure that an individual right will be violated than that the public will be benefited (Raphael, 149). It is indisputable that B will violate A's right to Justice if he fixes the wheel. But doubt about the social benefit of C giving his paintings to the National Gallery arises over such questions as what proportion of the public profess to like paintings, whether their professions are sincere or manifestations of cultural snobbery, and so on. Consequently, we are reluctant to allow that a man can act unjustly in respecting these rights; whereas we feel no such compunction at allowing that a man can forward the public good by acting unjustly.

But if Mill's Principle does not apply to Case (5), MacCormick's

Principle does apply. Who, then, has the moral obligation to compensate A, the bearer of the defeated right to Justice? In principle, it is always and only the maltreater, B, who can and ought to compensate the maltreatee, A.[21] Yet in Case (5) it would surely be unfair to leave the matter at that. Justice requires that B be reimbursed for compensating A by the beneficiaries of B's unfair treatment of A, namely, the general public.

5. Conclusion

The answers to the two questions posed in Sec. 1 are as follows. First, Woozley's criticism of Socrates' and Kant's Principles is justified — indeed justicized — since they contain much more falsity than truth. For, of the five species of Justice distinguished in Subsec. 2.2, only one, as several philosophers have recognised, is indefeasible, namely, Preliminary Justice. The work in Sec. 4 has consisted in showing in some detail how and why Non-preliminary Justice is not indefeasible, and in unearthing the probable causes of the false belief that it is so. Secondly, Mill's Principle does not give the true explanation of why Justice is indefeasible. Rather, it provides an interesting and significant part of the true explanation of why men falsely believe it to be so.

APPENDIX I: JUSTICE AND THE ALLOCATION OF BURDENS

There is no symmetry between Justice in the allocation of benefits and Justice in the allocation of burdens; just as, in general, there is no symmetry between giving pleasure and giving pain. This is reflected in the fact that, although the same Formal Principles govern Justice in both areas — viz., Simonides' Definition and Aristotle's Principle — the relevant Substantive Principles are different in the one area from what they are in the other.

I have said that the Substantive Principles which regulate the just allocation of benefits seem to me to be, for Reciprocative Justice, the Principle of Direct Proportionality to Contribution and the Principle of Complete Compensation; and for Non-reciprocative Justice, the Principle of Direct Proportionality to Need (Subsec. 2.3).

I shall indicate the Substantive Principles which regulate the just allocation of burdens by a very brief discussion of fairness in income tax. (See Lucas, Ch. 14.) The relevant Reciprocative Principles are, first, the Principle of Fair Exchange. This requires citizens to contribute to the exchequer in direct proportion to the benefit which they receive from the State. C, who has a large 'stake in the country', should contribute proportionally more than A, who has a small stake in it. For C, who is e.g. the owner of a large estate, derives much more benefit from the forces of law and order which maintain internal and external security than does A.[22] The second relevant Reciprocative Principle is another Principle of Complete Compensation. E.g., through a fault in the computer, the collector B demanded too little income tax from A last year. B therefore demands from A this year as much tax as will redress the situation taking both this year and last year into the account. In the allocation of benefits, the Principle of Complete Compensation requires B to return to A an equivalent good in consideration of the evil which B did to A. But in the allocation of burdens, the Principle of Complete Compensation requires B to return to A an equivalent evil in consideration of the good which B did to A. (See Eckhoff, p. 4.)

The relevant Non-reciprocative Principle is the Principle of the Fair Allocation of Pain. Because of the diminishing marginal utility of money, C, who is rich, can contribute more than A, who is not rich, yet suffer equal pain with A. Here, however, the view about Justice in income tax which prevails at present departs radically from Aristotle's Principle. That Principle requires contribution to be directly proportional to income. But the present view is that income tax ought to be progressive or graduated; i.e. that the proportion should increase as income increases. It may well be, nevertheless, that Aristotle's Principle is what Justice really requires, and that the prevailing belief that progressive income tax is fair is no more than a striking evidence of the great inroads which egalitarian ideas have made amongst us.[23]

APPENDIX II: THE INDEFEASIBILITY OF PRELIMINARY JUSTICE

My claim that the moral right to Equality of Consideration is absolute or unconditional is open to the objection that it may be practically impossible to give equal consideration to the claims of all concerned. E.g., if there are 200 applications for a university teaching post in Philosophy, it may not be possible for the selectors to give equal consideration to all of them in the time available. The right must therefore be understood to be subject to this important proviso.

Notes

1. I call this principle 'Kant's Principle' because he is its most eminent advocate, not because he originated it. It probably derives from the Old Testament (Vecchio, pp. 174 and 175).

2. But not things or events, or animals. 'Strictly speaking, only human conduct can be called just or unjust . . . Nature can be neither just nor unjust' (Hayek, pp. 31 and 32). 'Are we demanding too much of ourselves morally? Over two millennia ago the neo-Platonist Porphyry argued that human civilization would collapse if men were to try to extend justice to animals' (Passmore, p. 47).

3. Burke maintains that the latter is an artificial special relationship, because society is 'a partnership between those who are living, those who are dead, and those who are to be born' (*Reflections on the Revolution in France:* Barry, p. 69). But this inflates the workaday notion of a partnership into nonsense. What is the use of the concept of a partnership between doctors, some of whom are living, others of whom are dead, and yet others of whom are to be born?

4. On the resemblances between Plato's and Rawls' conceptions of Justice see Flew, Ch. III.

5. The word *opheilomena*, translated as 'due', has a strong suggestion of 'debt'. The concept is obviously reciprocative, because X is due to A from B *because*, e.g., B has borrowed X from A. Simonides' Definition is not to be found in the fragments of the poet Simonides. [See *Plato's Republic*, tr. Paul Shorey (London: Heinemann, 1937, p. 20, note c).] But it is to be found in the *Odyssey* of the poet Homer at 14, 84 (Pieper, p. 111, n. 3).

6. ' . . . there are two species of justice, distributive and commutative' (Thomas, p. 89).

7. A *piquant* feature of the story of the Judgement of Solomon in his pretending to treat as a divisible good something which is a paradigm of an indivisible one (I *Kings*, iii, 16-26).

8. Sometimes, however, B's recourse to dicing etc. is regarded not as a way of giving A and C an equal chance of obtaining X, but as a way of referring the decision to a supernatural power, who or which will certainly decide the matter justly. (See, e.g., Plato, *Laws*, 757.) Sometimes the two views are combined, when Chance is regarded as a supernatural agency, the goddess *Fortuna*. This view was held before the concept of Chance was understood, and Chance was regarded as a sort of cause rather than as the absence of a cause. (See Rescher, pp. 93-5; Eckhoff, pp. 215-18; Essay 2, Note 13.)

9. 'An act . . . can only be said to be just if it is based . . . on correct information' (Friedrich, p. 38).

10. 'Honest indignation is the voice of God' (William Blake).

11. Dr Johnson defended persecution on similar grounds. Indeed, we have just seen that persecution is the extreme form of Injustice. Cf. Stephen, pp. 93-113.

12. The useful distinction between 'to justify' and 'to justicize' is due to Frankena.

13. Thomas ranks Justice highest of the three cardinal moral virtues, the others being Fortitude and Temperance (Pieper, p. 42).

14. Berlin has drawn attention to a similar tendency to hyperinflate the ideal of Liberty into the only good (Berlin, pp. 167-72); cf. Flew, pp. 67 and 68; Passmore, pp. 47 and 48).

15. . . . justice, that chief law of nature and bond of every society' (Locke, p. 169; Hume, *Enquiry*, pp. 201, 203; cf Lucas, pp. 1, 18 and 19.)

16. Cf. the corresponding important distinction between Political Liberty and Social Liberty drawn most notably in Mill's *On Liberty*.

17. Mill uses the expression 'social and distributive justice' in Miller's sense (Mill, *Utilitarianism*, p. 58).

18. The meaning of Mill's Principle becomes clearer if his penultimate sentence is

rewritten as follows: 'In such cases, as we do not call anything unfair which is not morally wrong, we usually say, not that fairness must give way to some other moral principle (e.g. the obligation to save a life), but that what is unfair in ordinary cases (e.g. cheating) is by reason of that other principle, not unfair in the particular case.' C.L. Ten comments on this passage in his *Mill on Liberty* (Clarendon Press, Oxford, 1980, pp. 65 and 66). See also Frankena, pp. 5 and 6.

19. The expression 'a fair (= justicized) war' does indeed have a meaning, but it is a different meaning from that of 'a just (= justified) war'. The former means 'a fairly fought war' and relates to fairness *in* a war (*jus in bello*). It is a question of observing the prevailing rules respecting, e.g., the treatment of prisoners. The latter means 'a rightfully undertaken war' and relates to the rightfulness *of* a war (*jus ad bellum*). It is a question of, e.g., a war undertaken in self-defence. A just war can be unfair, and a fair war can be unjust. The explanation of this apparent paradox is that 'a just war' is a misnomer for 'a (morally) justified war'. (See Walzer, p. 21.)

20. Cf. 'The difficulties of translating the *Grundlinien der Philosophie des Rechts* begin with the title' (T.M. Knox, in Hegel, p. vi). Similarly, the French word *droit* has both the wide meaning 'right' and the narrow meaning 'just'.

21. Similarly, the only person who can apologise to A for having wronged him is B who wronged him. C can express regret to A at B's having wronged him, but C cannot, logically, apologise to A for this (Subsec. 3.1 of Essay 5). This is in fact another illustration of the compensation principle, since apology is a (very weak) sort of compensation.

22. Admittedly, this argument applies to property rather than to income. But the two are intimately connected, since (large) properties are usually sources of income. The owner of the large estate in the example will receive rent from his tenants. (See Benn and Peters, pp. 165-70.)

23. '. . . incomes above the limit (below which they should not be taxed at all) should be taxed only in proportion to the surplus by which they exceed the limit' (Mill, *Political Economy*, p. 831; see also pp. 805-13; cf. Benn and Peters, pp. 151-64; Friedman, pp. 133, 174-6).

References

The following abbreviations refer to books which are collections of articles:

'Brandt'. R.B. Brandt (ed.), *Social Justice* (Prentice-Hall, Englewood Cliffs, 1962).

'Cohen'. M. Cohen, T. Nagel and T. Scanlon (eds), *Equality and Preferential Treatment* (University Press, Princeton, 1977).

'Friedrich'. C.J. Friedrich and J.W. Chapman (eds), *Justice: Nomos* VI (Atherton Press, New York, 1963).

'Kamenka'. E. Kamenka and A.E. Tay (eds), *Justice* (Arnold, London, 1979).

'Kelbley'. C.A. Kelbley (ed.), *The Value of Justice* (Fordham University Press, New York, 1979).

'Pennock'. J.R. Pennock and J.W. Chapman (eds.), *Equality: Nomos* IX (Atherton Press, New York, 1967).

Aristotle, *Ethica Nicomachea*, tr. W.D. Ross in *The Works of Aristotle*, Vol. 9 (University Press, Oxford, 1915).

Barry, B., 'Justice as Reciprocity' in Kamenka.

Benn, S.I., 'Egalitarianism and the Equal Consideration of Interests' in Pennock.

Benn, S.I. and Peters, R.S., *Social Principles and the Democratic State* (Allen and Unwin, London, 1959).

Berlin, I., *Four Essays on Liberty* (University Press, Oxford, 1969).

Chapman, J.W., 'Justice and Fairness' in Friedrich.
Eckhoff, T., *Justice* (University Press, Rotterdam, 1974).
Feinberg, J., *Social Philosophy* (Prentice-Hall, Englewood Cliffs, 1973).
'Noncomparative Justice', *The Philosophical Review*, Vol. 83 (1974).
Fiss, O.M., 'Groups and the Equal Protection Clause' in Cohen.
Flew, A.G.N., *The Politics of Procrustes* (Temple Smith, London, 1981).
Frankena, W., 'The Concept of Social Justice' in Brandt.
Friedman, M., *Capitalism and Freedom*, Reissue (University Press, Chicago, 1982).
Friedrich, C.J., 'Justice: The Just Political Act' in Friedrich.
Gewirth, A., 'Political Justice' in Brandt.
Hare, R.M. *The Language of Morals* (Clarendon Press, Oxford, 1952).
Hart, H.L.A., *The Concept of Law* (Clarendon Press, Oxford, 1961).
Hayek, F.A., *Law, Legislation and Liberty*, Vol. 2 (Routledge and Kegan Paul, London, 1976).
Hegel, G.W.F., *Philosophy of Right*, tr. T.M. Knox (Clarendon Press, Oxford, 1942).
Hume, D., *A Treatise of Human Nature*, ed. L.A. Selby-Bigge (Clarendon Press, Oxford, 1896).
—— *An Enquiry Concerning the Principles of Morals* in *Hume's Enquiries*, ed. L.A. Selby-Bigge, 2nd edn (Clarendon Press, Oxford, 1903).
Justinian, *The Institutes*, tr. J.A.C. Thomas (North Holland, Amsterdam, 1975).
Kamenka, E., 'What is Justice?' in Kamenka.
Kant, I., *Perpetual Peace*, tr. M.C. Smith (Swan Sonnenschein, London, 1903).
Kelbley, C.A., 'Justice and Goodness' in Kelbley.
Locke, J., *Essays on the Law of Nature*, ed. W. von Leyden (Clarendon Press, Oxford, 1954).
Lucas, J.R., *On Justice* (Clarendon Press, Oxford, 1980).
MacCormick, D.N., 'The Obligation of Reparation', *Aristotelian Society Proceedings*, Vol. 78 (1978).
Mill, JI.S. *On Liberty, Utilitarianism*, both in *Utilitarianism, Liberty and Representative Government* (Dent, London, 1910).
Principles of Political Economy, ed. J.M. Robson (University Press, Toronto, 7th edn, 1965).
Miller, D., *Social Justice* (Clarendon Press, Oxford, 1976).
Passmore, J.A., 'Civil Justice and its Rivals' in Kamenka.
Perelman, C., *The Idea of Justice and the Problem of Argument*, tr. J. Petrie (Routledge and Kegan Paul, London, 1963).
Pieper, J., *Justice*, tr. L.E. Lynch (Faber and Faber, London, 1957).
Plato, *Crito*, tr. A.D. Woozley, in Woozley 1979.
—— *Gorgias*, tr. T. Irwin (Clarendon Press, Oxford, 1979).
—— *The Republic*, tr. F.M. Cornford (Oxford University Press, London, 1941).
Raphael, D.D., *Justice and Liberty* (Athlone Press, London, 1980).
Rawls, J., *A Theory of Justice* (Harvard University Press, Cambridge, Mass., 1971).
Rescher, N., *Distributive Justice* (Bobbs-Merrill, Indianapolis, 1966).
Richards, D.A.J., 'Reverse Discrimination and Compensatory Justice' in Kelbley.
Stephen, J.F., *Liberty, Equality, Fraternity*, 2nd edn (Smith, Elder, London, 1874).
Stone, J., 'Justice not Equality' in Kamenka.
Strawson, P.F., 'Freedom and Resentment', *British Academy Proceedings*, Vol. 48 (1962).
Tay, A.E. 'The Sense of Justice in the Common Law' in Kamenka.
Taylor, C., 'The Nature and Scope of Distributive Justice' in his *Philosophical Papers*, 2 (Cambridge University Press, Cambridge, 1985).
Thomas Aquinas, *Summa Theologiae*, Vol. 37, tr. T. Gilby (Blackfriars, London, 1975).
Vecchio, G. del, *Justice*, ed. A.H. Campbell, tr. Lady Guthrie (University Press, Edinburgh, 1952).
Vlastos, G., 'Justice and Equality', in Brandt.

Walzer, M., *Just and Unjust Wars* (Allen Lane, London, 1978).
Woozley, A.D., 'Injustice' in *Studies in Ethics, American Philosophical Quarterly Monograph No. 7* (Blackwell, Oxford, 1973).
—— *Law and Obedience* (University of North Carolina Press, Chapel Hill, 1979).

9 PROCEDURAL EQUALITY: A REPLY TO MR INGRAM

Introduction

The sort of procedural equality with which Mr Ingram is concerned is, naturally, *legal* procedural equality, i.e. the equal application of laws in individual cases, and in this I shall follow him. There are also, of course, questions of *non-legal* procedural equality. For example, there is the problem of applying the general rule that the competitors in a running race shall run equal distances to a particular case in which there are two competitors and the course is a circuit. The solution is not to start the competitors level, but to give the one in the outer lane such a start over the one in the inner lane as will equalise the distances that they have to run. By 'a law' Ingram understands a certain sort of general rule, and in this too I shall follow him.

The Application of General Rules

Ingram stresses the importance of 'the elaboration of what the application of law means'. This question does indeed provide an ideal point of entry into our topic. Consider, then, the following case. Rule 13 of the Drones' Club provides that every member shall pay his annual subscription to the Club on or before 1 January, on pain of expulsion in the event of non-compliance. On 2 January the appropriate Committee meet to consider the case of B. Wooster, whose subscription the Club has not received. Inquiry reveals the facts in the case to be as follows. On 1 January Wooster had written a cheque payable to the Club in the correct sum. But, being in a delicate condition after the New Year's Eve festivities, he had not delivered it in person, but had instructed his man, Jeeves, to do so. Jeeves, however — most uncharacteristically — had forgotten his instructions. The Committee are divided over the construction of the words 'pay his annual subscription to the Club' in Rule 13. The drys maintain that 'to pay' is what Ryle calls 'an achievement verb';[1] so that although Wooster had indeed *attempted to pay* his subscription, the fact that the Club did not receive it proves that he did not *pay* it. The wets, on the other hand, find nothing illogical in saying that *A* paid *X* to *B* although *B* did not receive *X*. They prevail, so that the minutes of the meeting of the Committee include the following sentence: 'The Committee decided not to apply Rule 13 in Wooster's case, since they considered that this rule did not apply to this case'.[2]

This compound sentence brings out some important points about the application of general rules in individual cases. First, there is an essential distinction of meaning to be made which, as is so often the case, is clearly indicated by a difference in a natural language. It is the distinction between *applying (transitive)* a general rule *in* a particular case and a general rule *applying (intransitive) to* a particular case. The former use of 'apply' is found in the simple sentence before the connective 'since' and the latter use of 'apply' is found in the simple sentence after it.[3] Secondly, the fact that the compound sentence is not a tautology of the form '*P* since *P*' shows that 'apply' does not mean the same thing in both its appearances. And this is indeed so. For in deciding not to apply Rule 13 in this case the Committee decided not to *execute* it. But in judging that Rule 13 did not apply to this case the Committee *interpreted* it. Thirdly, both executing a general rule and interpreting it are actions. In the case of execution this is obvious, but in the case of interpretation it is apt to be obscured by talk of particular cases 'falling under' general rules, which misleadingly suggests that this is something which simply happens. But it is not so. Individual cases do not just fall under general rules, they have to be deemed so to fall. Finally, the connective 'since' in the compound sentence reveals a vital connexion between the two concepts of application. Namely that, before applying a general rule in a particular case, one must always first satisfy oneself that this rule applies to this case. To fail to do so is to commit the fault of applying the rule 'mechanically'.

Three Theses on the Application of Laws

Using this distinction between the two concepts of application, Ingram's theses on the application of laws can be formulated as follows.

(i) *The Logical Thesis. Every law must, logically, be applied in every case to which it applies.* For any putative 'law' which is not so applied is not truly called 'a law'. There is only 'a statement on paper of prescriptive form'.

Here I disagree. For consider the following extreme case. A criminal statute provides that it shall be a capital offence to steal a sheep. But this barbaric law has never been applied, because juries have always refused to convict persons charged with this offence.[4] Moreover, it is inductively certain that they will continue to refuse to do so, so that it is certain that this law never will be applied. Nevertheless, until it is repealed, the law still exists, because it *can* be applied. Doubtless, in the circumstances described, the law would commonly be called 'a dead letter'. Yet the appellation would be inaccurate. For so long as it remains on the statute book, and so can be applied, it is not dead but dormant.

This important distinction between *being applied* and *being applicable* has an interesting parallel in a different field of philosophy. For compare (1) 'A law exists if and only if it is applied' (false) and 'A law exists if and only if it is applicable' (true) with (2) 'A material object exists if and only if it is perceived' (false) and 'A material object exists if and only if it is perceptible' (true).[5]

(ii) *The Practical Thesis. Every law must, practically, be applied in every case to which it applies.* For if it is not, people will not know for certain where they stand with respect to the laws, so that the laws will fail to fulfil one of their essential functions, which is to enable people to plan their affairs effectively.

This thesis seems to me to be important and substantially true, but to need modification in two significant respects. First, I think that the property of enabling persons to plan their affairs effectively, which is what Hayek and Raz understand by 'the Rule of Law', is a property of legal systems rather than of single laws.[6] Secondly, Ingram surely expects too much in demanding certainty. For it is *probability*, in the sense of the more-probable-than-not, and not its upper limit, certainty, which is the very guide of life.[7] So I suggest that the Practical Thesis be reformulated as follows: *Most of the laws of any legal system must, practically, be applied in most of the cases to which they apply.* For if they are not, there will no *Rule of Law* in the state in which the legal system in question obtains. The probability which is required for guiding action is provided by the two occurrences of the quantifier 'most'.

This reformulation allows to administrators a desirable discretion to forbear to apply some laws at all, on the grounds that they are immoral, or pointless, or unenforceable. For example, a law of New York State provides that it shall be a offence for anyone to hold a poker party in his private house. This law is broken many thousands of times every day, but an indifferent police exercise their discretion by turning a blind eye.[8]

The reformulation also permits a desirable exercise of prerogative power or administrative discretion in cases where equity or *clemency* require it. An example of the latter is the Home Secretary's power of pardon. As for the former, Aristotle recognised that *law* (*nomos*) ought sometimes to be overridden by *equity* (*epieikeia*) in order to achieve 'a correction of law where law is defective owing to its generality'.[9] For an illustration of this, let us return to the Drones' Club. On 2 January the Committee have to consider as well as Wooster's case that of the Father of the Club, whose subscription has also not been received. Inquiry reveals that this is because he has forgotten to pay it, which in turn is because he is so old that he habitually forgets to do most of the things which he has to do. The Committee exercise their discretion by deciding not to apply Rule 13 in his case. For they recognise that his case is 'special'. For Rule 13 is 'defective owing to its generality' because, applying as it does to every member, it fails to distinguish between members who suffer from incapacitating disabilities and members who do not. If Rule 13 had distinguished these two classes of members, it would have *discriminated between* them; which is a good thing to do. But by failing to discriminate between them, it *discriminates against* the former class; which is a bad thing to do. For *B* can discriminate against *A* by disregarding a relevant difference between *A* and *C* as well as by paying regard to an irrelevant difference between *A* and *C*, such as sex or skin-colour. The effect of paying regard to irrelevant differences is to treat differently those who are alike in relevant respects. The effect of disregarding relevant difference is to treat alike those who are different in relevant respects. By Aristotle's Rule of Justice (Sec. 4, below) both are unjust.[10]

Special cases are different from *hard cases*. The former arise when some general rule is 'defective owing to its generality'. But the latter arise when it is difficult to decide whether some general rule does or does not apply to an individual case; or when some individual case can be subsumed under two or more incompatible general rules. The second alternative is the legal analogue of the ethical problem of conflicting moral obligations. Wooster's case is a hard case because it exemplifies the first alternative, but it is not a special case. Conversely, the Father's case is a special case, but it is not a hard case. Nevertheless, the Committee might have dealt with the Father's case in the same way as they might have dealt with Wooster's case. That is, they might have found him in breach of Rule 13 but excused him on account of his disability.[11]

Ingram's remarks on administrative discretion and legal systems lead me to hope and to believe that he will be willing to accept my reformulation of his Practical Thesis.

(iii) *The Moral Thesis. Every law must, morally, be applied in every case to which it applies.* For if it is not, people will be less *happy* than if it is.

There seems to me to be important truth in this thesis too. But I think that it needs both modification and qualification. As to modification, I suggest that it needs to be reformulated in the same way as the Practical Thesis, thus: *Most of the laws of any legal system must, morally, be applied in most of the cases to which they apply.* For if they are not, there will be no Rule of Law in the state in which the legal system in question obtains. In consequence, there will be a general feeling of insecurity. This 'feeling' has propositional content, namely, that citizens will believe that they cannot rely on officials or on each other. But the result of this will be in turn that they will suffer a painful emotion, anxiety.

The vital qualification is this. Although it is true that the absence of the Rule of Law thus makes for unhappiness, it is also true that the presence of the Rule of Law makes for unhappiness, because it curtails *liberty.* The connexion between the Rule of Law and unhappiness is indirect but real, as follows. First, some (but not all) laws are backed by threats, and threats (if effective, as most legal threats are) curtail liberty. This is obviously true of criminal laws. But civil law is also coercive, since court orders are backed by threats of punishment for contempt in the event of recalcitrance. Enabling laws provide an example of laws which are not backed by threats and so do not abridge liberty. It must be remembered, however, that coercive laws can secure liberty as well as curtail it. A criminal law against kidnapping diminishes the liberty of potential kidnappers, but protects the liberty of potential kidnappees. Thus Locke: ' . . . liberty is to be free from restraint . . . from others; which cannot be where there is no law'.[12] Secondly, some (but not all) reductions of liberty cause a painful emotion, a feeling of frustration. But it is only those curtailments of liberty which restrain or deter a person from doing something *which he desires to do* which will cause him to feel frustrated.

The business world provides the classic illustration of how laws can enable citizens to plan their affairs effectively, which is the root idea of the Rule of Law. Consider the criminal laws against robbery and theft, which protect *private property.* They are specimens of what Hume and Smith call 'the rules of justice'. These positive laws provide a framework of order within which *entrepreneurs* can operate freely. These free operations produce a universal, self-regulating, economic system which is also ordered in a different way, namely, by scientific (economic) laws, such as Ricardo's Laws of Rent and of Comparative Advantage. The other salient features of this 'system of economic liberty', as Marshall calls it, besides private property and free enterprise, are the division of labour, competition, free contract, free trade and the unintended benefiting of others by acting in such a way as to benefit oneself (Smith's 'invisible hand'). This is a consequential argument of great weight in favour of these laws. For the system of economic liberty, to the existence of which they are indispensable, is a highly efficient means of production of wealth, so that they benefit all greatly.[13] They can also be defended on the ground that they safeguard a negative, general, moral right, namely, private property.[14] Furthermore, they illustrate vividly how laws can secure liberty by curtailing it. For by abridging the liberty of potential thieves and robbers they secure freedom of enterprise to businessmen. (Cf. the law against kidnapping, above.)

But if the Rule of Law, as it applies to the business world, requires businessmen to be legally protected from force and fraud by their fellow citizens, it also requires them to be legally protected from the depredations of governments. This might be achieved by, for instance, constitutional laws which made illegal capital levies, or taxes which are retroactive or too complicated to be intelligible.[15]

The unhappiness caused by the presence of the Rule of Law is by no means comparable to the unhappiness caused by its absence. We need shed no tears over the frustration suffered by would-be retroactive taxers, fraudulent operators, muggers and thieves who are deterred from their malpractices by laws. The insecurity suffered by honest toilers who are not protected from these malpractices by laws is quite another matter. Nevertheless, it is desirable to remember that, while the Rule of Law is undoubtedly on balance a good thing, it is not purely felicific.

The Relationship of Legal Procedural Equality to Justice

As Ingram truly says, 'in straightforward and typical cases' legal procedural equality is a necessary condition of justice. The nonstraightforward and atypical cases in which justice requires legal procedural inequality are precisely the 'special cases' discussed above. The reason why justice normally requires legal procedural equality is that the *Rule of Equal Legal Application* can be subsumed under *Aristotle's Rule of Justice*, which is best rendered: *Treat alike (equally) those who are alike (equal) in relevant respects, and treat differently (unequally) those who are different (unequal) in relevant respects in direct proportion to the relevant differences (inequalities) between them.*[16] This rule is correct. The Rule of Equal Legal Application comes under the first part of it.

That is, in applying a law, *L*, in the cases of *A* and *C*, justice requires *B* to apply *L* in both cases if *L* applies to both cases. For the relevant resemblance between *A* and *C* is precisely that *L* applies to both of them.

As Ingram also truly says, legal procedural equality is not the sufficient condition of justice. For there are other necessary conditions of justice. One is the non-legal procedural equality mentioned above. Again, as the second part of Aristotle's Rule shows, justice sometimes — indeed, far more often than not — requires inequality and not equality.[17]

But this is not the end of the matter. For, as the Rule of Equal Legal Application can be subsumed under Aristotle's Rule of Justice, so Aristotle's Rule can be subsumed under *Simonides' Rule of Justice*. This is best rendered: *Return to every man his due*.[18] The word *opheilomena*, translated as 'due', has a strong suggestion of 'debt'. It is a *reciprocative* concept, since *X* is due to *A* from *B* because, e.g., *B* has borrowed X from *A*. In general, *X* is due to *A*, not because of what *A is* (e.g. needy), but because of what *A has done* (e.g. contributed to the making of *X*) or *has had done to him* (e.g. *A* has been injured by *B*). It is therefore also a *retrospective* concept.[19]

Simonides' Rule is the correct *formal* rule of *reciprocative justice*. *Substantive* rules of reciprocative justice give content to it by specifying what is due to *A*, from whom, and why. For example, *Let B (the competent authority) punish A with degree of severity n because A has committed an offence with degree of gravity n!* This is the rule of making the punishment fit the crime. Aristotle's Rule follows from it because it requires that, if *A* and *C* are equal in respect of degree of gravity of offence, then *B* should treat them equally in respect of degree of severity of the punishment which he inflicts on them; but that if they are unequal in the former respect, then *B* should treat them unequally in the latter respect in direct proportion to their inequality in the former respect.[20] So, as (in normal cases) obeying the Rule of Equal Legal Application is a necessary condition of obeying Aristotle's Rule, and obeying Aristotle's Rule is a necessary condition of obeying Simonides' Rule; so (in normal cases) obeying the Rule of Equal Legal Application is a necessary condition of obeying Simonides' Rule.

Ulpian expanded Simonides' Definition thus: 'Justice is the settled and enduring intention of returning to every man his due' (*Justitia est constans et perpetua voluntas jus suum cuique tribuens*).[21] This brings out some crucial points about justice. First, that 'justice' means both '*just treatment*' and '*justness*'. Simonides' Definition is the true definition of the former in the reciprocative area. But *Ulpian's Definition* is a false definition of the latter in the reciprocative area. It is false because it is too narrow. For the *just will* of which he writes is not identical with justness. It is only one of the three necessary conditions of justness, the other two being *impartiality* and *judgement*.

However, justness and just treatment are closely connected. For 'justness' means 'the *moral virtue* which disposes a man to treat men justly'. Just treatment, on the other hand, is not a moral virtue, but (like life and liberty) a negative, general, *moral right*. Why, then, does justice not figure in the famous declarations of natural (human) rights? Because its place in them has been usurped by *equality*, as in the French Revolutionary slogan, 'Liberty, Equality, Fraternity!' But it is justice, not equality, which is the moral right; and, as we have seen, justice is not identical with equality, although it is closely connected with it.

Plato and Aristotle considered justness, not just action, to be the primary notion.[22] But in this they were mistaken. One might try to support their view by defining 'just treatment' as 'the treatment which the just man is disposed to accord to men'. But this will not do. For the just man will not *act* justly unless the information on which he acts is *true*. But a man can *be* just although the information on which he acts is false, so that he does not act justly and may *appear* to act unjustly. So it is just treatment which is the primary notion in terms of which justness must be defined.

As the will to be just is a necessary condition of justness, and the intention to be unjust is a necessary condition of unjustness; so *intention* is also necessary for just and unjust action.[23] This is conceptually connected with the fact that just treatment is a moral right. For one can neither respect nor violate a moral right unintentionally. In this respect justice resembles liberty. For as, in its full and proper sense, unfair treatment must be intentional; so, in its full and proper sense, *coercion* (= the violation of the negative, general, moral right to liberty) must also be intentional.[24]

APPENDIX I

I argue in Subsec. 3.1 that a law exists if and only if it is applicable (i.e. can be executed). The most obvious way in which a law can cease to be applicable and so to exist, and the way mentioned in the text, is by being repealed. But it is not the only way. For suppose that the penalty for stealing a sheep had been, not death, but transportation to Australia. Then the law would have been applicable so long as the Australian States were British colonies, since the British authorities could have sent convicts to Australia. But it would not have been applicable after the Commonwealth of Australia became an independent Dominion. For if the British authorities had attempted to send criminals to Australia after that date, the Australian immigration officers would have refused them permission to land. In these circumstances, if the 'law' had not been repealed and the words had still remained on the English statute book, they would have ceased to exist *as a law*. They would have become a dead letter.

APPENDIX II

In Sec. 4 I say that 'a man can *be* just although the information on which he acts is false, so that he does not *act* justly and may appear to act unjustly'. This needs elucidation.

First, 'just treatment' and 'unjust treatment' are contraries and not contradictories. E.g., if *B* treats *A* generously, then *B* does not treat *A* unjustly and *B* does not treat *A* justly.[25] So we need to distinguish unjust actions from just actions, from actions which are not just, and from actions which are not unjust. (Cf. the need to distinguish involuntary actions from voluntary actions, from actions which are not voluntary, and from actions which are not involuntary.)

Secondly, on how actions which are not just may appear to be unjust. Suppose that: (1) *B* is dividing *X* between *A* and *C*; (2) the only relevant resemblance or difference between *A* and *C* is contribution to making *X*; (3) *A*'s contribution is greater than *C*'s; (4) *B* is a just man who intends to treat *A* and *C* fairly; but (5) *B* believes falsely that *C*'s contribution is greater than *A*'s. Then *B* allocates more of *X* to *C* than to *A*, and thereby *unintentionally* does not treat *A* justly. *D*, however, believes falsely that *B* is acting on *B*'s true belief that *A*'s contribution is greater than *C*'s. So *D* infers wrongly that *B* is *intentionally* treating *A* unjustly, say because *B* is partial to C. 'Unjust treatment' *means* 'intentional treatment which is not just'. Similarly, 'coercion (= restraint)' *means* 'intentional prevention'. If *B* intentionally treats *A* unjustly, then *B* violates *A*'s moral right to justice. But if *B* unintentionally does not treat *A* justly, then *B* does not violate *A*'s moral right to justice. Similarly, if *B* intentionally restrains *A* from doing *X*, then *B* violates *A*'s moral right to liberty. But if *B* unintentionally prevents *A* from doing *X*, then *B* does not violate *A*'s moral right to liberty.

Notes

1. See G. Ryle, *The Concept of Mind* (Hutchinson, London, 1949), pp. 149-53.

2. Of course, even if the drys had prevailed Wooster need not have been expelled from the Club. The Committee might have found him in breach of Rule 13, but have considered that his attempt to pay was an exculpating circumstance.

3. Cf. with the verb 'to apply' the verb 'to fit'. 'After three fittings the suit fitted him perfectly' exemplifies both the transitive and the intransitive uses, in that order.

4. This sort of thing did in fact happen in England in the eighteenth and nineteenth centuries.

5. See Berkeley, *The Principles of Human Knowledge*, pt. 1, sec. 3; Mill, *Examination of Hamilton*, Ch. 11, appendix to Chs. 11 and 12.

6. See J. Raz, 'The Rule of Law and its Virtue' in his *Authority of Law* (Clarendon Press, Oxford, 1979).

7. This famous remark is usually attributed to Butler, and it is certainly to be found in the introduction to his *Analogy of Religion*. But a Latin scholar has told me that it is also to be found in, and probably originates with, Cicero. See also J.R. Lucas, *The Concept of Probability* (Clarendon Press, Oxford, 1970), Ch. 1.

8. On discretion, see H.L.A. Hart, *The Concept of Law* (Clarendon Press, Oxford, 1961), Ch. 7.

9. See Sec. 1 of Essay 7.

10. See Sec. 2 of Essay 5.

11. See R. Dworkin, *Taking Rights Seriously* (Duckworth, London, 1977), Chs. 2-4.

12. *Second Treatise of Civil Government*, sec. 57.

13. See F.A. Hayek, *Law, Legislation and Liberty*, Vol. 1 (Routledge and Kegan Paul, London, 1973), Ch. 2; Vol. 2 (Routledge and Kegan Paul, London, 1976), Ch. 10. Cf. Sec. 2 of Essay 12.

14. There is, of course,no inconsistency in advancing both *consequential (utilitarian) arguments* and *arguments from general (human) rights* in support of some value, such as justice, liberty or private property. In no classic philosopher is this clearer than in Locke, who habitually appeals to 'the public good' as well as to 'natural rights'.

15. See J.R. Lucas, *On Justice* (Clarendon Press, Oxford, 1980). Ch. 14.

16. *E.N.* 1131a 19-24. Cf. J. Feinberg, *Social Philosophy* (Prentice-Hall, Englewood Cliffs, 1973), p. 100.

17. Aristotle calls the ordinary equality mentioned in the first part of his Rule 'arithmetical equality' and the proportional equality mentioned in the second part of his Rule 'geometrical equality'. On the relationship of justice to equality see A. Flew, *The Politics·of Procrustes* (Temple Smith, London, 1981), Chs. 2-4; J. Stone, 'Justice not Equality' in E. Kamenka and A.E. Tay (eds.), *Justice* (Arnold, London, 1979).

18. Plato in fact renders this principle in the form of a definition, not of a rule, as follows: *Justice is returning to every man his due* (*To ta opheilomena ekasto apodidonai dikaion esti*(*The Republic*, 331E). See also Lucas, *On Justice*, Ch. 1 (Note 15 above). Simonides' Definition is not to be found among the fragments of the poet Simonides. But it is to be found in the *Odyssey* of the poet Homer at 14, 84.

19. On justice and reciprocity, see T. Eckhoff, *Justice* (University Press, Rotterdam, 1974), pp. 3-10 and part II; B. Barry, 'Justice as Reciprocity' in Kamenka and Tay, *Justice* (Note 17 above).

20. See D. Miller, *Social Justice* (Clarendon Press, Oxford, 1976), pp. 20-1. Aristotle's Rule is also formal, and needs to be supplemented by substantive principles specifying which resemblances and differences between *A* and *C* are 'relevant'. In my view, these are, in the domain of reciprocative justice, contribution and compensatibility; and in the domain of *non-reciprocative justice*, need.

21. Justinian, *The Institutes*, I, i.

22. See G. Del Vecchio, *Justice*, tr. Lady Guthrie (University Press, Edinburgh, 1952), Chs. 3, 4.

23. Suppose that: (1) *B* is dividing *X* between *A* and *C*; (2) the only relevant resemblance or difference between *A* and *C* is contribution to making *X*; (3) *A*'s contribution is greater than *C*'s and (4) *B* allocates more of *X* to *A* than to *C* because *B* is partial to *A*. Then *B* does not treat *A* justly because *B* does not act from a just will. Nevertheless, *B* acts as *B* would act if *B* were treating *A* justly. So if *D* believes falsely that *B* is a just man who intends to treat *A* and *C* fairly, then *D* will infer wrongly that *B* is treating *A* justly. Thus actions which are not just may appear to be just.

24. Thomas is particularly clear and convincing on the necessary intentionality of just and unjust action. See *S.T.*, 2a2ae. 59; 2-3; also J. Pieper, *Justice*, tr. L.E. Lynch (Faber and Faber, London, 1957), pp. 35-41. I maintain the necessary intentionality of coercion in Sec. 4 of Essay 7.

25. Suppose that: (1) *B* is dividing *X* between *A* and *B*; (2) the only relevant resemblance or difference between *A* and *B* is contribution to making *X*; (3) *B*'s contribution is greater than *A*'s; yet (4) *B* allocates more of *X* to *A* than to *B*. Then *B* treats *A* generously. But does *B* thereby treat *B* unfairly? No, because what happens is that *B* waives *B*'s moral right to the larger share of *X* in favour of *A*. (Perhaps this is what Aristotle has in mind when he says that a man cannot treat himself unjustly (*E.N.* 1136b 11-14).) (Cf. Subsec. 2.2 of Essay 8.) Although *B* can waive *B*'s moral right in favour of *A*, *B* cannot waive *C*'s moral right in favour of *A*. Consequently, generous treatment has to be a dyadic relation which involves only *A* and *B*. In the domain of *comparative justice*, however, just treatment is a triadic relation in which *B* mediates between *A* and *C*. See J. Feinberg, 'Noncomparative Justice',*The Philosophical Review*, Vol. 83, 1974.

10 IS THE CONCEPT OF FREEDOM ESSENTIALLY CONTESTABLE?

1. Introduction

In 1956 W.B. Gallie advanced the thesis that certain political concepts, such as that of social justice, are 'essentially contested'.[1] Since then, a considerable literature on the subject has developed, some of it in support of the thesis, some of it in opposition to it.[2] W.E. Connolly is a leading supporter of it, and John Gray is a leading opponent of it. However, Connolly's advocacy of it in the second edition of his book is significantly more moderate than that in the first (1974) edition of it. For whereas in the latter he maintains that 'definitive resolution of these controversies is usually impossible' (p. 3), in the former he wishes 'to deny that the definitional disputes persistently operative in moral and political philosophy are in principle irresolvable, and to deny that there are no criteria at all to illuminate these contests' (pp. 226, 230). Connolly claims that 'freedom is perhaps the most . . . controversial of the concepts we shall discuss' (p. 140), and it is this claim which I, like Gray, intend to dispute.

The important definitions of 'freedom' which have been propounded in widely different times and places are the following five.[3]

2. First Definition

'Liberty consists in doing what one desires.'[4] This is the opinion of the man in the street. The following example shows that it is false. A is B's slave, and B brainwashes A into desiring to be B's slave. Then, by this definition, A is free. But A cannot, logically, be both free and a slave. This disproof rests on the familiar and powerful logical principle that a proposition which implies a contradiction is false. It is much used in mathematical demonstrations.

3. Second Definition

A is free if and only if A is not 'a slave to his passions'[5] or in 'human bondage'.[6] On this view, the paradigm of the unfree man is the alcoholic. For with him the worst part of his nature (his passions) control the best part of it (his reason). But A is free if and only if A's reason and will control A's passions. This definition is false because liberty is a moral right, and A's moral rights must, logically, be held against B, who has the corresponding moral obligation. Liberty is therefore an interpersonal or interorganisational concept and not an intrapersonal or intraorganisational one.

4. Third and Fourth Definitions

Connolly considers the following problem in the definition of 'liberty' as 'the absence of coercion'. Namely, does 'B coerces A' mean (Third Definition) 'B prevents A from doing X', where 'prevents A from doing X' means 'makes A unable to do X'? Or does 'B coerces A' mean, as Bentham[7] maintains (Fourth Definition), 'B restrains A from doing X', where 'restrains' means 'intentionally prevents'? Connolly thinks that the question, which of these definitions is true, is essentially contestable (pp. 161-4). But in fact it is clear that the Third Definition is false and that the Fourth Definition is true.

For compare the following two cases. *Case (a)*. On finishing his work, a businessman, B, locks his premises and goes home. He thereby unintentionally locks in his secretary, A, who is working late, a fact which B has forgotten. A cannot communicate with the outside world and so has to spend the night in her office, which causes discomfort and inconvenience to her and anxiety to her family about her absence. On returning to work the following morning, B is aghast when he discovers the consequences of his forgetfulness. He apologises to A, assures her that his action was quite unintentional and the result of forgetfulness, and offers her in compensation two days' holiday with pay. A is mollified, accepts B's apology and offer of compensation, and the affair is closed. *Case (b)*. On going home, B intentionally locks A in his place of business because he considers that she has been slacking and he wants to force her to dispose of her arrears of work. On returning to work in the morning, B explains to A what he has done and why. A is furiously indignant, tells B that he has no right to treat her in this high-handed way, and informs him that she will report her detention both to the police and to her union, so that it can sue B for damages on her behalf. The utterly different conduct of both A and B in the two cases shows that they are as distinct as chalk and cheese. What is the essential difference?

Precisely that in Case (a), *B*'s unintentional action merely prevents *A* from leaving the premises and does not violate her moral and legal right to liberty, whereas in Case (b), *B*'s intentional action restrains *A* from leaving the premises and does violate her moral and legal right to liberty. (Cf. Sec. 4 of Essay 7.)

5. Fifth Definition

'Obedience to a law which we prescribe to ourselves is liberty';[8] e.g. *A* abstains freely from alcoholic drinks if and only if *A* obeys a rule so to abstain which *A* has imposed on *A*. So generally, *A* does *X* freely if and only if *A* does *X* *autonomously*.

That which is autonomous is either an individual (as in the above example), or, more usually, an organisation, e.g. the slogan 'a free church in a free state'. The most important 'opposite' of autonomy is *heteronomy*. *A does X* heteronomously if and only if *A* does *X* in obedience to a rule which *B* has imposed upon *A*. But *A* does *X anomously* if *A* does *X* neither autonomously nor heteronomously. 'Autonomous' and 'heteronomous' are therefore contraries and not contradictories. ('Restrained' and 'unrestrained', however, are contradictories.) *A* does *X aheteronomously* if and only if *A* does *X* either autonomously or anomously. The paradigm of the heteronomous organisation is the colony, which does not make its own rules (laws), but has them made for it by the colonial power of which it is a dependency. It is the 'negative' word 'heteronomy', not the 'positive' word 'autonomy', which wears the trousers.[9] (Similarly, with liberty, the 'negative' word 'restrained', not the 'positive' word 'free', is the trouser-word; and, with justice, the 'negative' expression 'unjust treatment', not the 'positive' expression 'just treatment', is the trouser-expression.)

To elucidate the notion of heteronomy it is necessary to explain its relations to *control, government* and *coercion* (restraint).

Control (direction) is a binary relation, the terms (subjects and objects) of which are *individual persons* or *organisations of persons*.[10] Control, like coercion, is necessarily intentional. Indeed, one reason why coercion is necessarily intentional is that coercion (restraint) is a species of control.

The species and sub-species of control which are important for present purposes are obtained by dividing it as follows. (1) *Political control v.* (2) non-political control. Political control is *government* (rule). A subject of government is *a government* and an object of government is either *a citizen* or *an organisation* of citizens, e.g. a trade union. An example of non-political control is parental control of children. Government is either (1.1) *coercive* or (1.2) non-coercive. Non-coercive government is government by e.g. advice, persuasion or warning. Coercive government is either (1.1.1) *coercive by law* or (1.1.2) coercive not by law. Coercive government not by law is government by e.g. decree, manipulation or incarceration. An object of coercive government by law is *heteronomous*. A heteronomous object is *unfree* (restrained) because the *threat* which backs the sort of law which we are considering here prevents its object from doing some *complex* (*conjunctive*) action, e.g. if murder is a capital offence, then a citizen is unable both to take a fellow-citizen's life and to keep his own life.[11] Both coercive and non-coercive government involves the exercise of *power*, since advising, persuading, warning, etc. are ways of influencing, and *influence* is a species of power. (Cf. Subsec. 6.1 of Essay 3.)[12]

Is the Fifth Definition true? There is truth in it, namely, that if *A* does *X* autonomously, then *A* does *X* freely. However, objection may be made to this as follows. Consider, e.g., *Case* (*c*). *A* imposes on *A* a rule to abstain from alcoholic drinks and backs it with a resolution to pay £100 to charity whenever he breaks it. The objection is raised that this abridges *A*'s liberty, because *A*'s resolution makes *A* unable both to break his rule and to keep (all of) his money. But the reply is that the objection is false. For when *A* breaks his rule, he can simply disregard his resolution, and so *can* both break his rule and keep (all of) his money. There is a crucial difference here between Case (c) and *Case* (*d*). *R* (*Rex*, a political authority) imposes on *A* and on all *A*'s fellow-citizens a rule to abstain from alcoholic drinks and backs it with a threat to fine any citizen £100 whenever he breaks it. If *R*'s threat is effective (as *R*'s threats usually are) then *A* and *A*'s fellow-citizens *cannot* both break *R*'s rule and keep (all of) their money. This is why heteronomy abridges liberty whereas autonomy does not do so.

But there is also falsity in the Fifth Definition. For it is not true that, if *A* does *X* freely, then *A* does *X* autonomously, i.e. it is false that *A* cannot do *X* freely and anautonomously. For *A* can do *X* freely and anomously. And when *A* does *X* anomously *A* does *X* anautonomously, since 'anomous' and 'autonomous' are contraries. (See above.) Suppose, e.g., *Case* (*e*), that *A* abstains from alcoholic drinks neither in obedience to a rule imposed on *A* by *A* nor in obedience to a rule imposed on *A* by *B* (e.g. by *R*). Then — provided that *A* is not constrained to abstain in some other way, such as by being forcibly deprived of alcoholic drinks — *A* abstains freely. The Fifth Definition is therefore false.

It is widely believed, on eminent authority,[13] that there are two concepts of liberty, the negative concept (unrestraint), and the positive concept (autonomy). (But the expression 'positive concept of liberty' is used for the Second Definition as well as for the Fifth Definition. See Sec. 1 of Essay 6.) However, we have just seen that it is not so. I think that *the cause* of the false belief that there are two concepts of liberty (or, better, that there are two meanings of 'free') is as follows. It is noticed that autonomous organisations and individuals are called 'free', e.g. 'the Irish Free State'. From this it is inferred erroneously that one meaning of 'free' is 'autonomous'. But this is wrong. For the unique, true definition of the *meaning* of 'free' is, as Bentham says, 'unrestrained' (the Fourth Definition, above). Autonomous organisations and individuals are *called* 'free' because they are, necessarily, aheteronomous (= unrestrained by threats which back rules imposed on them by others). This is because 'autonomous' and 'heteronomous' are contraries. (See above.) An analogy will clarify the point. *A* notices that persons who are under 18 are called 'minors'. From this *A* infers erroneously that 'minor' means 'person who is under 18'. But this is wrong. For the true definition of the *meaning* of 'minor' is 'person who is under age'.[14] Persons who are under 18 are *called* 'minors' because they are, contingently, under age. This is because the law has fixed the age of minority at under 18. The falsity of *A*'s belief can be seen very clearly from the fact that it entails the following paradox: the effect of reducing the age of minority from under 21 to under 18 was to change the meaning of the name 'minor' from 'person who is under 21' to 'person who is under 18'. But this is obviously untrue, since what the change in the law changed was the age of minority, not the meaning of the name 'minor'.[15]

There is another interesting connection, of a factual and not a conceptual kind, between autonomy and freedom. Certain liberties, notably those of expression, assembly and association, are in fact necessary conditions for the attainment of autonomy. Thus, a colony is most unlikely to achieve independence from a colonial power unless the colony's citizens are free to campaign for independence by speaking and writing for independence, by holding mass meetings to demand independence, and by forming a political party to work for independence. But the converse is not true. Autonomy is not in fact a necessary — or indeed a sufficient — condition of liberty, e.g. Indian citizens do not have more liberty under the Republic than they had when India was a Dominion of the British Commonwealth. (But cf. Essay 7, Sec. 2 and Appendix.)

Finally, a word on the relationship of autonomy to democracy. 'Self-government' means either 'autonomy (independence)' or 'democracy (representative government)'. These are logically distinct. But there is, again, an interesting factual connection between them. Namely that movements for independence tend to be accompanied by movements for representative government. For if a colony has representative government, then those citizens who desire independence can organise an independence party, some members of which will (with luck) be elected to the colony's legislature, and some of these will (with more luck) become ministers. This will greatly strengthen the hand of those citizens who desire independence. But the converse is not true. Movements for representative government do not tend to be accompanied by movements for independence. This is because movements for democracy occur in independent countries as well as in dependent ones.

6. Conclusion

In the expression 'essentially contestable' the word 'contestable' means 'can be contested', not 'ought to be contested'. In this respect 'contestable' is like 'visible' and unlike 'desirable'.[16] The modifier 'essentially' means 'necessarily'.[17] But we have seen in this essay that it is false that all definitions of 'free' are necessarily contestable. For it has been shown that one (and only one) definition of 'free', namely the Fourth Definition (Bentham's), is incontestably true.[18]

APPENDIX I

I say in note 5 that, for Plato, the free man is also the just man. Plato and Aristotle often use 'justice' in a very extended sense, such that justice (= justness) is not one moral virtue among others, but moral virtue itself; and that justice (= just action) is not one sort of morally right action among others, but morally right action itself. Plato's equation of the free man with the just man is important because it is the source of the paradoxical but influential doctrine that A does X freely if and only if A does X rightly, so that an immoral act is necessarily unfree. In fact, of course, the truth of 'A did X freely' is a necessary condition of the truth of 'A did X wrongly'. Cf. Oppenheim, *Political Concepts*, pp. 163-4. (See also Subsec. 3.2 of Essay 8.)

APPENDIX II

Here are three more arguments to show the falsity of the belief that one meaning of 'free' is 'autonomous' (Sec. 5). First, if it were true then the statement (1), 'Autonomous organisations and individuals are (called) free', would mean the same as the statement (2), 'Free organisations and individuals are (called) free', i.e. (1) would be a trivial tautology. But it is not. For someone could quite sensibly ask about (1), 'Why? Why are autonomous organisations and individuals (called) free?' The answer to which is, as is said in the text, 'Because they are not restrained by threats which back rules which have been imposed on them by others'.

Secondly, 'autonomous' and 'heteronomous' are contraries whereas 'free' ('unrestrained') and 'unfree' ('restrained') are contradictories (Sec. 5). So the first pair of words cannot be equivalent to the second pair of words.

Thirdly, if 'free' meant 'autonomous' then freedom would be an intrapersonal or intraorganisational concept. But in fact it is an interpersonal or interorganisational concept (Sec. 3).

Notes

1. W.B. Gallie, 'Essentially Contested Concepts', *Aristotelian Society Proceedings* Vol. 56 (1956). My essay is about freedom, but it is appropriate to record here my dissent from Gallie's contention that (social) justice is an essentially contested (or contestable) concept. See Secs. 1 and 2 of Essay 8.

2. See W.E. Connolly, *The Terms of Political Discourse*, 2nd edn (Martin Robertson, Oxford, 1983), p. 245.

3. These are not the same as the five definitions which Oppenheim proposes, though there is partial overlap. See F.E. Oppenheim, *Political Concepts: A Reconstruction* (Blackwell, Oxford, 1981), Chs. 4, 5. Oppenheim too opposes the thesis that freedom is an essentially contestable concept (pp. 182-5).

4. Mill, *Liberty*, v. This, however, is only one of Mill's views about the definition of 'liberty'. Most of the time he accepts Bentham's definition (the Fourth Definition, below). But sometimes he accepts the Second Definition (below). It is extraordinary that the author of the most famous philosophical work on liberty, who is usually so careful about questions of meaning, should apparently have been blind to the importance, and to the difficulty, of defining the word 'free'. See C.L. Ten, *Mill on Liberty* (Clarendon Press, Oxford, 1980), pp. 72-3.

5. Plato, *Republic*, pp. 430-48. For Plato, the free man is also the just man.

6. Spinoza, *Ethics*, IV, V.

7. See D.G. Long, *Bentham on Liberty* (University of Toronto Press, Toronto, 1977), pp. 54-5.

8. Rousseau, *Social Contract*, I, viii. Cf. Kant, *Foundations of the Metaphysics of Morals*, III, i.

9. See J.L. Austin, 'A Plea for Excuses', in his *Philosophical Papers*, J.O. Urmson and G.J. Warnock (eds) (Clarendon Press, Oxford, 1961), pp. 139-41.

10. We are not interested in, e.g., *A*'s control of his car. 'To control' also has the secondary meaning of 'to check', 'to verify', as in 'Comptroller and Auditor General, 'passport control' and 'control experiment'. See N. Rescher, 'The Concept of Control', in his *Essays in Philosophical Analysis* (University of Pittsburgh Press, Pittsburgh, 1969).

11. See Sec. 3 of Essay 3.

12. In his classic discussion 'of the grounds and limits of the *Laisser-Faire or Non-interference Principle*', Mill speaks of the vital distinction between coercive government and non-coercive government as that between 'authoritative governmental intervention' and 'unauthoritative governmental intervention' (*Political Economy*. 7th edn, V, xi, 1). But his terminology is uncharacteristically inept. First, because both coercive government and non-coercive government are authoritative for the very reason that they are governmental. Secondly, because the terms 'intervention' and 'interference' apply only to those acts of government which are designed to meet particular contingencies or emergencies and consequently have an *ad hoc* and 'one off' character, e.g., a government intervenes to prevent an Old Master from leaving the country by being sold to a foreign collector. (See F.A.Hayek, *Law, Legislation and Liberty*, II (Routledge and Kegan Paul, London, 1976), pp. 128-9.) These, however, form only a very small part of the acts of government. Government is mostly conducted by means of the public promulgation of general rules which are backed by threats, i.e. by coercion by law. The thesis that governments ought, as a general rule, to govern in this way is the *Principle of the Rule of Law*, but the words 'the Principle of Rule by Law' express the idea more accurately. For, obviously, laws cannot rule; only persons can do that. And one, preferable, way in which rulers can rule is by means of laws as opposed to by means of decrees, propaganda, etc. (See Sec. 1 of Essay 7.)

13. I. Berlin, 'Two Concepts of Liberty', in his *Four Essays on Liberty* (Clarendon Press, Oxford, 1969). Kant uses the expressions 'negative concept of liberty' and 'positive concept of liberty' (note 8, above).

14. See *The Concise Oxford English Dictionary*.

15. There are, of course, many words which do have more than one meaning, e.g. 'fast'. 'A fast ship' means 'a speedy ship'. But 'to make a ship fast' does not (usually) mean 'to make a ship speedy' but 'to make a ship secure'. It is possible, though needlessly mystifying, to describe this situation by saying that there are two concepts of fastness. But it is more natural, and more informative, to describe it by saying that there are two meanings of 'fast'.

16. Cf. Mill, *Utilitarianism*, iv. But Gallie claims 'to find *reasonableness* in the pursuit of inevitably endless conflicts' ('Essentially Contested Concepts', p. 196, emphasis added).

17. 'The thesis of essentially [contestable] concepts is a thesis about the *unrealisability* of rational consensus . . . ' (Connolly, *The Terms of Political Discourse*, p. 244, emphasis added). Connolly writes 'essentially contested concepts', but I take this to be a slip of the pen; see p. 225. Cf Gallie's '*inevitably* endless conflicts' (note 16, above, emphasis added).

18. Part of Sec. 4 of this essay forms part of a review of Connolly, *The Terms of Political Discourse* in *Political Studies* Vol. 32 (1984). I am grateful to the Editor for permission to reproduce it here.

11 COLLECTIVE LIBERTY AND RELIGIOUS LIBERTY

1. Introduction

An important but neglected problem in the philosophy of liberty is *collective liberty* and its relationship to *individual liberty*. In this essay I discuss it with particular reference to *religious liberty*. Religious liberty, or *toleration*, is itself of special interest, since it was in connexion with this issue that the philosophy of liberty originated.

2. Collective Liberty and Individual Liberty

The problems here are to distinguish two kinds of social collectives; and to see whether collective liberty can be reduced to individual liberty, or conversely.

2.1 Kinds of Social Collectives

Specimens of social collectives are women, tribes, political parties, churches, joint-stock companies ('companies', for short), trade unions ('unions', for short), municipalities and states. Names given to some or all of these are 'community', 'institution', 'association', 'class', 'group', 'organisation' and 'set'.

We need to distinguish and consider only two sorts of social collectives, namely, *social sets* and *social organisations*. 'A social set' means 'any kind of collection of individual persons'. All the specimen collectives listed above are sets. 'A social organisation' means 'an organised social set'. Excepting the first, all the specimen collectives listed above are organisations.

By Cantor's axiom for sets, the essential feature of a set is simply that all its members have some common attribute, e.g. that of being a woman. The essential features of an organisation are more complex. It has a *function* or purpose. One function of a union is collective wage-bargaining. In order to perform its functions, the union has an *organisation* or structure. It has a president, secretary and other officials who conduct the wage-bargaining on behalf of the ordinary members. Being president and being secretary are the distinct *rôles* or parts which these officials play. The union also has *procedures* governed by *rules*, such

185

as those for electing the president and secretary.

There are degrees of organisation. At one extreme, the French state is a highly organised set. At the other extreme, despite the existence of the International Labour Organisation, the workers of the world are not united or organised in any significant degree. Again, the same set can be organised at one time and unorganised at another time. In 74 BC the Roman slaves were unorganised. From 73 to 71 they were loosely organised under Spartacus. But after his defeat they were again unorganised.

Another vital difference between sets and organisations is that respecting their *identity conditions*. By the principle of extensionality for the identity of sets, a set is the same if and only if it has the same elements. But this is not true of organisations. 'The Catholic Church is not reborn every time a Catholic dies or is baptized' (Mellor, p. 61). The identity of an organisation consists rather in its fulfilling the same function or functions. Political England is the same state now as it was 500 years ago because it has the same essential functions (e.g. defence and internal security in geographical England), despite the facts that it is not the same set of citizens, that it has additional functions (e.g. the provision of welfare services), and that it now has rôles and procedures which it did not have then (e.g. a prime minister and the election of MPs by universal suffrage). Conversely, if a union were to change its sole function from collective wage-bargaining to missionary work, it would not be the same organisation as it was. So more than one organisation can be composed of one set, just as one organisation can be composed of more than one set (e.g. the Catholic Church, above).[1] (See Sec. 3.)

Again, *membership* of an organisation differs from membership of a set. As said above, one is a member of a set if and only if one *is* something, e.g. has the attribute of being a woman. But one is a member of an organisation if and only if one *does* something. One *is* a part *of* an organisation if and only if he *plays* a part *in* that organisation.[2] The minimum required of a member of a union is that he support it by paying his dues. If he does not, his membership lapses. The relation of a member to an organisation is a *causal part/whole relation*, like that of some part of a person's body to that person. I cause my hand to move, and it causes me to feel pain if it is injured. But more 'affecting or being affected by a part constitutes affecting or being affected by the whole. My hand is a part of me because some of its movements constitute actions of mine and some things done to it are *ipso facto* things done to me' (Mellor, pp. 63-4). The parts which individuals play in organisations are the causal relations which make these persons parts of those organisations.

The main problems of collective liberty arise over five kinds of organisations, namely, states, churches, companies, unions and municipalities. There are, first, the problems of *ecclesiastical liberty*, i.e. problems about the relationship of coercion between a state and a church. These problems are also called those of *toleration* or of church and state. Secondly, the problems of *economic liberty*, i.e. problems about the relationship of coercion between a state on the one hand and companies and unions on the other hand. These problems are also called those of free enterprise and free trade *versus* collectivism, and of the immunities of organised labour. Thirdly, the problems of *local liberty*, i.e. problems about the relationship of coercion between a state and local governments. These problems are also called those of decentralisation and of states' rights. Finally, the problems of *national liberty*, i.e. problems about the relationship of coercion between an independent state and its dependent states ('dependencies', for short). These problems are those of nationalism, imperialism and the right of self-determination.[3]

Since these four groups of problems are all about coercion by the state, they are problems of *political collective liberty*. This is the most important sort of collective liberty, because coercion by the state is much greater both in amount and in degree than any other kind of coercion. The problems of *ecclesiastical* liberty, *economic* liberty, *local* liberty and *national* liberty are also problems of *political* collective liberty. It is simply that the latter name considers the relationship of coercion from the standpoint of the subject or agent, whereas the former names consider this relationship from the standpoint of the object or patient.

Evidently, then, of these five kinds of organisations the independent state is supreme. Benn and Peters see the proper relationship between the state and other organisations within its jurisdiction as that of an arbiter between their conflicting claims. 'The government is . . . in the position of an umpire' (p. 275) (This is also Locke's view. *Second Treatise of Civil Government*, xix, 212.) However, as they point out elsewhere, the state is more than an umpire, because it not only enforces the rules, but also — and to an ever greater extent — makes them. But ' . . . once it is admitted that law can be made, and made specifically by the political authority, the political order no longer stands on an equal footing with other associations' (p. 257). The state is much more than *primus inter pares*.

2.2 *The Reducibility of Collective Liberty and of Individual Liberty*

Are statements about the collective liberty of states, churches, companies, unions and municipalities translatable into statements about the individual liberty of their members, or conversely? There are three fallacies to be avoided here, those of division, composition and equivocation. The fallacy of division is that of inferring that what is true of a whole is true of its parts. The fallacy of composition is the converse fallacy of inferring that what is true of its parts is true of a whole. The fallacy of equivocation is that of using a term in more than one sense in the course of an argument.

Respecting the possibility of equivocation, it must be remembered that there are attributes which can be predicated of organisations which cannot, logically, be predicated of their members. A union may be highly cohesive and mark that fact by naming itself 'Solidarity'. But its members cannot, logically, be cohesive. We speak of free states, free churches and free unions as well as of free men. But we have to bear in mind the possibility that 'free' does not mean the same when predicated of these organisations as it does when predicated of their members, and that 'free' in the former sense cannot, logically, be predicated of individual members. Conversely, we have also to bear in mind the possibility that organisations cannot, logically, be free in the sense in which their individual members can be free. Consider, then, the following inference. 'The USSR is free, therefore the citizens of the USSR are free.' First, it commits the fallacy of division. Secondly, it commits the fallacy of equivocation. For the premiss means that the USSR is an independent (autonomous) state. But the conclusion means that the citizens of the USSR have a considerable amount of individual political liberty (non-coercion). Thirdly, the premiss is true but the conclusion is false. Therefore, statements about the collective liberty of organisations are not always translatable into statements about the individual liberty of their members. Conversely, consider the following inference. 'The citizens of Bermuda are free, therefore Bermuda is free.' First, it commits the fallacy of composition. Secondly, it commits the fallacy of equivocation. For the premiss means that the citizens of Bermuda have a considerable amount of individual political liberty (non-coercion). But the conclusion means that Bermuda is an independent (autonomous) state. Thirdly, the premiss is true but the conclusion is false. Therefore, the inference is invalid and the corresponding implication is false. Therefore, statements about the individual liberty of members are not always translatable into statements about the collective liberty of their organisations.

Now for some clarification of the notions of collective liberty and individual liberty, and the relations between them.

Political control (*government*) is not, of course, the same thing as *coercion*. Neither 'all government is coercive' nor 'all coercion is government' are tautologies. Indeed, they are not even true. Today, governments control their citizens to an increasing extent by advice, warning and persuasion. Clerics are coerced by canon law just as citizens are coerced by criminal law.

Organisations are subject to coercion by criminal legislation just as individuals are. It can be an offence for an organisation to engage in restrictive practices, as companies do when they form cartels and unions do when they operate closed shops. This is achieved by treating organisations in law as individuals.[4]

Autonomy and *heteronomy* are contraries, not contradictories. A severe schizophrenic who is not in hospital neither has self-control nor is controlled by another. Similarly, a society which is in a state of anarchy neither has self-government nor is governed by another. There is not a dichotomy, autonomy or heteronomy. There is a trichotomy, autonomy or heteronomy or *anomy*. The bearing of this contrariety on the value of autonomy will appear later. As, in elucidating freedom, it is helpful to concentrate on unfreedom (coercion), and in elucidating justice, it is helpful to concentrate on injustice (unfair tratment); so, in elucidating autonomy, it is profitable to concentrate on heteronomy (subjection to rules imposed by another).

Heteronomy is a binary relation in which an individual or organisation, B, controls some other individual or organisation, A. E.g., a dependency is dependent *on* some other state, whereas an independent state is independent *of* all other states. But the relation, control, can be reflexive, when an individual has self-control and an organisation has self-government. This is autonomy (subjection to rules imposed by oneself).

The relationship of autonomy to *liberty* is as follows. Autonomous organisations and individuals are free because they are necessarily *aheteronomous* (unrestrained by *threats* which back rules imposed on them by others). This is because 'autonomous' and 'heteronomous' are contraries. (See above, and Sec. 5 of Essay 10.)

The terms of the relation, control, are individuals or organisations. The terms are not sets. In his *Subjection of Women*, Mill is not concerned about the control of one very large set, women, by another very large set, men. He is concerned about the control of women playing a certain rôle in a certain organisation (wives in a Victorian English family) by men playing another rôle in the same organisation (their husbands).

There are degrees of autonomy as there are of liberty. The Crown Colony of Bermuda is largely, but not completely, independent of the UK, in that it is self-governing in respect of its internal affairs.

The relations of the autonomy of organisations to the liberty of their members are interesting and significant. The UK might try to frustrate a Bermudian campaign for complete self-government by imprisoning the ringleaders (simple coercion), or by making it an offence punishable by a fine for any citizen to advocate complete self-government (complex coercion by legislation). In that case, it would be using individual unfreedom as a means to maintaining collective unfreedom.

'Self-government' means either 'independence (autonomy)' or 'democracy'. A move to abolish the office of Governor of Bermuda is a move to establish complete self-government in both senses. Similarly, abolition of the office of bishop in the Church of England would be a move both towards the Church's independence of the state[5] and towards its democratisation. Milton's pamphlets and speeches illustrate well how advocacy of self-government in both senses and of liberty can go together. In *The Reason of Church Government urged against Prelaty* he argues for an extreme form of ecclesiastical democracy in which there would be no hierarchy at all, let alone political bishops, and in which the Church would therefore be largely independent of the state.[6] But *Areopagitica* is a classic plea for the individual right of free expression; specifically, for the right to print pamphlets such as *The Reason . . .* without a licence.[7] So Milton aims to increase the individual liberty of its members as a means to increasing the collective liberty of the Church.

Different issues are therefore involved in religious, economic and national liberty. In religious liberty, the issue may be ecclesiastical liberty, i.e. a church's independence, notably from the state (autonomy). But the issue may also be the rights of members of a church to profess its faith and to practise its rites without restraint, notably by the state (individual liberties). Similarly with economic liberty. In the early, heroic stage of capitalism the issue was the right of the *entrepreneur* to produce and trade without coercion by state legislation, above all by having the freedom to make what contracts he chose with his customers, suppliers and employees (individual liberty). Today, however, the issue is at least as much that of companies preserving their independence from *the corporate state*. (See Tame.) In this, they have a common interest with the unions (collective liberty). Similarly, too, with national liberty. The main issue is the independence of the dependency from the colonial power (collective liberty). But, as a means to this, there is also the question of the rights of the citizens of the dependency to argue, protest and engage in civil disobedience as a means to obtaining national independence (individual liberties).

It is necessary to be clear about the limitations of what the foregoing argument has established. This is simply that statements about the *liberty* of organisations cannot always be reduced to statements about the *liberty* of their members, or conversely. It has *not* been claimed or shown, first, that statements about the freedom of organisations cannot be reduced to *any* statements about their members, or conversely. The former alternative is especially important. Consider, e.g., the statement 'Great Britain will[8] emancipate Bermuda'. It is possible, though laborious and pointless, to translate this into statements about individuals, as follows: 'The British Queen and MPs will make an Act of Parliament transferring to the Bermudian ministers and MPs responsibilities for defence and foreign affairs which are at present reserved to the Governor of Bermuda.'[9] Nothing in the preceding argument commits me in any way to what Quinton calls 'ontological collectivism' (Quinton, p. 3).

Again, what has been shown is that statements about the freedom of *organisations* cannot always be reduced to statements about the freedom of their members, or conversely. It has *not* been claimed or shown, secondly, that statements about the freedom of (unorganised) *sets* cannot be so reduced. 'Lincoln emancipated the slaves in 1862' means simply 'In 1862 Lincoln emancipated every member of the set possessing the attribute, American slave in 1862'.

Finally, it is not disputed that a change in the liberty of an organisation may result in a change in the liberty of its members. E.g., a state makes a heteronomous union autonomous, and the union takes advantage of its autonomy to introduce a closed shop. This diminishes the liberty of its members by making them unable both to leave the union and to keep their jobs. So an increase in the collective liberty of an organisation can cause a decrease in the individual liberty of its members. This is true and important, but it has nothing to do with the question of reducibility. For this is not any sort of *causal* question, but a *logical* question about meaning.

3. Religious Liberty

Here — as with economic liberty, local liberty, and national liberty — there are three problems, namely, those of meaning (or definition), of value (or justification), and of proper bounds (or distribution). Of these, the last is the most important.

First, then, as to meaning. 'Religious liberty' means three different things. (1) The autonomy of a church with respect to a state. This is *ecclesiastical liberty*, a question of the extent to which a church is controlled by, or is independent of, the state within the jurisdiction of which it wholly or partly lies. One meaning of 'a free church' is 'a church which is wholly or largely autonomous' in this sense. It is a matter of *collective liberty*. (2) The absence of coercion of churchmen (i.e. members of a church) by the state within the jurisdiction of which they reside. E.g., it is not an offence for them to profess any article of their faith or to practise any rite of their church. This is a matter of *individual liberty*. (3) The democratic organisation of a church. E.g., its government is congregational and not episcopal. This is *ecclesiastical democracy*, and a second meaning of 'a free church' is 'a church which is self-governing' in this sense. Of these three concepts of religious liberty, the first is the most important, and the problem of its proper bounds is 'the problem of church and state' *par excellence*.

The three concepts are related as follows. First, as to the relations between the first and the second concepts. If a church is independent of a state, then there can be no coercion of its members by the state, so that no question of the proper limits of such coercion presents itself. E.g., there cannot be a law making human sacrifice criminal. On the other hand, a church may be controlled by the state, and yet its members may have liberty with respect to the state in the profession of faith and the practice of works. E.g., this is the present situation of the Church of England.

Secondly, as to the relations between the first and third concepts. These two meanings of 'a free church' are logically independent. A church which is independent of the state may or may not be democratic. In principle, too, the same may be true of a church which is not independent of the state. In practice, however, state control and non-democratic organisation tend to go together. This is the truth in James I's saying, 'No bishop, no king'.

Next, as to the value of religious liberty. We have to appraise the value of these three kinds of religious liberty to the individual churchman, to his church, and to the state (Pennock).

The case for ecclesiastical democracy seems to me to be substantially the same as that for political democracy. To the individual churchman, the principle of 'one man, one vote' applies as a matter of the negative, general right to justice. Furthermore, ecclesiastical democracy has the same beneficial effects on individual churchmen as Tocqueville and Mill saw that political democracy has on individual citizens. It makes them active rather than passive, and makes them both to be and to feel genuine participants in their church. For, as we have seen, one is a part of an organisation if and only if he plays a part in that organisation (Subsec. 2.1). As for the churches, they too benefit from having members of this energetic and interested type. Another advantage to them is that, once the principle of ecclesiastical democracy is accepted, there is a settled and orderly procedure for deciding whether churches should be organised on, say, episcopal, presbyterian or congregational lines. Finally, the state benefits in the same way as the churches do. Actively participant churchmen, who are used to conducting their own affairs, are likely to display the same virtues in their capacity of citizens. Again, the state relies heavily on voluntary associations of many kinds for identifying social problems, suggesting or providing solutions to them, and supplying it with personnel to perform these tasks (Pennock). There is no reason why all of this should not apply to churches too.

As for the liberty of churchmen, their non-coercion by the state in professing their church's faith and in practising its rites is a negative, general right. This is because a churchman is harmed very grievously if he is restrained from doing so. For one who believes that his after-life depends on his doing these things will prize this right even more highly than his right to earthly life. But it does not follow from this that this right is absolute or unconditional. For instance, the state is morally justified in restraining the religious from child-sacrifice. (See below.)

As to ecclesiastical liberty, the chief advantage to a church of autonomy with respect to the state lies in the fact that, since autonomy and heteronomy are contraries, an autonomous church is necessarily independent of state control. The great danger in heteronomy, of course, is that of being used by the state for political purposes. E.g., in Imperial Russia, the Orthodox Church tended to be so used by the Tsars.[10] Similarly, in England in former times, the parson was widely regarded as the natural coadjutor of the squire in keeping the lower orders in their places. Figgis sees another great advantage to churches in their being autonomous with respect to the state. 'The advantage of toleration is that it acts automatically on the purity of religious bodies and the reality of their faith; and, where complete, it produces a temper which, annealed in the fires of constant criticism, is analogous to that produced by persecutions in the earlier days of the Church' (p. 119). I think that he has in mind the benefits which he believes would accrue to the Church of England if it were disestablished and had to compete on equal terms with the free churches and the freethinkers. 'Toleration' means, of course, 'autonomy'. A state tolerates the churches within its jurisdiction if and only if they are autonomous with respect to it.[11] E.g., it does not exercise control over dissenting sects by making it an offence for them to assemble.

It is sometimes claimed that autonomous churches benefit the state because they provide a valuable counterpoise to a powerful central government. On this view, the case for separating the spiritual and temporal powers is similar to that for separating the legislative, executive and judicial temporal powers. This argument will carry weight with those who accept the theory of liberal constitutionalism as expounded by Montesquieu and realised in the US constitution. But those who are unconvinced both by Montesquieu's theory and by its American exemplification will be less impressed by it.

Now for the central questions, that of the proper bounds of state control over a church within its jurisdiction; or alternatively, that of church control over a state. Naturally, extreme solutions are possible. One may maintain either that the church ought to be supreme over the state, or that the state ought to be supreme over the church. Bellarmine and Hobbes exemplify these two stances perfectly. But more moderate solutions are more interesting. The chief of these are the Church/State Identity Theory and the Church/State Duality Theory. As exponents of these theories I shall consider respectively Hooker, spokesman and apologist for the Elizabethan Settlement; and Locke, spokesman and apologist for the Revolution Settlement.[12]

The gist of Hooker's theory is contained in the following passages. (1) There ought not to be 'any man of the Church of England but the same man is also a member of the commonwealth; nor any man a member of the commonwealth, which is not also of the Church of England.' (2) 'When we oppose the Church . . . and the commonwealth in a Christian society, we mean by the commonwealth that society with relation to all the public affairs thereof, only the matter of true religion excepted; by the Church, the same society with only reference unto the matter of true religion, without any other affair besides.'

How might this theory be thought to solve the question at issue? In this way. If the ideal projected in passage (1) were realised, the following argument might be advanced. 'The English have solved the problem of church and state. For with them the church and the state are one. Hence the church cannot be heteronomous with respect to the state or conversely, since heteronomy is a binary relation.' The argument fails, however, because the premiss is false. If Hooker's plan were implemented it would indeed follow that the set, English churchmen, would be identical with the set, English citizens. But it would by no means follow that the organisation, the Church of England, would be identical with the organisation, the Kingdom of England. For although there is a principle of extensionality for the identity of sets, there is no such principle for the identity of organisations (Subsec. 2.1). That the Church and the Kingdom would still be different under Hooker's arrangement follows from the Principle of the Non-identity of Discernibles: *If it is not the case that every property of A is also simultaneously a property of B then A ≠ B.* It is easy to see that, on Hooker's scheme, the Church and the Kingdom would satisfy this principle. Thus, the state would have the property of being responsible for defence, but the church would not have this property. However, the church would be responsible for christenings, and the state would not. It is true that both church and state would have ministers. But the pastoral duties of ministers of religion are quite different from the executive duties of ministers of state. Again, the conditions of membership of the two organisations would be different. One becomes a member of the state either by birth or by naturalisation. However, one becomes a member of the church in neither of these ways, but by baptism.

What are the meanings of 'a Christian society' (Hooker, passage (2)) and of 'a Christian state' (otherwise, 'a Christian commonwealth' (Hobbes, Pt. III))? There are attributive uses of the adjective 'Christian' with either the definite or the indefinite article in which there is nothing to puzzle us. Such are 'the Christian religion', 'a Christian man'[13] and 'a Christian church' (e.g. the Roman Church, the Orthodox Church and the Lutheran Church). But 'a Christian society' and 'a Christian state' *are* puzzling. First, the term 'society', with either the definite or the indefinite article, means an organisation. E.g. 'the Society for the Promotion of Christian Knowledge'; or again, an Eccentrics Club might describe itself as 'a society of gentlemen for the fostering of innocuous eccentricities'. But for Hooker it clearly means a set, a set of Christian men, which he contrasts with an organisation, a Christian church-state. For he evidently does not think that, if his scheme were realised, there would be in England *two* organisations, a Christian society and a Christian church-state. Secondly, 'a Christian state' too is an organisation, since a state is necessarily organised. But the sort of organisation to which the adjective 'Christian' is properly attributed is a church, not a state. 'A Christian church' makes sense; 'a Christian state' makes no sense. The very expression 'a Christian state' discloses the essential confusion at the heart of the Identity Theory.[14]

The identity of church and state was the theory of Israel under the Mosaic Law, and of both the Western and the Eastern Roman Empires. It is still the theory of the Eastern Christian churches today, and in the West the idea has been revived in modern times by Eliot.

All this was crystallised in the idea of the *Holy Roman Empire*, the governing conception of a great Church-State, of which it is hard to say whether it is a religious or a temporal institution. Half the trouble came from the fact that popes and emperors were heads, in theory co-equal, of the same society. The argument so constantly repeated, that the unity of the society needs a single person as the centre, and that, therefore, the secular power must be subject to the spiritual, owes its force to the very fact that men were incapable of seeing two societies, and that the theory of two co-equal heads under Christ as King did not work in practice. (Figgis, pp. 205-6.)

The practical consequences of this failure to work was, in the West, the protracted conflicts, first between the popes and the emperors, and then between the popes and the kings or queens.[15] Its theoretical consequence was the uncompromising assertion either of state supremacy or of church supremacy by e.g. Hobbes and Bellarmine. Such were the dramatic effects of the failure of ancient and medieval minds to comprehend that more than one organisation can be made out of one set. (Cf. Quinton, pp. 21-2; Subsec. 2.1, above.)

The Church/State Duality Theory was the product of the Protestant Reformation. According to Figgis, Warburton was the first to propound it (pp. 108-10, 216-19). But the germ of it is to be found in a famous rule of the Author of Christianity himself: 'Render unto Caesar the things which are Caesar's; and unto God the things that are God's' (*Matthew* xxii, 21). The stock criticism of this rule is that it is purely formal, so that if it is to be of any help it needs to be supplemented by substantive principles specifying which things are Caesar's and which things are God's. On this, there are two things to be said. First, that it is not quite true, since the preceding verses show that Jesus held that one thing which was due to Caesar is tribute. This is a substantive point, and indeed a substantial one. Secondly, that the same stock criticism of formalism has been made of the scarcely less famous definition of 'justice' which Plato attributes to Simonides: 'Justice is rendering to every man his due' (*The Republic*, 331E). There is, indeed, so striking a resemblance between Simonides' Definition and Jesus' Rule that it is natural to wonder whether the Rule can be subsumed under the Definition by expanding the Definition as follows: 'Justice is rendering to every man and god his due'. In fact, however, the Rule cannot be so subsumed, because Jesus would not have agreed that his Rule is a Principle of Justice. This is because he would have held, rightly, that a man cannot treat a god fairly or unfairly, because he is in no position to do so; just as — to compare great things with less — a player cannot treat a referee fairly or unfairly, and a pupil cannot treat a headmaster fairly or unfairly.[16] Augustine, however, disagrees. He accepts Simonides' definition of 'justice' as 'returning to each his due', and maintains that Man ought to treat God justly in this sense. Indeed, he holds that 'true religion' consists in returning to God his due. E.g., since God loves Man, Man ought to love God in return. It is interesting that Augustine rightly accepts Simonides' true definition of 'justice', which Plato rejects, in preference to Plato's own false definition of it. (See Appendix 3 and Subsecs. 2.1 and 2.2 of Essay 8.)

Locke's problem is significantly different from Hooker's. For whereas Hooker is concerned about the proper relation to the state of the national church, Locke is chiefly concerned about the proper relation to the state of dissenters. His solution is that the state has a moral obligation to tolerate any church or sect so long as the latter confines itself to its proper function, which is the salvation of souls. The justification of this Principle of Toleration is that the proper functions of a state are quite different from those of a church, namely, first, maintaining the citizens' natural rights to life, security, liberty and property; and secondly, promoting the public good. He thinks that if church and state keep to their proper functions as he defines them there can be no conflict between them. Roman Catholics should not be tolerated because the Roman Church is really a political rather than a religious organisation, and should therefore be treated as a hostile foreign power.[17] This is therefore no exception to his doctrine of *religious* toleration. But he does make such an exception. The state, he says, is morally justified in legislating against religious practices, such as infant sacrifice, which are 'not lawful (i.e. morally permissible) in the ordinary course of life'.

However, this concession is fatal to his theory. For the high priest will of course defend child sacrifice on the ground that, if the god is not propitiated in this manner at regular intervals, he will in his rage consign the souls of the whole tribe to eternal perdition. Locke is mistaken in thinking that human thought and action can be divided into two mutually exclusive provinces, the spiritual (where the thought and action are directed towards the salvation of souls), and the temporal (where the thought and action are directed towards the maintenance of natural rights and the promotion of the public good). The distinction between 'temporal' and 'spiritual' is not in fact one between different *provinces* at all. It is a distinction between different *powers*. Moreover, it is a genuine distinction. Hobbes is wrong in saying that 'this distinction of Temporal, and Spiritual power is but words'. To be precise, it is a distinction between two different kinds of *sanctions* by means of which power is exercised. 'A man may be deterred either from theft or from heresy, either by a threat of excommunication or by a threat of imprisonment' (Stephen, p. 115).

It may be objected that what we have here are simply alternative descriptions of an action. The priest calls killing a child and Suttee 'sacrifices', i.e. means to saving the souls of the tribe by propitiating the god, and to ensuring that a husband is not deprived of his wife's company in the next life. The magistrate calls both 'murder'.[18] But this account of the matter will not do. For the priest's putative descriptions are not descriptions at all, since there is no irascible god to be propitiated and no next life to be enjoyed or endured. Here, as everywhere, the paramount question, which cannot be evaded, is truth.[19] This example again illustrates clearly how political control (government) and coercion are related. The suppression of Suttee and of human sacrifice are instances of morally justified state control over a church. The mode in which the control was exercised in India was coercion by legislation (cf. Subsec. 2.2).

According to Locke, ' . . . these two societies (namely, church and state) are in their original, end, business, and in everything perfectly distinct and infinitely different from each other'. The alleged difference of 'ends' is crucial. He is indeed right to stress the purposes or functions of organisations. But he seems to assume that, if church and state have any common functions, they will conflict, so that they ought to be denied any common functions. However, this does not follow. Certainly, as we have seen, state and church have and ought to have some different functions, such as defence and christening. But it does not follow that they ought to have no common functions, e.g. education and welfare. For if they do have such common functions, they will not necessarily be in harmful conflict. First, the conflict may take the beneficial form of competition. If there are both church schools and state schools in competition with each other, the result is likely to be a raising of the standard of the education provided by both sorts of schools, to the general advantage. Secondly, if both church and state provide welfare services, they may well co-operate rather than compete. (Cf. Benn and Peters, pp. 289-92.)

Both the Church/State Identity Theory and the Church/State Duality Theory have obvious analogues. Locke's account of what the relationship of the church to the state ought to be parallels his and Descartes' substantial dualist account of what the relationship of the mind (or soul) to the body is. Similarly, Hooker's account of the former relationship parallels the Mind/Brain Identity Theory. Again, Locke's attempt to define the proper bounds of ecclesiastical liberty by one simple principle resembles Mill's attempt to do the same thing for individual liberty. (See Sec. 3 of Essay 6.)

But neither theory succeeds, nor do Bellarmine's and Hobbes' supremacist theories succeed, because no such final solution is possible. For, as church and state do and will compete and co-operate in such matters of common concern as welfare and education, so they do and will conflict in such areas of common concern as war and peace, marriage and divorce. I agree with Eliot that there will always be, and ought always to be, not merely a certain distance, but also a certain *tension* between the two organisations (pp. 53-5). The problem is to prevent this tension from becoming excessive, and eventuating in such extremes as the catacombs on the one hand or Canossa on the other.

APPENDIX 1

In Sec. 3 I say *à propos* of ecclesiastical democracy that 'a second *meaning* of a "free church" is "a church which is self-governing" ' (emphasis added). But this needs expansion, since the true situation is as follows. Democratic organisations, such as states with representative governments, are *called* 'free' because they are *believed* to be autonomous and so necessarily aheteronomous and unrestrained by threats which back rules imposed on them by others. But this belief is false, for reasons which Mill makes clear:

> . . . such phrases as 'self-government', and 'the power of the people over themselves', do not express the true state of the case. The 'people' who exercise the power are not always the same people with those over whom it is exercised; and the 'self-government' spoken of is not the government of each by himself, but of each by all the rest. The will of the people, moreover, practically means the will of the most numerous or the most active part of the people; the majority, or those who succeed in making themselves accepted as the majority; the people, consequently *may* desire to oppress a part of their number; and precautions are as much needed against this as against any other abuse of power. The limitation, therefore, of the power of government over individuals loses none of its importance when the holders of power are regularly accountable to the community, that is, to the strongest party therein. (*On Liberty*, i)

The expressions 'free state' and 'autonomous state' can be interpreted either collectively or distributively. E.g. respectively 'The Irish Free State' and 'Great Britain is a much less free country today than it was 100 years ago'. The former celebrates the independence of the Southern Irish State from Great Britain, whereas the latter laments the decrease in the individual liberties of the citizens of Great Britain. In the false belief that democratic states are autonomous, the expression 'autonomous state' is construed distributively to mean a state in which there is, in Mill's words, 'government of each (citizen) by himself'. It is not construed collectively, as in 'The Irish Free State'. (Cf. Oppenheim, pp. 131-2.)

APPENDIX 2: ORGANISATIONS, SETS AND GROUPS

In note 13 I comment on the failure to distinguish organisations from sets. I think that one cause, or effect, of this failure is the fact that the word 'group', which is used extensively in these contexts, is ambiguous between 'set' and 'organisation'. Thus, Glazer understands by 'group rights' the rights of, e.g., Francophone Canadians and black Americans. So to him 'a group' means 'a set'. On the other hand, those sociologists who study their subject from the standpoint of social psychology understand by 'a group' 'an organisation'. Thus, for Levy Brühl, a tribe is a typical group, and for A.F. Bentley a typical group is the Anti-Saloon League.

The concept, *family*, also illuminates the distinction between a set and an organisation. It might be thought sufficient for *A, B* and *C* to constitute a family that *C* should be the offspring of *A* and *B*. In that case, a family would be a set determined simply by what *A, B* and *C* are, namely, parents and offspring respectively. But in fact this condition is necessary and not sufficient. For suppose that parents *A* and *B* and offspring *C* never communicate with each other and never take any interest in each other, to the extent of not knowing or caring whether the others are alive or dead. In this case, they would be said not to constitute a family but to be simply a trio of individuals. To be a part of a family one must play a part in a family. E.g., if *C* is a child, *A* and *B* must support *C*, and *C* must recognise *A*'s and *B*'s authority over *C*. As everyone recognises, therefore, the family is no mere social set, but a social organisation, indeed a very important one.

APPENDIX 3: THE GROUNDS AND SIGNIFICANCE OF THE CHURCH/STATE IDENTITY THEORY

Two notable exemplifications of the Church/State Identity Theory are the Holy Roman Empire, a catholic-empire-church, and the Church of England, a nation-state-church. The theorist of the latter is Hooker in his *Laws of Ecclesiastical Polity*, and the theorist of the former is Augustine in his *City of God*. In Bryce's words, 'it is hardly too much to say that the Holy Empire was built upon the foundation of the *De Civitate Dei*' (p. 93, note).

The grounds of the theory appear to be the following three. First, the fallacy that out of one set only one organisation *can be* made. (Cf. Figgis on the Holy Roman Empire in Sec. 3 of the text.) This, of course, involves difficulties. In particular, ought the head of the catholic-empire-church to be the Pope, or the Emperor; or ought they to be co-equal heads, as in the 'diarchy' theory of Pope Gelasius I? In fact, there is no difficulty. The set, all persons, can be organised in one way as the catholic church with the Pope as head, and in another way as the universal empire with the Emperor as head.

The converse fallacy is that one organisation *can be* made out of only one set. Hume shows the falsity of this belief in his discussion of personal identity, where he points out that 'the same individual republic . . . may change its members' (*A Treatise of Human Nature*, I, iv, 6). This is as true of a church as it is of a state (republic). (Cf. Mellor on the Catholic Church in Subsec. 2.1 of the text.)

Secondly, the belief that all persons *ought to be* organised in a single church-state and not in a distinct church and a distinct state, because this is necessary in order to assure the *unity* of mankind. Bryce brings out clearly the obsession with unity in what he calls the 'theory of the medieval empire'. (Cf. again Figgis on the Holy Roman Empire.)

Thirdly, the thesis of Augustine and Hooker, that persons *must be* organised in a single state-church in order to constitute a 'true republic (commonwealth)' (Augustine; cf. Barker, pp. xxx-xxxi). The premiss of Augustine's argument is Cicero's definition of *res publica*, which he accepts as true. It is *res populi*, and *populus* is 'the union of a number of men associated by the common acknowledgement of *jus* and common pursuit of interest' (*Republic*, I, 25). By *jus* Cicero understands simply 'justice'. But Augustine understands by it *vera justitia* or 'true righteousness', and argues accordingly that 'where there is no true righteousness there cannot be a union of men associated by a common acknowledgement of *jus*'. He argues further that *vera justitia* means, as Simonides says, 'returning to each his due'. This includes especially returning His due to God, so that 'true justice' means 'true religion', since only true religion returns to God His due. He concludes accordingly that the presence of true religion (i.e. Christianity) is necessary for the existence of a true commonwealth, so that the Roman Republic and Empire were not true commonwealths.

The significance of the theory consists in the following three points. First, the argument of the theorist of the Church of England (Hooker) is the same as that of the theorist of the Holy Roman Empire (Augustine). Secondly, the argument is invalid because it equivocates on the meaning of *jus*. The cause of this equivocation is the fact that Plato and Aristotle also equivocate on *dikaion* and *dikaiosune*; for Augustine was particularly influenced by Plato (Barker, p. viii). Sometimes they mean by 'justice' 'justness' or 'fairness', which is one moral virtue among others. But at other times they mean by it 'righteousness', i.e. moral virtue itself. Similarly, they sometimes mean by 'justice' (= 'just action') 'fair treatment', which is one sort of morally right action among others. But at other times they mean by it 'morally right action' itself. (Cf. Essay 8, Subsecs. 3.2 and 4.1; and Essay 10, Appendix I.) Thirdly, this invalid argument nevertheless provides the supposed justification for the Church of England being an *established* church. It is hardly too much to say, therefore, that the case for the establishment of the Church of England rests on the unsatisfactory account of justice which Plato presents in his *Republic* or *On Political Justice*.

Notes

1. But as is usual with questions of identity, there are difficulties. E.g., a union has two functions, collective wage-bargaining and ensuring safety at work. It exchanges safety at work for missionary work, but retains wage-bargaining. Is it the same organisation as it was?

2. Presumably this is why rôles are also called 'parts', as in 'the leading part' in a play. This example shows that, although there cannot be organisations without rôles, there can be rôles without organisations. For a play is not an organisation.

3. There is, of course, the complication that a state is not the same thing as a nation, despite the existence of nation-states.

4. In 1886 the US Supreme Court declared that the corporation is a person in constitutional law (Miller, p. 236).

5. Today, bishops of the Church of England are still political in that they are appointed by the Crown on the advice of the Prime Minister and are members of the House of Lords.

6. The Church's independence would still not be complete because the Head of the Church would still also be the Head of the State. This Erastian arrangement was instituted by an Act of Parliament of 1534.

7. It anticipates in a most interesting way some of the main points in Ch. 2 of

Mill's *On Liberty*.

8. Or will not, as the case may be.

9. Even this rigmarole falls far short of a complete individualist reduction. 'Making an Act of Parliament' needs to be translated into statements about draftsmen drafting, MPs voting, royalty assenting, and so forth.

10. For instance, C.P. Pobedonostsev used his position as Procurator of the Holy Synod (1880-1905) to uphold the autocracy of Alexander III. In return, he took strong measures against all forms of dissent from the Orthodox Church.

11. A leading difficulty in the relations between the Roman Catholic Church and nation-states such as England was precisely that the former is, at least in aspiration, catholic (i.e. universal), whereas the jurisdictions of nation-states are of course restricted. But this problem did not present itself in the relations between that Church and the Empire, since the latter was also, at least in aspiration, universal. See Figgis on the Holy Roman Empire, below.

12. The Toleration Act of 1689 was of course a vital part of that settlement.

13. 'A Christian man' does not mean the same as 'a Christian churchman'. For, first, an isolated individual, such as Robinson Crusoe, can be a Christian man although he cannot be a Christian churchman. For a churchman is a member of a church, a church is an organisation, and an organisation — herein differing again from a set — must have more than one member. Secondly and conversely, the career of Cesare Borgia shows clearly that one can be a Christian churchman without being a Christian man. A classic example of failure to distinguish an organisation from a set is Mill's *mot*, 'The Tory party is the stupid party'. For he explained to the House of Commons that he meant by this, not that all Tories are stupid, but that all stupids are Tories; at which the House was much amused. But the gloss is not about the organisation, the Tory party, at all. It asserts that the set, stupids, is included in the set, Tories. (See M. St J. Packe, *The Life of John Stuart Mill* (Secker and Warburg, London, 1954), pp. 454-5).

14. ' . . . there is absolutely no such thing . . . as a Christian commonwealth' (Locke). For all that, Locke alludes approvingly to 'the judicious Hooker'.

15. For instance, in 1245 Pope Gregory IX excommunicated Emperor Frederick II for the third time, and in 1570 Pope Pius V excommunicated Elizabeth I of England and released her subjects from their allegiance to her. Cf. Note 6.

16. But the converse is of course possible. A god can treat a man fairly or unfairly, just as a father can treat his child fairly or unfairly. Nor is this possibility of unfair treatment excluded if the god is morally perfect, as the Christian god is by definition. For it can be morally justifiable, indeed morally obligatory, for B to treat A unfairly. See Essay 8.

17. Cf. note 15. The position on this issue of Milton, who also advocated religious toleration, is the same as Locke's.

18. In the last century the Government of India, which was then British, made Suttee and human sacrifice criminal (Stephen, p. 61).

19. ' . . . the British Empire in India . . . governs, not indeed on the principle that no religion is true, but distinctly on the principle that no native religion is true' (Stephen, p. 60).

References

The following abbreviations refer to books which are collections of articles.

'Kamenka'. E. Kamenka and A.E. Tay (eds), *Human Rights* (Arnold, London, 1978).

'Pennock'. J.R. Pennock and J.W. Chapman (eds), *Voluntary Associations: Nomos XI* (Atherton Press, New York, 1969).

Augustine, Saint, *The City of God*, tr. J. Healey (Dent, London, 1945), Bk. 19, Ch. 21.

Barker, Sir Ernest, Introduction to Augustine, *The City of God*.

Bellarmine, R.F.R., Cardinal, *On the Power of the Supreme Pontiff in Temporal Matters*, 1610.

Benn, S.I., 'Freedom, Autonomy and the Concept of a Person', *Aristotelian Society Proceedings*, Vol. 76 (1976).

Benn, S.I. and Peters, R.S., *Social Principles and the Democratic State* (Allen and Unwin, London, 1959), pp. 13-29, 235-96.

Black, M., *Critical Thinking* (Prentice-Hall, New York, 1946), pp. 209-24.

Brodbeck, M., (ed.), *Readings in the Philosophy of the Social Sciences* (Macmillan, New York, 1968), pp. 239-44, 280-8.

Bryce, Viscount James, *The Holy Roman Empire* (Macmillan, London, 1904).

Day, J.P., 'Individual Liberty' in A. Phillips Griffiths (ed.), *Of Liberty* (University Press, Cambridge, 1983).

—— 'The Indefeasibility of Justice', *Cogito*, Vol. 3 (1985).

Eliot, T.S., *The Idea of a Christian Society* (Faber and Faber, London, 1939).

Figgis, J.N., *Churches in the Modern State* (Longmans, Green, London, 1913).

Glazer, N., 'Individual Rights against Group Rights' in Kamenka.

Hobbes, T., *Leviathan*, 1651, Pt. III.

Hooker, R., *The Laws of Ecclesiastical Polity*, pp. 1594ff.

King, P., *Toleration* (Allen and Unwin, London, 1976).

Locke, J., *A Letter concerning Toleration*, 1689.

McConnell, G., 'The Public Values of the Private Association' in Pennock.

Mellor, D.H., 'The Reduction of Society', *Philosophy*, Vol. 57 (1982).

Mill, J.S., *On Liberty*, 1859.

—— *Representative Government*, 1861.

—— *The Subjection of Women*, 1869.

Miller, A.S., 'The Constitution and the Voluntary Association' in Pennock.

Milton, J., *The Reason of Church Government urged against Prelaty*, 1641.

—— *Of Reformation touching Church-discipline in England*, 1641.

—— *Areopagitica*, 1644.

—— *A Treatise of Civil Power in Ecclesiastical Causes*, 1659.

Montesquieu, Baron C. de, *The Spirit of the Laws*, 1748.

Oppenheim, F.E., *Political Concepts* (Blackwell, Oxford, 1981).

Pennock, J.R., 'Epilogue' in Pennock.

Quinton, Lord, 'Social Objects', *Aristotelian Society Proceedings*, Vol. 75 (1975).

Sisson, C.H., 'Richard Hooker and the *Ecclesiastical Polity*', *The Salisbury Review*, Issue No. 2 (1983).

Spinoza, B. de, *A Theological-Political Treatise*, 1670.

Stephen, Sir James F., *Liberty, Equality, Fraternity*, 2nd edn (Smith, Elder, London, 1874), pp. 114-33.

Suppes, P., *Introduction to Logic* (Van Nostrand, Princeton, NJ, 1959), pp. 101-8, 177-228.

Tame, C., 'Against the New Mercantilism: The Relevance of Adam Smith', *Il Politico*, Vol. 43 (1978).

Tocqueville, A. de, *Democracy in America*, Pt. I 1835, Pt. II 1840.

12 ECONOMIC LIBERTY AND ECONOMIC JUSTICE

1. Introduction

Like *religious liberty, economic liberty* is primarily a question of *collective liberty* rather than of *individual liberty*. This is because the main issue is the proper bounds of the coercion of *businesses* and *trade unions* by *governments*. As religious liberty was the chief problem of collective liberty in the sixteenth and seventeenth centuries, so economic liberty has been the chief problem of collective liberty from the eighteenth century to the present time (Essay 11).

2. Free Businesses

Three different questions are discussed under the heading 'economic liberty'. (1) The autonomy of businesses with respect to governments. By 'a business' is meant, e.g., a one-man band, a tenant farm, a co-operative insurance society or a multinational corporation. All businesses except one-man ones are organisations. This is a question of the extent to which businesses are controlled by, or are independent of, the government or governments within the jurisdiction of which they lie. It is a matter of *collective liberty*, because when a government *controls* a business it exercises its control for the most part by *coercion by law*.[1] It can do this because businesses are persons in law. (2) The absence of coercion of economic men by the government within the jurisdiction of which they reside. By 'economic men' is meant individual persons considered in their roles of producers, distributors or exchangers of *wealth*, i.e., of goods or services. E.g., it is not an offence for them to change their employment, or to make purchases from persons other than their employers. This is a matter of *individual liberty*. (3) The democratic organisation of a business. This is a matter of *economic democracy*, which is discussed under such titles as 'workers' control and self-government in industry'. Of these three questions the first is the most important, and the problem of the proper bounds of the autonomy of businesses with respect to governments is the problem of economic liberty *par excellence*.

The three questions are related as follows. First, as to the relations between the first and second concepts. If businesses are independent of government then there cannot, logically, be coercion of their members by government, so that no question of the proper limits of such coercion arises. E.g., there cannot be a law making it an offence for an individual to leave the employment of one business and to take up employment with another business. The relation between the first and third concepts is logical independence. A business which is autonomous with respect to government may or may not be democratically organised.

Respecting the *value* of economic liberty, it is necessary to appraise the value of these three kinds of economic liberty to the individual economic man, to his business and to the state.

The individual liberty of economic men is a negative, general, moral right. For persons are harmed gravely if they are restrained or deterred from working at what they want, or from working for whom they want, or from being self-employed. It is a matter of what Mill calls 'the liberty of tastes and pursuits'. To most people, few if any pursuits are more important than their work. This liberty rests in turn on *free contract*, and illustrates Maine's famous generalisation, 'the movement of progressive societies has hitherto been a movement from Status to Contract' (Maine, p. ix). Consider the plight of a serf who is tied to the land, or of an employee under the truck system who can buy goods only from his employer. This liberty also benefits an individual's business and the state. It makes for efficient production, since men do well what they like doing, and since shrewd shopping by consumers exposes producers to keen competition. Naturally, this liberty only *tends* to produce these desirable results. A man may choose the wrong job, or make a bad buy. He may be free to cease to be a farm worker and to become a doctor, but the freedom will be of no use to him if he cannot afford a doctor's long and expensive training.

The value of economic democracy can be discussed fruitfully by a consideration of Mill's view of 'the probable futurity of the labouring classes' (*Political Economy*, IV, vii). Initially, the form of economic democracy which he favoured was *partnership* between capitalists and labourers. This form prevails today in the German Federal Republic, where there are an ideal of *Mitbestimmung* and the institution of worker-directorships. Later, however, he came to feel that partnership was insufficient, and that the ideal form was *co-operative associations of producers* who would both own the capital and produce the goods or services. He was converted to this idea by experiments on these lines in France and by the success of the Rochdale Pioneers in England; and also by a reform of the law of partnership (in which he himself played a part) whereby the managing members of such an association could be made responsible for malversation of its funds.

The advantage to the individual of this mode of production is that it eliminates one of the most harmful features of capitalism, namely, *the division of labour* between the organisers of production (owners, directors and managers) on the one hand and the organised (operatives) on the other. This heteronomy of the latter deprives them of responsibility and initiative, and makes them both to be and to feel themselves 'hands' or 'cogs in a machine'. The first benefit of economic democracy is that it excludes economic autocracy.[2] The importance of *work* and of conditions of work was preached by William Morris and Ruskin. They considered that capitalism saw things exclusively from the standpoint of the consumer, and that it was inferior in this respect to the pre-capitalist system which, through its guilds, took effective care of the producer's interests.

The co-operative mode of production is also advantageous to the associations. Like political democracy and ecclesiastical democracy, economic democracy makes the individual energetic and self-reliant. Since his own prosperity depends on that of the association, he will be interested in it, and apt to provide suggestions for improvements in the organisation and methods of production. Conversely, since, if the association loses or fails, he too will lose or fail, he will behave responsibly.

Finally, there are substantial benefits to the state in co-operative production. It combines the advantages of large-scale production with a diffusion, as opposed to a concentration, of wealth. Further, wealth will be distributed among the producers according to contribution, thus satisfying the soundest substantive principle of justice. (See Essay 8; M. Friedman, pp. 161-2, 166-7.) Above all, it averts a conflict between the capitalist interest and the labouring interest, since in this system the set, capitalists, is identical with the set, labourers.

Such is the ideal. But the reality presents a sorry contrast. Both in France and in Britain producers' co-operatives have a record of virtually unbroken failure. It seems that a system of production in which the organisers are responsible to and controlled by the persons whom they organise does not work. This failure of co-operative associations of producers (sellers) contrasts strikingly with the success of co-operative associations of consumers (buyers), such as the British C.W.S., where the organisers are responsible to and appointed by the customers.

However, Mill's ideal of co-operative production differed from that of other contemporary advocates of it in one crucial respect. Whereas the Owenites and Christian Socialists rejected *competition*, Mill insisted on it. On his scheme, producers' co-operatives were to compete with one another. So while the producer's interest was to be assured by co-operative association, the consumer's interest was to be assured by competition between the associations. And there is evidence that this system *does* work. For it has been tried in contemporary Yugoslavia — a country which from the first has worn its Communism with a difference —, apparently with success. Presumably the spur of competition produces in the co-operatives the discipline which is indispensable if they are to flourish or at least survive.[3]

The value of the autonomy of businesses with respect to governments, and the proper bounds of this autonomy, cannot be assessed without an understanding of its nature.[4]

Suppose that all governments were to confine their relationships to the businesses within their jurisdiction (excepting taxation) to the making and administration of general rules (laws) of the following kinds: criminal laws against theft, fraud, etc. to protect private property; tort laws to ensure compensation for damage to property; enabling laws to facilitate the transfer of property, e.g. by bequest; and contract laws to ensure that valid contracts are enforceable by the courts.[5] Then the businesses of the world would spontaneously interrelate in what I shall call 'The Universal Self-regulating Economic System' (USES).[6] The chief features of this system would be as follows.

Businesses would be formed on the principle of *free enterprise*; i.e. any citizen would be free to set himself up in any kind of (legal) business if he judged that it would be profitable to do so. Businesses would *compete* with each other both in the *production* of goods and services and in the *consumption* of the *factors of production* (*land, labour* and *capital*). They would *exchange* goods and services on the principle of *free contract*. E.g., a retailer would purchase so much of a certain commodity from a wholesaler at a certain *market price*. The same principle would govern the relationship between businesses and consumers generally. An especially important case of it would be that of *free wage-contracts* between employers and their employees. (See Sec. 3.) There would be world-wide *free trade*, since it would be advantageous for businesses in every country to specialise in the production of those products which they could produce with the greatest relative efficiency, and for businesses in other countries to purchase these from them. For free trade is simply an application of the principle of specialisation or *division of labour*.[7]

Ideally, the USES is indeed universal. But there can be considerable catallaxies of narrower scope. E.g., the USA has been called the greatest free-trade area in the world. (This, of course, is as viewed from the inside. Viewed from the outside, such a catallaxy may be protected by high tariffs.)

The principle by which the USES regulates itself is that of negative feed-back. E.g., a manufacturer over-produces his product, so that its price falls. He responds to this indication by reducing his output, so that its price rises again to its original level. The process is similar to that by which the temperature of the air in a room is kept constant by a thermostat.[8]

The USES is a hybrid system. To a limited extent, it is an organisation, in that its constituent businesses are regulated by positive laws (framework-rules). But to a greater extent it is not an organisation, but a spontaneous order regulated by scientific laws (e.g. Ricardo's Laws of Rent and of Comparative Advantage, Say's Law, Gresham's Law, etc). This raises the great question, What would be the effect on the spontaneous operation of the USES of certain changes in the framework-rules? I shall revert to it later.

Smith observes that, in the USES, the businessman 'is . . . led by an invisible hand to promote an end which was not part of his intentions,' viz., the public interest (p. 456). One must distinguish how the businessman sees his actions from how the economist sees them. Consider one who speculates in futures in some commodity market. As he sees it, his *purpose* (= his intention) is to maximise his profit. But as the economist sees it, his purpose (= his function) — provided that he knows his job — is to reduce fluctuations in the price of that commodity, which is in the public interest. These descriptions of his 'purpose' are not, of course, incompatible.

The USES is, as Hayek puts it, 'abstract'. In favourable conditions, quite large social collectives can be observed. On a clear day and in open country, an armoured division can be seen from the air. The existence and nature of the UNO cannot be similarly established by observation. But they can be established by reading its Charter and Bulletin. The USES, however, has no Charter or Bulletin. Moreover, it is immense in size and complexity. It took the genius of Hume, Smith and other pioneer political economists to descry its *modus operandi* and indeed its very existence.

These considerations make it possible to distinguish significantly different kinds of social collectives. It is instructive to compare the following three, all of which are in aspiration universal. (1) A universal ordered set, the elements of which are individuals, and which is an organisation. E.g., the RC Church, a religious social collective. (2) A universal ordered set, the elements of which are organisations and which is an organisation. E.g., the UNO, a political social collective.[9] (3) A universal ordered set, the elements of which are organisations (businesses), and the order of which is partly organised but mainly spontaneous. E.g., the USES, a political-economic social collective.

An autonomous business *is* a part *of* the USES if and only if it *plays* a part *in* the USES by engaging in business transactions with other autonomous businesses. So the relationship of an autonomous business to the USES is a causal part/whole relation which is in some respects like that of an individual member to an organisation such as the RC Church. (See Subsec. 2.1 of Essay 11.) Yet there are crucial differences. For a businessman need not know that he is playing a part in the USES. Indeed, he can be ignorant of its very existence. Compare, in this respect, a businessman heading an autonomous business and a diplomat heading his country's delegation at the UNO. The latter must, of course, know of the existence of the UNO, of its purposes and of its organisation. He will also know the part which he has to play in it, on which he will have been given explicit instructions by his government.

The situation of a businessman in the USES, Hayek observes, is like that of a player in a non-zero-sum competitive game, in that his success will depend partly on his skill and partly on chance.[10] That is how the economist sees it. But the businessman may well see it differently. If he is successful, he is likely to ascribe his success entirely to his skill. If he is unsuccessful, he is likely to ascribe his failure entirely to bad luck.

Businesses can be more or less autonomous with respect to governments; the USES requires that they should be completely so, except to the extent that they are coerced by framework rules and by taxation. Like the Catholic Church, or the Universal Empire of which Dante dreamed, it is therefore an ideal which is unlikely to be fully realised in practice. Smith was well aware of this. 'To expect . . . that the freedom of trade should ever be restored in Great Britain, is as absurd as to expect that an Oceana or Utopia should be established in it' (p. 471).[11]

If the ideal of the USES is not fully realised, this is not because *the USES* is coerced by some government. It is because some of its constituent *businesses* are so coerced. The USES cannot be so coerced because it is neither an individual person nor an organisation. Consequently, it cannot be subjected to, notably, coercion by law. Autonomy and heteronomy are contraries and not contradictories. Businesses, then, can be autonomous or heteronomous with respect to governments, but the USES is necessarily anomous in this respect.

We are now in a position to assess the value of the autonomy of businesses with respect to governments. Since autonomy is contrary to heteronomy, one great value of this autonomy is that it excludes the harms inflicted by heteronomy. The first of these is that Mercantilism, old and new, is motivated by what Smith calls 'the wretched spirit of monopoly'. Indeed, an alternative name for Mercantilism is 'the system of monopoly'. Under it, 'occupations were the monopoly of gilds and corporations which restricted entrance to them, methods of production were dictated by State or gild officials, and the flow of trade was confined . . . by prohibitive tariffs, tolls and export duties to certain selected channels' (Clay, p. 62). Under this system, merchants and manufacturers *exploited*, i.e. took unfair advantage of, all consumers, thereby violating their negative, general right to justice.

A second harm inflicted by heteronomy is due to its inefficiency as compared with free enterprise. Mill gives three reasons for this. First, citizens tend to understand their own interests better, and to care for them more, than any government can. Secondly, 'even if a government were superior in intelligence and knowledge to any single individual in the nation, it must be inferior to all the individuals of the nation taken together'-(*Political Economy*, p. 942). Thirdly, reflection on the principle of the division of labour reminds us that 'every additional function undertaken by the government is a fresh occupation imposed upon a body already overcharged with duties' (ibid., p. 940). Under heteronomy, therefore, the standard of living of all citizens will be lower than under autonomy, and will fail to rise with economic growth as rapidly as it will under autonomy.

A third harm inflicted by heteronomy is similar to that inflicted by governmental control over churches; viz., that businesses, like churches, may be used for political purposes. Consider, e.g., Hitler's abuse of the German economy as an instrument of war. Obviously, all citizens are impoverished by such unproductive expenditure.

A fourth harm which counted for much with Mill was the danger to the individual liberty of all citizens in increasing excessively the power of government.

The problem of economic liberty is seen today as primarily that of preserving the autonomy of businesses (and of unions too) from *the corporate state* (Sec. 3). Miller views the situation as follows. 'The demise of *laissez-faire* has undermined the individualistic base of contract . . . Maine's . . . assertion that the "movement of progressive societies has hitherto been a move from Status to Contract" . . . has now been soundly repudiated. A new form of status has arisen, a "new feudalism" in which "contracts of adhesion" tend to be the norm. Freedom remains, but it is the attenuated liberty of choosing which contract or group to "adhere to''. (p. 238)[12] There is 'capitalism without competition, a combination of state support and private control' (Tame, p. 6). The USA is seen as as providing the most complete exemplification of this 'technocorporate state.' It need not be totalitarian, as Mussolini's Italy was. It is rather — to adapt Figgis's words about the Holy Roman Empire — the . . . conception of a great Business-State, of which it is hard to say whether it is an economic or a political institution. (See Sec. 3 of Essay 11.)

The benefits conferred by economic liberty are *claimed* to be as follows. First, its efficiency as a method of production assures to all consumers severally the blessings of 'cheapness and plenty' (Smith). Under it '. . . supply and demand tend to reach an equilibrium at which the efforts and sacrifices which lie behind supply are exactly balanced by the satisfactions which lie behind demand; thus present market values (i.e. prices) represent a maximum economy of the application of means to ends, a maximum of satisfactions and a minimum of cost' (Clay, p. 409; parenthesis added). The chief reason for this efficiency is specialisation, i.e. the division of labour. Another important reason for it is that the existence in the USES of a framework of stable rules (positive laws) enables businessmen to *plan* their operations effectively. This is a special case — the application to businessmen — of the benefit conferred on all citizens by the Rule of Law (Essay 7).

Economic liberty also benefits all consumers collectively. The increase in wealth created by efficient production means that government can collect more in taxes to pay for 'service' (non-coercive) functions (such as the provision of roads, sewerage and education) which private enterprise finds it not worth while to provide either at all or in adequate quantities.

The benefits conferred by economic liberty as a method of distribution are *claimed* to be as follows. It is to the advantage of all consumers because it is the *most efficient* mode of distribution. For services *tend* to be educed by the prospect of wealth, so that all the things that people desire will be produced or provided in proportion to the strength of the desire for them. It is to the advantage of all producers because it is the *most just* mode of distribution. For under this system wealth *tends* to reward service, and distribution according to contribution (service) is one of the two acceptable substantive principles of reciprocative justice. (See below.)

On this older view, economic liberty as a mode of distribution of wealth yields what Rawls calls 'imperfect procedural justice'. There is an independent criterion for the just result (distribution according to contribution), but no guarantee that adherence to the procedural rules will lead to a just outcome in a particular case. As said above, what is claimed is only that under this system wealth *tends* to reward service. On a modern view, that of Hayek, economic liberty as a mode of distribution of wealth yields what Rawls calls 'pure procedural justice'. Here, there is no independent criterion for the just result. 'Instead . . . the outcome is . . . fair, whatever it is, provided that the procedure has been properly followed' (Rawls, p. 86; cf. Hayek, Vol. 2, pp. 126-8; Feinberg, pp. 117-19). (Compare with this notion of procedural justice the notion of procedural equality which is treated of in Essay 9.)

Are these claims justified? The claim that the present system of economic liberty benefits all consumers both severally and collectively because of its productive efficiency is mainly sound, though in need of substantial qualification. (See the end of this Section.) Even the present system's severest critics, such as Marx, show reluctant admiration for the achievements of capitalism as a method of production. But the claims that it is both the most efficient and the just method of distribution are dubious, to say the least. The alleged tendency of services to be educed by the prospect of wealth is only very approximately true, and the alleged tendency of wealth to reward service is barely a half-truth. Consequently, a leading reason why governments have found it necessary to coerce businesses has been to correct the operation of the USES where this works against human rights or the public interest. This leads naturally into a consideration of the proper bounds of the liberty of businesses.

It is necessary to distinguish three questions. First, what control governments *can or cannot* exercise over businesses, and in what forms. Secondly, what control governments *may or may not* exercise over businesses, and in what forms. Thirdly, what control governments *ought or ought not* to exercise over businesses, and in what forms.

Respecting forms of control, the important divisions are the following ones. (1) *Coercive vs.* non-coercive control. (1.1) Coercive control *by law vs.* (1.2) Coercive control *by administrative powers.* We are primarily interested in coercive control because non-coercive control does not affect freedom.[13]

On the first question, it is necessary to remember that the control which governments can exercise over businesses is limited. E.g., it is beyond the capacity of any government to tax a very large and very rich multinational corporation which is based in a secure tax-haven. On the other hand, governments have sometimes extended economic liberty on a very large scale. E.g., the 'opening up' of Japan. Beginning in 1853, the American, British, French and German governments used the threat of military force to coerce the Japanese government into opening its ports, which had been virtually closed for two centuries, to European and American trade. The justification for this action was that diminution of the Japanese government's liberty by the threat of force was far exceeded by the benefit to all Japanese, European and American citizens which this extension of economic liberty entailed. If this justification is acceptable, here is an example of permissible coercion by government — the second question, above.

Governments do not only control businesses which supply goods and services. They themselves sometimes also supply goods and, more especially, services. It is necessary to distinguish three cases of this, which I shall do taking education as an example.

First, governments may supply education in competition with other suppliers, e.g. churches. This does not abridge liberty, and the effect of the competition is likely to be beneficial. (See Sec. 3 of Essay 11.) Secondly, governments may supply education because there are no or not enough other suppliers. One basic assumption of the theory of the system of economic freedom is that services are educed by the prospect of wealth. But with education it can happen that there is no prospect of wealth because citizens are unwilling to pay for it or for enough of it. This too does not abridge liberty and is highly beneficial since it is in the interests of all citizens that all citizens should be educated.[14] Thirdly, governments may monopolise the supply of education, say by making illegal the supply of it by alternative agencies such as churches and private schools and universities. This abridges the freedom of enterprise of would-be alternative producers and the freedom of choice of consumers. It is bad for these reasons and also because it eliminates beneficial competition. (See above.)

I turn now to the third question, taking first what control governments *ought not* to exercise over businesses and in what forms.

First, governments ought not to attempt to control ('plan') all, or even the most important businesses ('the commanding heights of the economy'). For they either cannot do it all, or only extremely inefficiently.

What are regarded as extreme positions respecting economic liberty are significantly different from extreme positions respecting religious liberty. Extreme collectivists do not hold that the state should be supreme over the economy, as Bellarmine held that the church should be supreme over the state. They regard some economic liberty as necessary. Thus, agriculture in the USSR is by no means completely collectivised. Similarly, extreme economic liberals do not maintain that the economy should be supreme over the state, as Hobbes held that the state should be supreme over the church.[15] (See Sec. 3 of Essay 11.) They regard the positive laws which are the framework-rules as essential. Economic liberals are more or less so accordingly as they advocate more or less of such laws.[16]

Secondly, as a general rule, governments ought not to engage in *coercive administrative* actions. I.e., speaking generally, they ought to forbear from economic interventions or interferences by means of *specific commands*, such as compulsory purchase orders. In economic, as in other affairs governments ought usually to govern by means of *general rules* (laws). (See above.)[17]

Let us consider now the question of what control governments *ought* to exercise over businesses and in what forms.

First, governments ought to *establish and facilitate* the operation of the USES by enforcing and, if necessary, making the framework-rules (*laws*). As said above, these are criminal laws, tort laws and contract laws, all of which curtail freedom. But they are also enabling laws, e.g. to facilitate the transfer of property. These do not abridge liberty, and the provision and execution of them is a very important service function of government.[18] Governments ought also to impose taxes to pay for the armed forces, police and law courts which are needed to execute the framework-rules. Taxes are also needed to enable governments to discharge their service functions in such matters as education, roads and sanitation. Taxation curtails liberty greatly.[19]

Secondly, governments ought to *correct* the operation of the USES when it goes against individual moral rights or the public interest. The following are important and familiar examples. In the interest of *producers*, governments have restricted the freedom of wage-contracts by Factory Acts. The justification of this curtailment of liberty has been that one basic assumption of the system of economic freedom is often false. This is that each is not only the best *judge* but also the best *guardian* of his own interest. This is false when the bargaining positions of the contracting parties are very unequal, as when a rich employer drives a hard wage-bargain with an unemployed pauper.

In the interest of *consumers*, governments have enacted Anti-Trust laws. The justification of this abridgement of producers' freedom of association is that restriction of competition, especially in the extreme form of *monopoly*, deprives the consumer of his safeguard. The root difficulty here for the system of economic freedom is that free enterprise includes freedom to combine as well as freedom to compete. This is a basic difficulty for trade unions also, since their aim, like that of trusts and cartels, is to restrict competition between producers by means of combination. (See Sec. 3.) Again in the interest of consumers, governments have passed Adulteration Acts to ensure the quality of foodstuffs. The justification of this curtailment of vendors' free enterprise is again that the Principle of Rational Self-interest tends to be false, since consumers are apt to lack the knowledge needed to be competent judges of the quality of the commodity. (But cf. Lepage, pp. 127-31.)

In these three — and other — cases of governmental correction of the operation of the USES, Freedom is diminished to achieve Fairness. For the aim is to ensure that neither producers nor consumers are *exploited*, i.e. taken unfair advantage of.

Thirdly, it is arguable that governments ought to *improve* the operation of the USES by making fundamental changes in the framework-rules, especially laws relating to private property. Eminent Liberals, past and present, are interestingly divided on this supremely important question. I shall illustrate this division by contrasting the positions on it taken by Hayek and by Mill.

We have seen that the system of economic freedom has succeeded better in the production of wealth than in its distribution. Consequently, those who advocate changes in the framework-rules do so mainly, but not exclusively, to improve the operation of the system in respect of distribution. The sort of changes in these positive laws which they recommend relate mainly, but not exclusively, to private property. On the whole, Hayek is opposed to such changes. His position is that 'the aim of law should be to improve equally the chances of all,' and that 'the chances of all will be increased most if we act on principles which will result in raising the general level of incomes without paying attention to the consequent shifts of particular individuals or groups from one position on the scale to another' (II, pp. 129-32, 188-9). That is, the efficiency of the system in the production of wealth will also take care of the problem of its distribution.

Mill, on the other hand, advocates changes in the framework-rules, those relating to property and the distribution of wealth being very radical.[20] Respecting the production of wealth, we have seen that he not only advocated, but himself played a part in, a reform of the law of partnership which would make possible the mode of production which he thought offered the brightest prospects to the working class, viz., cooperative associations of producers.

Respecting the distribution of wealth, he favoured a radical change in the law relating to inheritance. Namely, that it should restrict *A*'s right to inherit from *B* more than a reasonable start in life (*Political Economy*, pp. 218-26). His objection to the existing law was moral, in that it was unjust. For he believed that the true substantive principle of justice was return according to contribution; i.e., like Locke, he thought that the producer has a moral right to property in his product. But under the existing system 'those who did least work were most highly rewarded . . . This injustice was the result of inequalities in the ownership of wealth, and these in turn were the result of the laws concerning inheritance' (Ryan, pp. 165-6).

His *most* radical proposals for changes in the framework-rules, however, relate to private property in land. He holds that such property is not justified by the above substantive principle of justice since 'no man made the land', and concludes accordingly that 'when private property in land is not expedient, it is unjust' (*Political Economy*, pp. 226-32; *Dissertations and Discussions*, IV).[21] He proposes accordingly (1) that the landlord should continue to own his land provided that he improves it; (2) that the State should appropriate land, with due compensation to the landlord, if productivity would be increased thereby; and (3) that the State should appropriate the future 'unearned increment' in the rent received by the landlord which is caused by social changes, such as the growth of towns.

The most interesting of these proposals is the last. For it places Mill in a tradition which, beginning with the *Physiocrats* in France and Spence in England, passes through Ricardo's Law of Rent to Spencer's *Social Statics*, and culminates in the *Progress and Poverty* of the 'single-taxer,' Henry George, with whom Mill exchanged views about Chinese immigration into California. In modern times, George's theory has been viewed sympathetically by Mill's 'godson', Russell, and by Dewey (Russell, pp. 239-41; Dewey).

Living in California in the 1870s and 1880s, the problem which exercised George was 'the persistence of poverty amid advancing wealth'. His solution of it was that this phenomenon was caused by private property in land.[22] For this gave to landlords a monopoly which enabled them to exact from both capitalists and labourers in the form of rent all the increased wealth created by economic growth. His remedy was to abolish private property in land, without compensating landlords, and to allow individuals and organisations to rent land from the State on payment of a 100 per cent tax on the rent. There should be no other tax besides this single one.

Following this programme would be immensely beneficial. Regarding the distribution of wealth, it would ensure perfect Economic Fairness. For the substantive principle of Reciprocative Justice, distribution in direct proportion to contribution, would be fully satisfied.

Negatively, those who produced nothing, namely landlords (since 'no man made the land'), would receive nothing. Positively, those who produced something, namely capitalists and labourers, would receive the whole product of their labour, since they would not be exploited by landlords.

Regarding the production of wealth, it would ensure complete Economic Freedom and, consequently, maximum Economic Efficiency. The result of 'in effect putting up the land at auction to whoever would pay the highest rent to the State' would be complete Free Enterprise. Marx's generalisation, that leadership of industry is an attribute of capital, just as in feudal times the functions of general and judge were attributes of landed property, would cease to be true. The abolition of all taxes except the single one would relieve industry and trade of a heavy burden and stimulate production vastly. It is an accepted canon of taxation that it ought not to reduce the national income or check its growth, and the single tax on land meets this requirement perfectly (George; Clay, p. 393).

It is not surprising that political economists have found George's analysis of and remedy for the problem of poverty despite progress too simple and too good to be true. Their commonest criticism is that private property in land is not the only monopoly. Great capitalists are also often monopolists, and elements of 'rent' or 'unearned increment' can be detected in e.g. the wages of workers whose unions operate a closed shop. (See Sec. 3.)[23]

But, whatever the interest of George's analysis and proposal for economists, its interest for the present inquiry is clear and great. For it is the most extreme system of Economic Freedom ever proposed,[24] and it brings out vividly the points of central philosophical importance. First, as to the rights to Fairness and to Private Property. The producer's right to property in his product, or to distribution according to contribution, is fully respected.[25] Secondly, as to the right to Freedom. The right to Free Enterprise in production is fully respected.[26] Economic Freedom is maximised because coercion by law is minimised. For only two (though extremely radical) changes in the framework-rules are required, viz., the expropriation of landlords and the imposition of the single tax. Thirdly, as to the public good. First, the effect of respecting the above three rights is to maximise productive efficiency, thereby conferring on all the great benefits of cheapness and plenty. Secondly, the yield of the single tax (which will be very great) is to be applied to the public benefit in maintaining law and order, caring for the old and infirm, etc. (George, 1880, p. 311).

The essential difference between Liberals and Collectivists respecting Economic Freedom is therefore as follows. Liberals aim to improve, indeed to perfect, the operation of the USES by maximising its spontaneous order (Hayek's *cosmos*) and minimising its artifical order (Hayek's *taxis*) (Hayek, pp. 1,35-54). So coercion by positive law (the framework-rules) is to be minimised and Economic Freedom correspondingly maximised. Collectivists, on the other hand, aim to maximise artificial economic order and minimise, ideally indeed eliminate, spontaneous economic order. So coercion by positive law is to be maximised and Economic Freedom correspondingly minimised. This essential difference shows itself in all major economic issues. For instance, in the different conceptions of the problem of the distribution of wealth. As just said (note 25), for the Liberal, this problem is that of how, given certain framework-rules (e.g. laws maintaining private property in land), *wealth does distribute itself* (e.g. according to Ricardo's scientific Law of Rent). But for the Collectivist, this problem is that of how *government ought to distribute wealth* (e.g. by means of positive laws intended to implement an 'incomes policy').

Collectivists are apt to complain that the trouble with Socialism is that it has never yet been given a full and fair trial. But the Liberal can make the same complaint. In Mill's words 'the principle of private property (i.e. the system of economic freedom) has never yet had a fair trial in any country' (*Political Economy*, p. 982).[27] His point is, of course, that it will only be given a fair trial when the sort of radical changes in the framework-rules which he advocated have been effected. Perhaps, indeed, we are too unimaginative in this matter. We are so dazzled by what the capitalist method of production has achieved when running with the brakes on that we fail to appreciate what far greater success in production, as well as justice in distribution, it would achieve if it were allowed to run with the brakes off.[28]

Notes

1. Governments also exercise non-coercive control over businesses, e.g. by providing 'guide-lines'.

2. Smith opens his *Wealth of Nations* with the words 'the greatest improvement in the productive powers of labour, and the greater part of the skill, dexterity, and judgement with which it is anywhere directed, or applied, seem to have been the effects of the division of labour'. But he was as well aware of its disadvantages as of its advantages.

3. Besides partnership between capitalists and labourers and producers' cooperation there is another pretended system of economic democracy, viz., militant syndicalism. Sorel had a vision of 'the free producers of tomorrow working in manufactories where there

are no masters' (VII, iv). But this movement, with its advocacy of violence, revolution and the general strike, provides a recipe for economic anarchy rather than economic democracy.

4. The same is true of the autonomy of trade unions. See Sec. 3.

5. These rules are called by Hume and Smith 'the Rules of Justice'. I shall call them 'framework-rules'.

6. Alternative names are 'the system of natural liberty' and 'The Great Society' (Smith), 'the system of economic freedom' (Marshall), 'The Open Society' (Popper), 'The Catallaxy' (Hayek), and 'the capitalist method of production' (Marx).

7. This Law of Comparative Advantage was one of Ricardo's great analytical discoveries (Samuelson, pp. 662-5).

8. The germ of this idea is already to be found in Smith. Malthus, however, questioned it (Barber, pp. 68-72).

9. The name 'United Nations Organisation' is of course a misnomer, since the elements of this organisation are states, not nations. An essential difference between these is that nations are sets whereas states are organisations. States are, indeed, the largest, most powerful and most complex organisations that we have. It is not surprising, therefore, that the question of their proper relationship to the USES is both so important and so difficult. (On sets and organisations see Subsec. 2.1 of Essay 11.)

10. A central error of the Mercantilists was to regard economic transactions as like zero-sum games. This was because they conceived of *wealth*, not in the modern manner as a flow, but as a stock, especially of valuables. Thus, if Spain acquires all the gold and silver, England cannot acquire any of them; and conversely (Bonar, p. 131; Cannan, pp. 10-11).

11. Yet the word 'restored' sounds oddly, for when was it ever so? But the remarkable fact is the extent to which free enterprise and free trade did prevail in Great Britain and her Empire in the last century, especially under Gladstone; and on account of her economic supremacy, throughout the world.

12. Cf. the 'new tribalism' of contemporary trade unionism (Sec. 3).

13. Here I follow Mill and Hayek. See note 1.

14. Cf. the principle of the coincidence of particular and general interests (Essay 6). Such cases are also referred to as 'neighbourhood effects' (M. Friedman, pp. 30-3, 85, 93, 178, 191).

15. Lenin, indeed, maintains that in democratic states businessmen do control the government. But he does not think that this is how things ought to be.

16. Thus, Smith and Spencer are extreme economic liberals. The former writes: 'According to the system of natural liberty, the sovereign has only three duties to attend to . . . first, the duty of protecting the society from the violence and invasion of other independent societies; secondly, the duty of protecting, as far as possible, every member of the society from the injustice or oppression of every other member of it . . .; and, thirdly, the erecting and maintaining certain public works and certain public institutions, which it can never be for the interest of any individual, or small number of individuals, to erect and maintain . . .' (pp. 687-8). We have seen above that the third, 'service', function of government does not affect liberty. Cf. Mill on the inadequacy of the thesis that the province of government should be restricted to the protection of person and property against force and fraud (*Political Economy*, pp. 800-4, 936).

17. We touch here on the thorny problem of *administrative discretion* and the threat which it poses to liberty and other moral rights. For a balanced view of it, see Benn and Peters, pp. 127-33. It is interestingly discussed with particular reference to economic issues by Shonfield, pp. 385-427. Administrative discretion can work for liberty as well as against it, as when the police turn a blind eye. See Sec. 3 of Essay 9.

18. See Hart, pp. 27-8.

19. How businesses, as opposed to individuals, ought to be taxed is too complex a question to be treated here. But liberal principles require departure from current

practices. E.g., M. Friedman advocates abolition of corporate income tax (p. 132).

20. A — perhaps the — fundamental thesis of Mill's *Political Economy* is that whereas the laws of the production of wealth, like other scientific laws, cannot be changed by Man, those of its distribution can. On this see Ashley, pp. xxi-iii; Day (1975), pp. 10-16; Barber, pp. 99-101; Keynes, pp. 36, 42-3, 84-111.

21. Locke, on the other hand, holds that the principle does justify private property in land, because working land is just one way of mixing one's labour with something. See Day (1966).

22. The term 'land' is used to cover all natural resources. The crucial distinction is between this and artificial goods which, in Locke's terms, have had labour mingled with them.

23. The Single-Taxer's reply to this objection is that the land-monopoly is the basic one on which all others rest. Abolish it, and they too will vanish. For George, the landlord, not the capitalist, is the villain of the piece, who exploits both capitalists and labourers. It is not surprising, therefore, that Marx's comment to Hyndman on *Progress and Poverty* was 'the capitalists' last ditch'. For other objections to George's remedy see Clay, pp. 374-8. Clay's whole discussion of 'rent' (pp. 350-78) is very clear and judicious. It is essential for an understanding of George to appreciate that, living in California in the 1870s and 1880s, he was ideally placed to observe the processes which he analysed. His prediction in 1871 that free ('no-rent') land would cease to exist about 1890 was astonishingly accurate, since this is the date generally accepted by American historians as marking the end of the frontier.

24. A possible exception is the 'anarcho-capitalism' of the 'new Libertarian movement'. See D. Friedman; Lepage, pp. 157-9.

25. There are two uses of the verb 'to distribute'. (1) 'To distribute' means 'to allocate'. E.g., *B* distributes *X* between *A* and *B*. This requires at least one distributor (*B*) and at least one distributee (*A*) who is not identical with the distributor. (2) The reflexive use. E.g., iron filings distribute themselves along the lines of force around a bar-magnet. This does not require at least one distributee who is not identical with the distributor. In classical economics, distribution is understood in sense (2). So a typical question about the distribution of wealth is: Given the institution of private property in land, what proportion of the product (say, Ricardo's 'corn') goes to (distributes itself to) the landlord as rent? See note 20 above.

26. These arguments from rights, as well as consequential arguments from the public interest, are very conspicuous in Mill, Spencer and George.

27. Here is a contemporary expression of the same thought: 'If the West is "sick", if our rivers are becoming sewers and our cities uninhabitable, if poverty and misery survive here despite the overall rise in the standard of living, despite political efforts at wealth distribution, it is not because our society is capitalist but because it is not and never has been capitalist' (Lepage, p. 24). He is reporting the views of 'the New Economists', principally the members of 'the Chicago School'.

28. 'We should never lose sight of the fact that a program for removing institutional barriers to human liberty may be just as revolutionary as, and possibly more revolutionary than, the program that installed such barriers' (Buchanan, p. xi).

References

Ashley, W.J., Introduction to J.S. Mill, *Principles of Political Economy* (Longmans, Green, London, 1909).

Barber, W.J., *A History of Economic Thought* (Penguin Books, Harmondsworth, 1967).

Benn, S.I., and Peters, R.S., *Social Principles and the Democratic State* (Allen and

222   *Economic Liberty and Economic Justice*

Unwin, London, 1959).
Birnie, A., *Single-Tax George* (Nelson, London, 1939).
Bonar, J., *Philosophy and Political Economy* (Swan Sonnenschein, London, 1909).
Buchanan, J.M., Foreword to Lepage, *Tomorrow Capitalism*.
Cannan, E., *A Review of Economic Theory* (King, London, 1930).
Clay, H., *Economics* (Macmillan, London, 1916).
Day, J.P., 'Locke on Property', *The Philosophical Quarterly* (1966). Reprinted in *Life, Liberty and Property*, ed. G.J. Schochet (Wadsworth, Belmont, 1971).
—— 'The Uniformity of Nature'. *American Philosophical Quarterly*, Vol. 12 (1975).
Dewey, J., Foreword to Geiger, *The Philosophy of Henry George*.
Feinberg, J., *Social Philosophy* (Prentice-Hall, Englewood Cliffs, 1973).
Friedman, D., *The Machinery of Freedom* (Arlington House, New Rochelle, 1973).
Friedman, M., *Capitalism and Freedom*, Reissue (University of Chicago Press, Chicago, 1982).
Geiger, G.R., *The Philosophy of Henry-George* (Macmillan, New York, 1933).
George, H., *Progress and Poverty*, 1880.
Gide, C. and Rist, C., *A History of Economic Doctrines*, tr. R. Richards (Harrap, London, 1915).
Gray, A., and Thompson, A.E., *The Development of Economic Doctrine*, 2nd edn (Longman, London, 1980).
Hart, H.L.A., *The Concept of Law* (Clarendon Press, Oxford, 1961).
Hayek, F.A., *The Road to Serfdom* (Routledge and Kegan Paul, London, 1944). *Law Legislation and Liberty* 1 (Routledge and Kegan Paul, London, 1973). 2 (ditto, 1976).
Keynes, J.M. *The Scope and Method of Political Economy*, 4th edn (Macmillan, London, 1917).
Lenin, V.I., *State and Revolution*, 1917.
Lepage, H., *Tomorrow, Capitalism*, tr. S.C. Ogilvie (Open Court, La Salle, 1982).
Maine, H.S., *Ancient Law*, 1861.
Malthus, T.R., *The Principles of Political Economy*, 1820.
Marshall, A., *Principles of Economics*, 9th edn, ed. C.W. Guillebaud (Macmillan, London, 1961).
Marx, K., *Capital*, 4th edn, tr. E. and C. Paul (Everyman's Library, 1930).
Mill, J.S., *On Liberty*, 1859.
—— *Principles of Political Economy*, 7th edn, ed. J.M. Robson (University of Toronto Press, Toronto, 1965).
—— *Dissertations and Discussions* 4 (1875).
Miller, A.S., 'The Constitution and the Voluntary Association', *Voluntary Associations: Nomos XI*, ed. J.R. Pennock and J.W. Chapman (Atherton Press, New York, 1969).
Nozick, R., *Anarchy, State and Utopia* (Blackwell, Oxford, 1974).
Popper, K.R., *The Poverty of Historicism* (Routledge and Kegan Paul, London, 1961). *The Open Society and its Enemies*, 5th edn (Routledge and Kegan Paul, London, 1966).
Rawls, J., *A Theory of Justice* (Clarendon Press, Oxford, 1972).
Ricardo, D., *On the Principles of Political Economy, and Taxation*, ed. P. Sraffa and M.H. Dobb, (University Press, Cambridge, 1951).
Russell, B., *Freedom and Organisation 1814-1914* (Allen and Unwin, London, 1934).
Ryan, A., *J.S. Mill* (Routledge and Kegan Paul, London, 1974).
Samuelson, P.A., *Economics*, 6th edn. (McGraw Hill, New York, 1964).
Schwartz, P., *The New Political Economy of J.S. Mill* (Weidenfeld and Nicolson, London, 1972).
Shonfield, A., *Modern Capitalism* (Oxford University Press, London, 1965).
Smith, A., *The Wealth of Nations*, ed. Campbell, Skinner and Todd (Clarendon Press, Oxford, 1976).
Sorel, G., *Reflections on Violence*, tr. T.E. Hulme (Allen and Unwin, London, 1916).
Spencer, H., *Social Statics*, 1850.
Tame, C.R., 'Against the New Mercantilism', *Il Politico*, Vol. 43 (1978).

13   PROFESSOR TAYLOR ON LIBERTY AND JUSTICE

Professor Charles Taylor's views on liberty and justice are presented in the following substantial and impressive essays: 'What's Wrong With Negative Liberty', 'The Nature and Scope of Distributive Justice' and 'Kant's Theory of Freedom'. They are published or republished in his *Philosophical Papers*, 2 (Cambridge University Press, Cambridge, 1985).

Taylor is concerned with modern views of liberty, not the ancient one, in which liberty was a matter of status. A freeman was a man who was not a slave. The modern view which Taylor rejects is 'the Hobbes-Bentham view', which is 'negative', in that 'A is free to do X' is analysed as 'A is not stopped from doing X by some external obstacle'. He accepts instead the 'positive' view, in which 'A is free to do X' is analysed as 'A is not stopped from doing X by some internal obstacle', such as fear.

In criticism, first, Bentham's view is not the same as Hobbes'. For Hobbes, there is no difference between a jailer stopping a prisoner from leaving his cell by locking the door and a jailer stopping the water from leaving his bath by plugging the hole. According to Bentham, however, the jailer restrains the prisoner but stops the water. Restraint is the special sort of stopping which is intentional and of which both the subjects and the objects are persons. Taylor's criticisms, e.g. of 'the untenable Hobbesian reductive-materialist metaphysics' (p. 222) apply to Hobbes' view but not to Bentham's. Again, the expression, 'positive' view of liberty, is commonly applied to two different views. One is that 'A is free' means 'A is not a slave to his passions'. This is the view of Plato, Spinoza and Taylor. The other is that 'A is free' means 'A is autonomous'. This is the view of Rousseau and Kant. It has a stronger claim to the name, because Kant uses the expressions 'positive' and 'negative conceptions of liberty', whereas Plato and Spinoza do not. (See Secs. 3, 4, 5 of Essay 10.) Although there are similarities between the two views, there are also obvious and essential differences. The former mentions the emotions, but the latter does not. The latter mentions rules, but the former does not.

The chief weakness of Taylor's view is that it fails to capture the real objects of concern. When people are worried about liberty, the sort of things that they are worried about are governments arresting and detaining citizens without trial, jamming foreign broadcasts, and making it an offence to consume alcoholic drinks in public houses after 11 p.m. Taylor's man 'who is prevented by unreasoning fear from taking up the career he truly wants' (p. 227) certainly has a problem. But it would never occur to the average reasonable person, untutored in philosophy, to see it as a problem about the man's freedom. As Taylor himself observes, if the man is not restrained from taking up the career, we can say of him (and can say correctly of him) that 'he is not capable of taking proper advantage of his freedom' (ibid.).

The sort of justice with which Taylor is concerned is distributive justice, not retributive justice, which is about 'due restoration' for injury (p. 312). He distinguishes two questions, the nature of distributive justice, and the criteria of justice which are current in Western societies today. On the first question, he distinguishes further distributive justice, which is socially and historically relative, from absolute justice. He instances the dispute between Agamemnon and Achilles over Briseis. 'Achilles holds that she was part of his share; Agamemnon holds that the ruler cannot be left with less than the followers' (p. 301). According to Taylor, by the standards of Mycenaean warrior society, it was fair that Achilles (say) should have her; but by the standards of absolute justice it was unfair that either of them should have her, because 'people should not be allocated like this as spoils of war' (ibid.). But, first, this issue is not about justice; it is about whether the rightful owner of Briseis was Agamemnon, or Achilles, or neither. Secondly, the only things that matter are surely, in Taylor's terms, the 'absolutely just' and the 'absolutely right'. The true formal principles of justice are Simonides' 'justice is returning to each his due', and Aristotle's principle of equality and 'proportionate equality' (p. 290). These are, in Taylor's terms, 'trans-societal and ahistorical'.

On the question of the criteria of distributive justice which are current in Western states today, Taylor discerns two principles: 'the contribution principle' and 'the republican principle' (p. 315). The former asserts that 'highly talented people ought to be paid more than the ordinary' (p. 306). The reason underlying this 'widely felt intuition' is 'the principle of equal fulfilment', which rules out 'treating me as though my exceptional capacity were not my own, but in some way belonged to society' (ibid.). His target here is Rawls. The republican principle asserts that 'a common citizen-ship . . . cannot consist with too great inequalities . . . and . . . the balance of mutual indebtedness [in] maintaining together institutions of common deliberation is much more [nearly] equal' than it is in the economic domain (pp. 311, 314). '(Distributive) justice involves giving appro priate weight to both of these principles' (p. 313). Every society ought to combine them 'in a weighting that is appropriate for the particular society, given its history, economy, degree of integration' (ibid.). But in fact people are rejecting this plurality of principles and maintaining one of them exclusively. Consequently '(these principles) are in great and increasing tension' as economic growth slows down (p. 315). 'So on both sides there grows the sense of being imposed on by sheer force, and the principles of justice invoked seem sham . . . A reasoned debate about distributive justice becomes impossible' (p. 307).

Taylor's formulation of the contribution principle is incorrect because, as he himself says, 'contribution is a joint function of capacity and effort' (p. 308). But that principle is indeed a true substantive principle of justice. It gives content to Simonides' formal principle. The republican principle, however, is superfluous. For the excessive inequalities against which it is directed are already debarred by the contribution principle. E.g., the latter justifies the chairmen of large and successful companies being paid considerably more than the headmasters of good schools. But not ten times more. So there is nothing wrong in maintaining the contribution principle to be the sole substantive principle of distributive justice for benefits. The explanation of the present discontents in Western states which Taylor describes is that this principle is more honoured in the breach than in the observance.

INDEX OF NAMES

226

INDEX OF NOTIONS

identity
  church/state 194-6, 198, 201-2
  conditions of social collectives 186
  mind/brain theory 198
impartiality 146-7, 152-3, 173
  see also fairness; injustice; justice
imperative theory of law 56-7, 120
indefeasibility of justice *see under* justice
individual liberty 60, 101-17, 205
  definition, problem of 101-5
  distribution, problem of 107-12
  justification, problem of 105-7
  legal paternalism and 108, 111, 112-13
  qualified freedom 113-14
  rule of law and 122-3
  see also autonomy *and under* collective
    liberty
ineligible alternatives 44-6
inequality of consideration 146
influence 52-5, 180
injury, averting 105
injustice 134-6, 138-40, 150, 154, 174
  comparative discrimination and 87
  feelings of 151
  types of 134-5, 142-3, 147, 150,
    155
  as vice 153
  see also fairness; justice; unfairness
intention 173, 174
  coercion and 125-30, 148
justice and 147-8
interpersonal concept of liberty 102-3
intimidation *see* threats and offers
intrapersonal concept of liberty 48, 101-2
irresistible motives 46-7

judgement 152-3, 173
  knowledge and 147
justice/just
  action 30, 134-8, 147, 153
  civil 140-1
  distributive 71-2, 94, 224-5
  economic *see* under economic liberty
  equality and 73, 90, 143-7, 171-3
  indefeasibility of 156-60
    allocation of burdens 160-1
    preliminary justice 161
    by public good 159-60
    by rights 156-9
    see also meaning; value *below*
  intention and 147-8
  liberty and 223-5
  meaning of 134-48
    equality and 73, 143-7
    intention and 147-8
    just action 134-8, 147, 153
    principles and species of 138-43
  political 141
  rule of 171-2
  value of 148-56

public good and 154-6
  rights and 148-52
  virtue of 152-4
will 152, 153, 172
  see also fairness; injustice; justness;
    reciprocative; unfairness
justiced *see* justified
justification
  of compensation 89,92
  of individual liberty 105-7
  problem of retributive punishment 65,
    66, 70-2, 74-5
justified and justicized, confusion between
  157
justness 152-3, 172,174
  freedom and 182
  reciprocative 152
  as virtue 153-4, 173
  see also justice

knowledge 123
  judgement and 147
  just action and 153
  liberty and 11-15

laisser-faire see economic liberty
law/s
  application of theses on 167-73
  civil 72-3, 78, 111-12
  criminal *see* criminal law; retributive
    justice
  desire and 56
  economic liberty and 215-16
  imperative theory of 56-7, 120
  liberty and 56-7
  philosophy of *see* logic of will
  politics and 37
  praemiary 56, 58
  of tort 73, 78, 124
  see also government; rule of law
legal paternalism 108, 111, 112-13
legal equality *see* procedural equality
legislation
  coercion by 103-5, 106, 126
  collectivist 3
  Good Samaritan 108-9
  moralistic 111-12
  paternalistic 110-11
  utilitarian 109-10
liberal constitutionalism, traditional 119,
  121-2, 130
liberties to do sorts of actions 106-7
liberty
  ability and 4, 17, 42-4, 49
  as absence of coercion 52, 102, 121,
    125, 178
  and actions 106-7
  acts, consequences and 5-6
  autonomy and 189-90
  collective *see* collective liberty

For Product Safety Concerns and Information please contact our EU
representative GPSR@taylorandfrancis.com
Taylor & Francis Verlag GmbH, Kaufingerstraße 24, 80331 München, Germany

www.ingramcontent.com/pod-product-compliance
Lightning Source LLC
Chambersburg PA
CBHW070403270326
41926CB00014B/2673